LEARNING

AND

BEHAVIOR

■

Second Edition

LEARNING
AND
BEHAVIOR

■

Second Edition

PAUL CHANCE
Chesapeake College

Wadsworth Publishing Company
Belmont, California
A Division of Wadsworth, Inc.

Psychology Editor: Kenneth King
Production Editor: Jerilyn Emori
Managing Designer: Donna Davis
Print Buyer: Barbara Britton
Designer: Richard Kharibian
Copy Editor: Thomas L. Briggs
Technical Illustrator: Joan Carol
Cover: Donna Davis
Cover photographs: Dede Hatch and Jaye R. Phillips/The Picture Cube

Printed in the United States of America 19

4 5 6 7 8 9 10---92 91 90

Library of Congress Cataloging-in-Publication Data

Chance, Paul.
  Learning and behavior.

  Includes bibliographies and index.
  1. Conditioned response.   2. Learning, Psychology of.
I. Title.
BF319.C45   1988   153.1'5   87-15967
ISBN 0-534-08508-3

For Arno H. Luker

Contents

■

THREE
PAVLOVIAN PROCEDURES   46

EIGHT
EXTINCTION AND FORGETTING 205

NINE
THINKING 239

TEN
THE LIMITS OF LEARNING 265

Preface

■

This second edition of *Learning and Behavior* differs from its predecessor in several important ways. The chapters are shorter, for example, and there are more of them. There is a longer introduction; a chapter on research methodology and one on thinking; and there is considerably more material on reinforcement schedules, extinction, and forgetting. The text also discusses certain phenomena, such as peak shift, transposition, and the matching law, not covered in the first edition. I had some ambivalence about covering these topics in an introductory text, but included them on the grounds that instructors who find them unsuitable can direct students to skip over them.

The theme that runs through this edition is different from that in the earlier book. Whereas the previous edition focused on the role learning plays in individual development, the present text focuses on the role of learning in the adaptation of humans and other animals to a changing environment. Although this theme lent itself more readily to some chapters than others, I have tried to incorporate it throughout.

Some instructors may be puzzled by the changes in the titles of chapters dealing with classical, instrumental, and vicarious conditioning. The term *conditioning* is used in the text, but the term *procedures* is used in the chapter titles. Conditioning refers to a set of procedures, analogous to natural experiences, that change behavior. All too often, though, students get the idea that conditioning refers to something going on inside an organism. While certain kinds of physiological and cognitive events may occur during conditioning, the term ordinarily refers not to these events but to events occurring in the organism's environment. The use of the term *procedures* in the chapter titles draws attention to this fact.

Another change in the text is the addition of review questions at the end of each chapter. Many of these questions are quite familiar in form, requiring students to recall or look up some fact in the chapter. But other questions require a different kind of answer. The students may be asked to give an example of a phenomenon from their own experience, or they may be asked to design an experiment to test a hypothesis. Such questions require students to think about what they have read, to put what they have learned to use, much as a researcher might. Answering such questions may be a useful learning exercise, especially if it encourages students to share their views with others.

While the differences between the first and second editions are substantial, the two have much in common. The second edition, like its predecessor, is intended for use by undergraduate students taking a first course in learning. The first edition found use as a text in courses on learning and cognition, experimental psychology, and research methods. This edition may see similar use, but it was expressly written for introductory courses in learning principles, courses that focus in large part on conditioning.

Like the first edition, the second is not encyclopedic. My aim was not to provide a state-of-the-art summary of research on learning, but to produce a text that will effectively assist the instructor in teaching the basic principles of learning. As in the first edition, I have tried to achieve this end by writing in a simple, straightforward way, with lots of examples and illustrative studies; by using both human and animal examples and studies, in the hope that students will more clearly see the relevance of "rat psychology" to their own behavior; by organizing the material so that each idea is logically connected to those that precede it; by avoiding technical terms that are not part of the course content; by including review questions that encourage students to think about what they have read rather than merely memorize selected sentences; and, most importantly, by covering only as much material as students might reasonably be expected to master in a one-semester course.

The learning course is one in which the student comes to understand some of the most important ideas of human and animal nature, ideas that provide immediate insight into our daily experience. In this edition, as in the first, I have attempted to write a text that will help the instructor convey the vital importance of these ideas.

Many people assisted me in this endeavor. A number of them pointed out flaws in the first edition or made useful comments on the manuscript of this edition. My thanks to John M. Knight, Central State University; George Marsh, California State University, Dominguez Hills; Marion Pelchat, Washington College; Howard Rachlin, State University of New York at Stony Brook; John C. Ruch, Mills College; Jack Sherman, University of California at Los Angeles; W. Scott Terry, University of North Carolina; Ronald Ulm, Salisbury State College; Robert Yaremko, San Diego State University; and Eugene B. Zechmeister, Loyola University of Chicago. I owe a special debt to Jerry Venn of Mary Baldwin College for his encouragement and for his good advice on reaching students.

I also want to thank the folks at Wadsworth for their help, especially Donna Davis, Jerilyn Emori, Ken King, and Peggy Meehan. A special thanks to Tom Briggs, who edited the entire manuscript and caught many flaws in the writing that had slipped by other eyes, including my own.

Much of the credit for what is worthwhile in this edition of *Learning and Behavior* goes to those just mentioned. As for the book's shortcomings, the credit for those is all mine.

ONE

■

Introduction: Nature, Nurture, and Behavior

Change, said the Roman philosopher Lucretius 2,000 years ago, is the only constant. Yet we tend to regard change as an aberration, a brief disruption in a normally constant world. When a great volcano such as Mount Saint Helens in Washington erupts, knocking over thousands of trees and covering the earth for miles around with a blanket of volcanic ash, we think how strange it is that nature should misbehave so. It is, we tell ourselves, a momentary lapse, a kind of geological tantrum; soon our old planet will regain its composure, its sameness.

But the truth is that it is only our short tenure on earth that deludes us. In the course of an individual human's lifetime, volcanic eruptions are rare, but in the life of the earth, they are the very stuff of existence. Our time here is too brief to see continents crash together and tear apart, mountains rise and fall, vast deserts replace oceans; too brief to see thousands of animal and plant species come and go, like the ever-changing, varicolored crystalline shapes of a kaleidoscope.

Change is not the exception to the rule, then, but the rule itself. Throughout nature, the struggle to prevail is a struggle against change: Food supplies dwindle, prey animals become faster, predators become more formidable. Some changes, such as the movement of continents, take place over eons; others, such as the advance of glaciers, take thousands of years; still others, such as the weather or the appearance of a hungry predator, occur daily. The one constant is change. Any individual or species must be able to cope with change if it is to survive. But how? By what mechanisms can we and other organisms deal with such a fickle world?

NATURE: ADAPTATION THROUGH EVOLUTION

One mechanism for coping with change is genetic evolution. In *On The Origin of Species*, published in 1859, the English naturalist Charles Darwin proposed that species arise through the process of natural selection. There is, he argued, tremendous variation among the members of any given species. Some of these variations are relevant to features in the environment; others are not. Those features that are relevant are either beneficial to the species or harmful. Not only are individuals with favorable variations more likely to survive and hence to reproduce, but their offspring are more likely to show this helpful variation, so future generations will increasingly display this characteristic. Evolution is therefore the inevitable product of variation and natural selection.

Although Darwin did not understand the genetic basis for variation (the work of Gregor Mendel was not then widely known), he knew from direct observation that variation among the members of a species was common. He also knew that selective breeding of farm animals with a specific variation often resulted in offspring that resembled their parents in that characteristic. And he knew that selective breeding of individuals with a given characteristic would, over several generations, result in a high proportion of animals with that characteristic.

Darwin went beyond the animal breeders, however, by proposing that this same sort of selection process took place throughout nature. A characteristic, perhaps the thickness of a mammal's fur, varies widely among the members of the species. If the climate turns gradually colder, those individuals with thick coats will have an advantage over those with thin coats and will live longer and produce more thick-coated offspring. With each succeeding generation, there will be proportionally more animals with thick coats.

Darwin's theory does not require the involvement of any intelligent agent; we need not, for example, imagine God as animal husbandryman. The slow-witted and the slow afoot are culled by natural predators. Those that are not suited to a change in climate, a change in the food supply, a change in predators, perish.

```
W1520100029770      52010029770000
W1520300029770      52010029770000
W1520100029889      52010029880000
W1520100029954      52010029950000
W1520100030028      52010030020000
W1520100030143      52010030140000
W1520100030283      52010030280000
W1520100030309      52010030300000
W1520100030341      52010030340000
W1520200030381      52010030380000
W1520200030514      52010030510000
W1520100030663      52010030660000
W1520100030747      52010030740000
W1520100031265      52010031260000
W1520100031356      52010031350000
W1520100031372      52010031370000
W1520100031406      52010031400000
W1520100031505      52010031500000
W1520100031620      52010031620000
W1520200031751      52010031750000
W1520200031769      52010031760000
W1520100031778      52010031770000
W1520100031935      52010031930000
W1520100031976      52010031970000
W1520200032015      52010032010000
W1520100032081      52010032080000
W1520100032099      52010032090000
W1520100032149      52010032140000
W1520200032221      52010032220000
W1520200032346      52010032340000
```

QL 751 A6443, 1994

QL 751 S616 1999

QL 750 A5...

Reserve — Animal behavior: an evolutionary approach
John alcock. 5th edtn.

(www.sciencedirect.com/science/journal/000 33

Research on *Biston betularia,* one of the many large moths found on the British Isles, supports Darwin's theory nicely. *Betularia* feeds at night and rests during the day on the trunks and limbs of trees. Its survival depends in large part on its ability to escape detection by the birds that find it an appetizing food. Several decades ago, nearly all *betularia* were a mottled light gray color, closely resembling the lichen-covered trees on which they rested. A rare black variation of the moth stood out against this background like coal against snow. But when pollutants in certain industrial areas killed the lichen and darkened the bark, the light-colored moths increasingly fell prey to birds, while the dark moths tended to survive and reproduce. An examination of *betularia* collections reveals that in forests near industrial centers, the black *betularia* has increased and the light-colored variety has declined. In some areas, 90 percent of the *betularia* are of the once-rare black variety (Kettlewell, 1959).

It is likely that the same sort of process that affected the coloration of *betularia* has affected the skin color of humans living in very different climes. A natural substance in the skin, melanin, screens out the sun's rays. The more melanin, the darker the skin and the more sunlight is screened out. The people of Scandinavia and Northern Europe, where there is relatively little sunlight, are characteristically fair-skinned, which allows them to absorb the sunlight needed to produce vitamin D. People who live nearer the equator, where there is an abundance of sunlight, are characteristically dark-skinned, which provides them with protection against the hazards of too much sun. Like *betularia,* the human species takes on the coloration that survival in a given environment requires.

Evolution would be of limited importance to the study of behavior if it applied only to physical characteristics such as coloration. But the principles of variation and natural selection also apply to behavior; as the environment changes, those individuals that behave in adaptive ways are favored. Variations in behavior and the process of natural selection produce a repertoire of innate, adaptive behavior. Such genetically based forms of behavior can be classified as reflexes, fixed action patterns, and inherited behavior traits.

Reflexes

A **reflex** is a simple, involuntary reaction to a specific event (see The Reflex Arc box). Reflexes are either present at birth or appear at predictable stages in development. They are part of the inherited adaptive equipment of the organism. All animals, from amoebas to college professors, have reflexes.

THE REFLEX ARC

Reflexes are mediated by (carried out by means of) a relatively simple set of interconnected units called the **reflex arc.** Take, for example, the patellar reflex. A sharp blow to the patellar tendon, just beneath the knee cap, causes the foot to swing forward. What happens is this: The blow excites receptors at the tendon. This electrochemical excitation is transferred to nearby sensory neurons (nerve cells), which carry the impulse to the spinal cord, where interneurons are activated. The interneurons carry the impulse to motor neurons, which convey the excitation to muscles in the leg. The muscles contract, pulling the leg forward. In other reflexes, the sequence ends with the excitation of glands rather than muscles, so the reflex arc is said to consist of receptors, sensory neurons, interneurons, motor neurons, and effectors (muscles or glands).

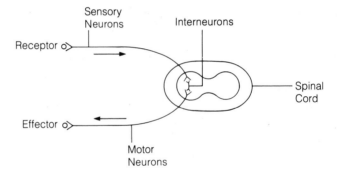

Figure 1-1   Reflex arc.

Notice that the reflex arc does not require any willful, conscious act. We do not have to think about jerking our leg when rapped on the knee. We are ordinarily aware that the knee has been struck because sensory nerves in the spinal cord carry impulses to the brain. The impulse that reaches the leg muscles does not emanate from the brain, however, but from the spinal cord. Thus, we respond reflexively *and* become aware that we have been hit at about the same time.

Many reflexes serve to protect the organism from injury. The amoeba is an irregularly shaped, one-celled animal that travels by extending a part of its perimeter forward and then pulling the rest along after. When the amoeba encounters a toxic substance, it immediately withdraws from it; this reflex minimizes the harmful effects of the noxious substance. Larger animals do much the same thing when they withdraw a limb from a painful object. The professor who absentmindedly picks up a very hot skillet will immediately release it and withdraw the injured hand. Other protective reflexes in humans include the eyeblink, in which the eye closes when any object approaches it; the pupillary reflex, in which the iris contracts or relaxes in response to changes in light; the sneeze, by which irritants such as dust and pollen are expelled from the nose and lungs; the patellar reflex, or knee jerk, which keeps us on our feet when something trips us up; and the vomit reflex, which removes harmful substances from the stomach in an efficient, if indelicate, manner.

Other reflexes are important in food consumption. When an amoeba encounters some edible object, say a dead bacterium, it immediately responds to the object by engulfing it; it can then begin making a meal of it. Humans have a number of such reflexes. Touch a baby's face and he or she will turn toward what touched him or her; this rooting reflex, as it is called, is useful in finding the mother's nipple. When the nipple touches the baby's lips, this evokes the sucking reflex, which brings milk into the baby's mouth. Food in the mouth elicits the salivary reflex, the flow of saliva that begins the process of digestion. Swallowing triggers peristalsis, the rhythmic motion of the lining of the esophagus that carries food to the stomach. Food in the stomach prompts yet another reflex, the flow of digestive juices.

Reflexes are highly stereotypic; that is, they are remarkably invariant in form, frequency, strength, and time of appearance during development. This is not to say, however, that they do not vary at all. The rooting reflex, for example, may first appear in one infant at the age of 7 days, but may not show up in a second infant for another week.

Reflexes are also subject to modification by experience. Repeated exposure to a stimulus that evokes a given reflex will result in a reduction in the strength of the reflex, a phenomenon known as **habituation** (see Figure 1-2).

Wagner Bridger (1961) studied habituation in infants. You already know that a loud noise will make you jump; another part of this startle reflex is the quickening of the heartbeat. Bridger found that

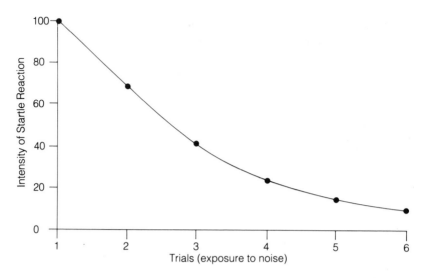

Figure 1-2   Habituation of the startle reflex. The intensity of the startle response declines with each exposure to the noise. (Hypothetical data.)

when babies first heard a noise, they responded with an increase in heart rate, but with repetition of the noise at regular intervals, the change in heart rate became less and less pronounced until, in some cases, the noise had no measurable effect at all.

Sensitization is the counterpart of habituation. In this case, the likelihood that an event will evoke the reflex is increased by experience. If, for example, you are startled by a loud noise, you are then more likely to jump when you hear a soft noise. The loud noise sensitizes you to the soft noise.

Though reflexes are more complex and variable than most people imagine, they nevertheless represent the simplest and most uniform kind of innate behavior. Other forms of inborn behavior are more complex and more variable.

Fixed Action Patterns

Fixed action patterns are series of interrelated acts. They resemble reflexes in that they are innate; display little variability from individual to individual, or from day to day in the same individual; and often are reliably elicited by a particular kind of event. They differ from reflexes in that they involve the entire organism rather than a few muscles or glands; are more complex, often consisting of long series of reflex-like acts; are more variable, though still very stereotypic; and are less likely to be evident at or soon after birth. Fixed action patterns used to be called *instincts*, but this term has fallen out of favor lately, partly because it came to refer to any more or less automatic behavior (as in, "he knew *instinctively* what to do").

Some fixed action patterns protect the animal from predators. When confronted by a threatening dog, the housecat arches its back, hisses, growls, and flicks its tail. These acts make the cat appear larger and more formidable than it really is and may therefore serve to put off an attacker. The armadillo responds quite differently to predators: It coils itself into a ball, its armor-like shell forming a nearly impregnable barrier to its enemies. And the opossum plays dead if it cannot escape an attacker.

Other fixed action patterns provide protection against the elements. Geese and many other birds migrate to warmer climes in the fall, while many insects, amphibians, reptiles, and small mammals respond to the approach of winter by hibernating.

Some fixed action patterns are useful in procuring food. Pigs root for worms and larvae buried in the ground, some spiders build webs with which to capture their prey, and woodpeckers tap holes in tree bark to get at the insects that live there.

Many fixed action patterns involve courtship and mating. The male western grebe, a water bird, attracts a mate by running on the water, while the male bighorn sheep wins a partner by bashing its head against that of its rival. In most animals, the mating act itself involves characteristically stereotyped behavior. When the female chimpanzee is capable of conceiving, she approaches an adult male and presents her swollen and inflamed genitals; the male responds to this display by mounting the female. The act may be repeated numerous times while the female is receptive, but each performance is a nearly identical repetition of the last.

Fixed action patterns also govern the care and rearing of the young (see Figure 1-3). After mating, the female of certain species of wasp builds a nest, places a paralyzed spider into it, lays an egg on top of the prey, closes the nest, and goes on its way, leaving the young wasp to fend for itself after it has hatched and has eaten its first meal. The newborn of many higher species of animals require greater nurturance, for which task their parents are genetically equipped. Birds work slavishly to feed their ever-hungry young. The brown-headed cowbird cares for its young by depositing its eggs in another bird's nest, often tricking an unsuspecting sparrow into making a heroic effort to feed a youngster twice its own size.

Figure 1-3   Young of mouth-breeding fish return to the safety of the female's mouth when danger threatens. (After Tinbergen, 1953/1962, figure 12, p. 20. Reprinted by permission of Metheun & Co., London.)

We saw that reflexes are reliably elicited by specific kinds of events. Fixed action patterns are also initiated by certain events, called **releasers.** For instance, male rats ordinarily will mate only with females that are in estrus (i.e., in heat). The estrous female produces pheromones (odorous chemicals) that act as releasers for sexual behavior in the male. The pheromones trigger mating; in their absence, the male will not usually attempt to mate. Similarly, a nesting gray lag goose responds to an egg that has rolled out of the nest by "stretching the neck towards it, bringing the bill behind the egg and with careful balancing movements rolling it back into the nest" (Tinbergen, 1951, p. 84). An egg, or almost any more or less round object near the nest, will release this fixed action pattern.

Because of their complexity and their utility, many fixed action patterns appear to be willful, intelligent acts. The truth is that they are no more voluntary or purposeful than is the behavior of a person who responds to a rap on the knee by jerking a leg. Take, for instance, the brown-headed cowbird's practice of placing its own eggs into another bird's nest and throwing out one or more of the nesting bird's eggs, an apparently intelligent, intentional act. The cowbird seems to do this *in order* to save itself the trouble of rearing its young. Further, the casual observer might reasonably infer that the bird *knows* what it is about, that it understands the logic in what it does. But there is, in reality, no reason to believe that this behavior reveals avian cleverness. The fact that the behavior occurs throughout the species, but not among other, apparently equally intelligent birds, indicates that it is a fixed action pattern, as much a product of genetic evolution as the color of its feathers is.

Another illustration of the unthinking nature of fixed action patterns is provided by the tropical army ant. Entire colonies of these ants charge across the forests in what may appear to be a highly organized, intelligently directed campaign. In fact, the ants are merely following a chemical trail laid down by the ants ahead of them. T. C. Schneirla (1944) demonstrated that on a flat surface, such as a road, where no obstacles direct the course of the march, the lead ants tend to move toward the ants beside them. Thus, the column turns in on itself, and the ants soon march around in a circle. Again, not very thoughtful behavior.

Despite such evidence, some people persist in believing that fixed action patterns are learned behavior. They argue that the behavior is so complex that it could not possibly be the product of genetic evolution. How, for example, could genetic variation and selection account for the fact that a cowbird removes eggs from another bird's nest and replaces them with its own? How could genes for such a complex behavior suddenly emerge? The answer is that they probably do not "suddenly emerge." What we see in fixed action patterns may well be the product of thousands, perhaps millions, of years of evolution. B. F. Skinner (1975, 1984; see also Carr, 1967) has theorized that complex fixed action patterns may be selected by gradual changes in the environment, changes that take place over eons. Take, Skinner suggests, the salmon's migration upstream to breed. This act often requires the fish to ascend steep cliffs and swim against rushing currents. How could such complex and difficult behavior be the product of evolution? Skinner notes that at one time, returning to the breeding grounds might have constituted a relatively easy swim up a gently rising stream. As geological changes gradually increased the steepness of the slope, those fish with the ability to make the trip bred successfully and reproduced their kind, while those not up to the challenge failed to reproduce and so were selected out. As geological changes continued to increase the difficulty of the task, the process of natural selection produced salmon capable of mastering it. Skinner suggests that other complex fixed action patterns were molded by the environment in much the same way.

Are there any fixed action patterns in human beings? It is hard to say. Several decades ago, textbooks listed hundreds of human instincts, including the sex instinct, the social instinct, the maternal instinct, and the territorial instinct (see, for example, McDougall, 1908). But the list has shrunk in recent years. Some psychologists today maintain that there are no fixed action patterns in human beings, that the supposed instincts lacked the monotonous character of, say, nesting birds and foraging ants. For example, people, like chimpanzees, approach prospective sexual partners from time to time, but the method of approach varies tremendously from culture to culture, from individual to individual, and even within the same individual from time to time. Humans have invented marriage, dating services, prostitution, and all sorts of rules and customs for defining how, with whom, and under what circumstances sexual acts are to be performed. The complexity and variability of mating among humans does not closely resemble the stereotypic mating behavior of lower animals.

Much the same sort of case can be made against the so-called maternal instinct. True, many women do desire to have children and to protect and nurture them. But, again, there is tremendous variation in how mothers perform these tasks. In some societies, for example, young children are fondled and held constantly, and their slightest need is met immediately; in other societies, children of the same age are left pretty much to their own resources. Moreover, women in western societies increasingly delay or forego altogether the traditional maternal role. True fixed action patterns are not so readily discarded.

On the other hand, sociobiologists and ethologists note interesting similarities between the behavior of humans and the fixed action patterns of lower animals. People may not be territorial in the same sense as chimpanzees, but there is no denying that neighbors and nations often quarrel over boundary lines. Perhaps the best case for a fixed action pattern in humans is the incest taboo. E. O. Wilson (1978) argues that people have an innate aversion to mating with members of their own family. In support of this, he cites research (Shepher, 1971) showing that children reared in Israeli kibbutzim (large, family-like communal groups) almost never marry within the kibbutz. Even this "instinct" is, however, suspect. Sigmund Freud (1913/1918) pointed out that if there really were a natural aversion to incest, there would be no need for an incest taboo. The taboo, he argued, was a cultural invention designed to avoid problems caused by incest. Further doubt about Wilson's view is raised by recent studies showing that incestuous behavior is much more common than had been thought (Russell, 1986). Fixed action patterns are generally found in virtually all members of a given species.

But even if we accept the view that incest, territoriality, and perhaps a few other patterns of behavior have genetic bases, it is clear that they are nowhere near as stereotypic as the fixed action patterns of so many lower animals. In humans, the role of genetics in behavior is generally more subtle and takes the form of inherited behavior traits.

Inherited Behavior Traits

Over the past few decades, a great deal of research has been done on the role genes play in determining general behavioral tendencies, or traits. Many of these traits fall under the heading of personality characteristics: activity level, aggressivity, neuroticism (i.e., the tendency toward various deviant behavior patterns), and so forth. Others are more narrowly defined: taste preference, hoarding (of food, for instance), and sexual preference. Such tendencies, which will be referred to here as **inherited behavior traits,** were once classified as instincts, but they differ from fixed action patterns in important ways.

As noted previously, fixed action patterns are elicited by fairly specific kinds of environmental events, called releasers. The gaping mouth of a fledgling induces the parent bird to provide food, while a closed mouth does not have this effect. Inherited behavior traits, on the other hand, are elicited by a wider variety of events. For instance, under certain circumstances, aversive (painful or unpleasant) events will reliably elicit aggressive behavior in many animals and in humans (Berkowitz, 1983). But the term *aversive event* covers a lot of territory: It can refer to an electric shock, a pin prick, a spray of cold water, an air temperature above 80 degrees, and so on. Such events lack the specificity of events that elicit fixed action patterns.

Another difference between fixed action patterns and behavior traits concerns the degree of fixedness of the behavior. Each web-spinning spider instinctively spins a web with a particular pattern, and it goes about the task with a remarkable sameness, like someone living a recurrent dream. But the rat that attacks its neighbor goes about it in a far less stereotypic manner; further, there may be considerable difference between the attack of one rat and another.

While behavior traits are more elusive than fixed action patterns, there is no doubt about their heritability. Selective breeding can, for example, produce strains of both very active and very inactive rats (Rundquist, 1933). Similarly, experimenters have bred strains of animals differing in fearfulness (Hall, 1937), aggressiveness (Fuller & Scott, 1954), and addiction proneness (Nichols & Hsiao, 1967; see Figure 1-4).

Numerous studies have demonstrated that humans, too, inherit many behavior traits. Studies of identical twins separated soon after birth reveal that their adult personalities have much in common (Far-

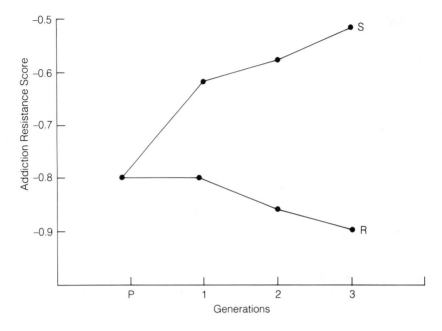

Figure 1-4   Inherited behavior trait. There is no instinct for addiction, but heredity plays a role in its development. From an unselected population of rats (P), rats susceptible (S) or resistant (R) to morphine addiction were interbred for three generations. Susceptible rats became increasingly susceptible, while resistant rats became increasingly resistant, to addiction. (After Nichols & Hsiao, 1967. Copyright 1967 AAAS. Reprinted by permission.)

ber, 1981). They often have similar career interests, wear the same styles of clothes, enjoy the same kinds of art, music, entertainment, and hobbies, and so on. Studies comparing different racial groups also show the role of heredity in behavior traits. Daniel Freedmand (1974; reported in Wilson, 1978) compared Chinese-American infants with Caucasian-American infants and found marked differences in disposition. The babies with Oriental ancestry were less disturbed by noise, less irritable, and less likely to object to being restrained than were those with Caucasian backgrounds.

Similarly, although people do not have a social instinct (in the strict sense of fixed action patterns), they do have a strong, apparently innate tendency toward affiliating with other people. True hermits are rare, if not nonexistent. A sense of group membership seems to be an inevitable consequence of this trait. The famous psychoanalyst Erik Erikson (1968) was among those who observed that group members tend to demean outsiders. Groups, he said, engage in *pseudospeciation:* Members of other groups are considered inferior, as though they were subhuman species. Certain hunter-gatherer tribal groups refer to themselves by a word that in their language means merely *human being.* The word *Cheyenne,* for example, means *the people.* The implication, of course, is that members of other tribes are something less than people. Members of sophisticated Western societies have by no means outgrown this tendency (Bandura, 1973; Keen, 1986).

It is easy to see how inherited behavior traits, like reflexes and fixed action patterns, may be products of natural selection. Rabbits are not well equipped for fighting, so the more combative among them are apt to be short-lived. The rabbit that flees the fox may escape, while the rabbit that stands and fights is unlikely to mate again. The same evolutionary forces no doubt have had their influence on human behavior: Individuals who preferred isolation to the security of the crowd were more likely to become some predator's meal.

Thanks to genetic variation and the process of natural selection, then, adaptive forms of behavior—reflexes, fixed action patterns, and inherited behavior traits—evolve. As the environment changes, new adaptive forms of behavior appear in the species and old forms of behavior that are no longer adaptive disappear. Genetic evolution is therefore a marvelous invention for coping with a variable environment, but it has its limits.

Limits of Genetic Evolution

The chief problem with genetic evolution as a way of coping with change is that it is slow. Changes in the environment do not produce changes in the genes that are helpful to individuals now living; they merely give a reproductive advantage to those individuals with adaptive characteristics. Suppose, for example, that the winters became gradually more severe in North America's Rocky Mountains. The bears that lived in this region would have to adapt to colder winters to survive. Contrary to popular belief, bears are not true hibernators. They do spend much of their winters sleeping in caves or dens, but they awaken periodically and emerge occasionally from their dwelling to feed. If the winters grew colder, the supply of available food might be reduced, and the cold might make foraging and hunting too expensive in terms of calories expended. Those bears that were genetically inclined to sleep for long periods and to stay within their lairs would therefore have an advantage over those that stirred about more frequently. (This assumes, of course, that the warmer months offer the bears the opportunity to gorge themselves with food and store up large amounts of fat.) These animals would be more likely to survive and reproduce, so over a period of many generations, the bears in this region might evolve into true hibernators.

But the evolution of adaptive behavior is a slow process, measured not in days or months but in generations. Genetic evolution is therefore of no value in helping individuals adapt either to cataclysmic changes or to the minor variations in daily life. Evolution will do nothing to help the current generation of bears meet the challenge of suddenly colder winters. And if a given bear is able to endure the cold, but finds in the spring that its traditional food supply has been destroyed by the bulldozer, evolution does not give it an appetite for another kind of food, or the skill to obtain it. Genetic variation and natural selection make it possible for the *species* to adapt to change, but they do not help the living *individual* to adapt.

As a consequence, evolutionary change is always "behind the times." Individuals are born with particular characteristics not because those characteristics will help them survive, but because, in the past, they helped that individual's *ancestors* to survive. As the environment changes, what was for one generation a very adaptive characteristic may become irrelevant or even injurious for the next.

B. F. Skinner (1983b) has pointed out that human beings also can become hostages to their genetic history. He notes, for example, that humans evolved in a world in which salt and sugar were not readily available. Those individuals who had a natural preference for these foods were more likely to get the sodium and the calories needed for survival. We have, as a consequence, evolved into a species with strong likings for both salty and sweet foods. But our world has changed. In industrial societies, salt and sugar are abundant, and we consume too much of them, endangering our health in the process. Similarly, Skinner notes, a strong appetite for sexual contact favored the survival of our species during most of its evolution. Until recently (in evolutionary terms), childhood diseases killed most children before they reached reproductive maturity; others died in early adulthood from starvation, disease, childbearing, or the routine hazards of an untamed world. Consequently, those individuals who were most virile and most fertile were favored. But in the last 200 years, advances in medicine, sanitation, and food production have so greatly reduced the mortality rate of our young that we no longer need to be so fertile for our species to survive. Yet we retain our antiquated sexual appetite, with the result that we are seriously in danger of overpopulating the planet. This is not to say that genetic evolution is intrinsically self-destructive, nor that it is unimportant to survival. But evolution is limited by its sluggishness. Fortunately, another mechanism for adapting to rapid changes in the environment is available, the mechanism of learning.

NURTURE: ADAPTATION THROUGH LEARNING

A second mechanism for adapting to a variable environment is learning. Actually, learning is itself a genetically evolved biological mechanism, a kind of fixed plasticity (Skinner, 1984). It is an inborn ability to adapt to changes in the environment. Learning takes up where reflexes, fixed action patterns, and inherited behavior traits leave off by helping the organism adapt to situations for which its innate behavior is inadequate.

Consider, for example, how animals come to avoid eating poisonous foods. In some species, there is an innate tendency to avoid certain tastes. This tendency has survival value in that many bad-tasting objects are harmful. But the inborn taste preferences are not perfect; many items that taste good are deadly. How then does an animal (or a person)* survive this danger? By learning to avoid eating the harmful items.

Poisonous foods are not the only hazards, of course, and learning plays an important role in protecting humans and many animals from such dangers as fire, water, storms, and natural predators. Cities provide any number of examples of the adaptive value of learning. Mice, raccoons, opossums, pigeons, foxes, coyotes, and many other animals evolved in a world in which humans played an insignificant part and cities did not exist. They have managed to adapt to the very different world of modern cities partly through learning. Pigeons, for example, have learned to take food from the hands of humans. The peregrine falcon, which once made its home on the cliffs above the Hudson River, now resides among the cliffs of New York's skyscrapers. Humans also have adapted to the new landscape: Where they once carried bow and arrow and stalked deer, they now carry briefcases and hunt the mighty dollar.

Learning, like evolution, is an adaptive mechanism, a way of coping with a changing environment. In a sense, learning is a kind of

---

* People are, of course, animals. I distinguish between animals and people to avoid the impression that we are concerned only with "lower" species.

THE SUPERIOR ANIMAL

Humans spend an amazing amount of time trying to prove their superiority over other species. Part of this effort has been devoted to finding some uniquely human characteristic, some quality that sets our species apart from lower organisms. We used to say, for example, that *homo sapiens* was the only animal that reasoned, but studies of animal learning raised serious doubts about that. We said that we were the only creature to make and use tools, but then we discovered that chimpanzees make and use tools all the time. We said that humans were the only animals capable of learning language, but then we taught apes to communicate.

One by one, the characteristics that we have held to be uniquely human have been taken away from us. Perhaps the only uniquely human characteristic is this: So far as we know, we are the only creature that spends time trying to prove its superiority over other creatures. The ultimate futility of this endeavor was pointed out by the British philosopher Bertrand Russell: "Organic life, we are told, has developed gradually from the protozoon to the philosopher; and this development, we are assured, is indubitably an advance. Unfortunately, it is the philosopher, not the protozoon, who give us this assurance" (quoted in Durant, 1927, p. 523).

---

evolution; through it, adaptive behavior is "selected" and nonadaptive behavior "dies out" (Skinner, 1981, 1984). Genetic, or **endogenous** (in the genes), evolution and learning, or **exogenous** (outside the genes), evolution are merely two different ways of dealing with a changing world. Typically, the two processes work together, as we shall now see.

THE NATURE-NURTURE DEBATE

One of the longest-running arguments in the study of behavior concerns the roles of heredity and environment in behavior. Basically, the debate is over the extent to which behavior is due to heredity (nature) as opposed to experience (nurture). Do we, as individuals, behave the way we do because it is our *nature* to do so or because of the *nurturance* we have received? The question applies not only to individuals but also to human beings in general: Is human behavior dictated by genetics, or is it the product of learning? The same sort of question can be asked about other species as well. Is the gorilla naturally very gentle, or is it gentle because it has learned to be so? Of course, no advocate of the genetic view denies that learning occurs, and no one who leans toward the role of learning ignores the role of heredity. Nevertheless, for centuries, people have lined up on one side or the other of this debate, according to what they believed was the more important determinant of behavior.

The trouble with the nature-nurture debate is that it creates an artificial division between the adaptive mechanisms of genetic evolution and learning. The fact is that evolution and learning work together to increase the organism's chances of survival.

Consider, for example, aggression among rats. Researchers have found that rats can be induced to attack their peers if they are given an electric shock. Even if the rats are in different parts of a cage, the shocked rat will run over to its roommate and attack it (Ulrich, 1966; Ulrich & Azrin, 1962). This response to pain seems to be innate, but aggression is not the inevitable response to pain. In one early study, Nathan Azrin and his colleagues (1966) found that if rats learned how to escape from a situation in which they were shocked, they were far less likely to attack their fellows. In another study, researchers found that when rats were first taught to be aggressive toward other rats, they were far more aggressive when shocked than were rats that had not had this training (Baenninger & Ulm, 1969). Other studies showed that animals rarely fought when shocked unless they had had fighting experience (Powell & Creer, 1969). Thus, the likelihood that aversive stimulation, such as that from electric shock, will induce aggressive behavior depends on both the rat's genetic history and its learning history.

Other forms of behavior reflect the same sort of nature-nurture synergy. Harry and Margaret Harlow (1962a, b) reared infant monkeys in isolation to see how their development would be affected. They found, among other things, that as adults these monkeys were socially inept and rather neurotic. When given the opportunity to mate with a normally reared monkey, they sometimes showed an interest, but were at a loss as to how to proceed. Further, if an isolation-reared female monkey managed to get pregnant, she made a poor mother.

The relative importance of nature and nurture is even more difficult to determine when it comes to human behavior. E. O. Wilson (1978) notes that among the !Kung San, the aboriginal people of Australia, violence against their fellows is now almost unknown. But

Wilson points out that a half century ago, when the population density among these people was greater and when there was less governmental control over their behavior, their per capita murder rate rivaled that of America's most dangerous cities.

Wilson (1978) notes that the Semai of Malaya also have demonstrated the capacity for both gentleness and violence. Murder is unknown among these people; they do not even have a word in their language for the concept of killing. Yet when the British colonial government trained Semai men to fight against Communist guerrillas in the 1950s, the Semai became fierce warriors. One anthropologist wrote that "they seem to have been swept up in a sort of insanity which they call 'blood drunkenness'" (Dentan, 1968; quoted in Wilson, 1978, p. 100). Wilson concludes from such evidence that "the more violent forms of human aggression are not the manifestations of inborn drives . . . [but are] based on the interaction of genetic potential and learning" (Wilson, 1978, p. 105).

Genetics and learning also interact in more amorous situations. The mistaken ideas that children (and some uneducated adults) have about reproduction make it clear that learning is very important in the development of human sexual behavior. But human sexuality is not entirely the product of learning. Numerous studies have suggested that heredity may play an important part, for instance, in determining the frequency of adult sexual activity, the number of sexual partners a person has in a lifetime, and even the kinds of sexual practices an individual finds acceptable (Eysenck, 1976). As in the case of aggressive behavior, sexual behavior is the product of both genetic evolution and experience.

Almost any form of behavior reflects the same sort of interaction between nature and nurture. Take the nocturnal habits of certain animals. Animals that once hunted by day, such as the North American puma and the bobcat, now hunt by night. Perhaps this shift to a nocturnal lifestyle first occurred because animals learned to avoid humans by staying hidden during the day. But genetic evolution also may have played a part: Those animals with a strong innate tendency to roam about during the day were more likely to be killed by hunters than were those that preferred to hunt at night. The same sort of interaction between learning and genes can be seen in territoriality, language, superstition, religion, hunting, food preferences, and many other forms of behavior. Genetic evolution and learning both play a part in adaptation. They are merely different ways of adapting to the environment, different ways of coping with life's one constant—change.

SUMMARY

Change is the only constant, and the ceaseless struggle for existence is the struggle to adapt to an ever-changing world. In the animal kingdom, adaptation is accomplished by two mechanisms, evolution and learning.

Charles Darwin's theory of evolution states that genetic adaptation depends upon variation and natural selection. A given characteristic varies within a species, and those variations that are adaptive are selected because they contribute to the survival of individuals with that characteristic. Inherited characteristics include physical attributes, such as size and weight, and certain kinds of behavior: reflexes, fixed action patterns, and inherited behavior traits.

Reflexes are simple responses to specific events and are involuntary and largely invariable. Examples include the eye blink and the knee jerk.

Fixed action patterns, which used to be called instincts, are a series of reflex-like acts in response to a particular event. Like reflexes, fixed action patterns are involuntary and relatively invariable. Unlike reflexes, fixed action patterns usually involve the entire organism rather than a few muscles or glands, and they may be fairly complex. The event that sets a fixed action pattern into motion is called a releaser. Examples of fixed action patterns include the armadillo's habit of rolling into a ball when attacked, web spinning in certain spiders, and the migration of salmon.

Inherited behavior traits are general tendencies. They differ from reflexes and fixed action patterns in that they are far more variable and are elicited by a wider variety of events. Examples include activity level, aggressivity, and fearfulness.

The evolution of adaptive forms of behavior plays an important role in the survival of a species. But genetic evolution is a slow process that does nothing to aid the individual organism faced with a new challenge. A mechanism by which the individual organism may adapt to sudden change is learning.

The capacity for learning is itself a biological characteristic of the species and is the product of genetic evolution. Through learning, an organism can cope with aspects of its environment for which its innate behavior is inadequate.

The nature-nuture debate—the argument over the relative importance of genetics and learning in determining behavior—is an ongoing one. But this debate obscures the underlying fact that both genetic evolution and learning typically contribute to the survival of the individual and the species. They are merely different ways of adapting to change.

REVIEW QUESTIONS

Warning to Students: Many of the questions that appear here (and in subsequent chapters) cannot be answered merely be searching through the chapter and copying a line or two from the text. The answers to such questions are not to be found in the text in this literal sense. To answer them properly, you may have to apply information in the text in imaginative ways.

1. Define the following terms. Give an example or illustration of each that is *not* taken from the text.

genetic variation	fixed action pattern
natural selection	releaser
evolution	nature-nurture debate
reflex	inherited behavior trait

2. What are the twin mechanisms of genetic evolution?

3. Why is the process of evolution still going on today?

4. Why has the field mouse not evolved into an animal as large and ferocious as the grizzly bear?

5. In what sense is evolution the product of experience?

6. How are reflexes like the ROM (read only memory) of a computer, that part of the computer's memory that is built in?

7. A person is asked to blink his eyes and does so. Is this a reflex act? Justify your answer.

8. Invent a new reflex, one that would be helpful to humans.

9. One learning specialist (Rachlin, 1976) refers to fixed action patterns as complex reflexes. Do you favor this idea? Explain your answer.

10. Speculate on whether humans *lost* fixed action patterns they once had as their learning ability evolved, or whether their learning ability evolved because they *lacked* adaptive fixed action patterns.

11. Do you think that the human tendency to believe in some sort of religion is an inherited behavior trait? Why or why not?

12. During wars, some soldiers sacrifice themselves to save their comrades. Some scientists believe such altruistic behavior is the product of natural selection. How can this be, when the altruistic act ends the person's opportunities for reproduction?

13. How are reflexes, fixed action patterns, and inherited behavior traits alike? How do they differ?

14. Some scientists have suggested that much innate human behavior has outlived its usefulness. The gravest threats to our survival, they say, now come from innate behavior that is no longer adaptive. What evidence (*not* provided by the text) can you muster to support this view?

15. In what sense is it true that learning does for humans what fixed action patterns do for animals? In what way is learning superior to fixed action patterns? In what way is it inferior?

16. In what sense is learning the product of evolution? In what sense is evolution the product of learning?

17. How can it be said that in an unchanging world, an organism with appropriate innate behavior would have no need of learning?

18. Learning ability is usually considered to have survival value. Under what circumstances might learning be nonadaptive?

19. Caged animals behave very differently than animals in the wild. In which circumstance is their "true" nature revealed? Where should one look to see "true" human nature?

20. Suppose a dozen young children were placed on an island and provided with food and shelter but no opportunities to learn from other human beings. What would they be like as adults? Would they have a language? Laws? Marriage customs? A religion? Government? Which would be more important in determining how they turned out, innate behavior or learning?

SUGGESTED READINGS

It is hoped that reading this chapter has left you wanting to know more about the topics covered. If it has, you may want to read one or more of the following works. You will find even the more technical among them surprisingly readable.

The classic work on biological adaptation through evolution is Darwin's *On the Origin of Species,* originally published in 1859. Several very entertaining and informative books on evolution are available, including *The Immense Journey* (1957) by anthropologist Loren Eiseley. *The Origin* (1980) by novelist Irving Stone is a fictional account of Darwin's life and work.

Reflexes were first described by the 17th century French philosopher René Descartes in *Treatise of Man* (1662/1972). Fixed action patterns are discussed in E. O. Wilson's *Sociobiology: The New Synthesis* (1975).

The role of experience in adaptation is, of course, the subject of this book, so relevant readings will appear at the end of each chapter. However, it may be useful to mention certain general references here. Numerous introductory learning texts are available that offer a kind of counterpoint to this one. Among the more popular are Barry Schwartz's *Psychology of Learning and Behavior* (1984) and *Behaviorism, Science and Human Nature* by Barry Schwartz and Hugh Lacey (1982). Perhaps the most sophisticated introductory text is *Behavior and Learning* (1976) by Howard Rachlin, one of the leading researchers in the field.

The interaction of nature and nurture in behavior is the subject of an excellent article by B. F. Skinner, "Selection by Consequences" (1981). And, although E. O. Wilson is often accused of neglecting the role of experience in behavior, readers of *On Human Nature* (1978) will see that he fully appreciates its importance. The nature-nurture debate has interested novelists and philosophers, and some of their work on the subject is provocative as well as entertaining. Examples include William Golding's *Lord of the Flies* (1962) and Aldous Huxley's *Ape and Essence* (1948).

TWO

■

The Study of Learning
and Behavior

We have seen that learning is an adaptive mechanism, a way of coping with a changing world. The study of learning, then, is the study of the way an organism's behavior changes in response to changes in its environment. An organism is constantly interacting with, one might say *communicating with,* its surroundings: A rat wanders down an alley in a maze; the alley divides; the rat turns to the right; the alley leads to a dead end; the rat goes back to the choice point and takes the alternate alley; the alley leads to another choice point; and so on. The question to be considered in this chapter is, How is this process of adaptation—this communication—to be studied? Let us begin by examining what psychologists mean by the term *learning.*

DEFINING LEARNING

Learning is often defined very simply as a relatively enduring change in behavior due to experience. The apparent simplicity of this definition is, however, illusory.

Consider, for example, the phrase *change in behavior.* Why should learning be said to be a change in behavior? Why not say, for example, that learning is the *acquisition of knowledge?*

The word *change* is preferred over *acquisition* because learning does not always appear to involve acquiring something, but it does always involve some sort of change. For instance, domesticated hens, and certain other birds that live in groups, have an innate tendency to establish a pecking order, a kind of rank based partly on fighting ability. When a new bird joins a flock, it fights with the other birds until it establishes its proper rank. Then it will dominate those birds beneath it in rank and defer to those above it. Although the tendency to establish a pecking order is innate, learning appears to be involved in determining a given individual's rank. Learning in this case means that the bird continues to peck certain birds, but *gives up* pecking others. In this instance, learning seems to mean that something is lost rather than gained.

What does the phrase "due to experience" mean? This phrase is necessary to our definition because, while learning involves changes in behavior, not all changes in behavior involve learning. Fatigue, injury, drugs, disease, and maturation change behavior, but these changes are not considered learning. Learning refers only to changes in behavior due to experience.

Experience refers to "an event or series of events participated in or lived through" (American Heritage Dictionary, 1971). Notice that this use of the term *experience* focuses on events taking place in the organism's environment. When we say that learning is a change in behavior due to experience, then, what we mean is that the change in behavior was brought about by some change in the organism's surroundings. The study of learning is thus the study of different kinds of events—those involving the behaving organism (response events) and those involving the organism's environment (stimulus events).

Response Events

There are two kinds of behavior. When behavior is mediated by smooth muscles or glands, it is called **respondent behavior.** Smooth muscles and glands are ordinarily not under voluntary control: Most of us cannot make the muscles lining our esophagus (gullet) contract, or make our adrenal glands secrete less adrenalin into the bloodstream. (At least, not directly. We can, of course, swallow, which induces the esophageal contractions known as peristalsis, and we can reduce our blood level of adrenalin by taking a nap.) Respondent behavior typically involves reflexes such as the knee jerk and the eye blink.

Operant behavior is mediated by striated muscles, those that are usually under voluntary control. Such behavior is called operant because it is said to operate on the environment; that is, it has some effect upon the environment. In many experiments, a rat is placed in a cage that contains a lever. Pressing the lever is operant behavior because it has the effect of moving the lever. Operants also differ from respondents in that operants are less stereotypic. The reflex action of the eye's pupil to light is quite monotonous, but lever pressing can take a myriad of forms.

In studying the changes in respondent and operant behavior associated with learning, it is necessary to define behavior in some precise way. It is to such specific kinds of behavior that psychologists refer when they use the term *response*. A **response** is any specified action, or set of actions, by muscles or glands.

We may wish, for example, to study how a child comes to fear dogs. But *fear* is a vague term; it means different things to different people. To study fear scientifically, we must define it in terms of some specific action of muscles or glands, some response. Fear may be defined as the production of vocal sounds greater than 90 db (decibels, a unit of loudness). This sort of precision may seem unnecessary. Why not just define fear as crying? After all, everybody knows what crying is. But experience has shown that judgments about what qualifies as a given response can differ. Suppose a child whimpers softly; is that crying? Or suppose the child yells very loudly, but there are no tears; is that crying? By defining fear as vocal sounds greater than 90 db, there is no doubt about what is and is not to be considered crying.

Similarly, we may wish to study lever pressing in the rat. But what is a lever press? If the rat touches the lever with its nose, is that lever pressing? What if the rat stands on the lever while sniffing the ceiling of the cage and, in the process, "accidentally" depresses the lever? What seems to be a clearly defined response—lever pressing—proves to be open to interpretation. To get around this problem, the psychologist may define lever pressing as any act sufficient to activate an electrical recording device connected to the lever. Thus, if the rat touches the lever, but does not exert sufficient pressure to activate the recording device, the rat has not made a lever press response. If, on the other hand, the rat presses the lever with enough force to activate the recorder, then the rat has made a lever press response.

One criticism of studies that define behavior in such highly specific ways is that the behavior studied is not representative of behavior in general. Lever pressing and other such simple responses are said to be fundamentally different from everyday, complex acts such as studying, working, dating, quarreling, or going to the dentist. But we cannot assume that two kinds of behavior are fundamentally different merely because one is more complex than the other. The question must be submitted to empirical test, that is, to direct observation. This is often done by establishing a principle in the laboratory using some very simple response, such as lever pressing, and then applying the principle to more complex behavior, such as dating. In general, such studies suggest that the principles that apply to simple responses also apply to more complex forms of behavior.

Learning involves a change in behavior that is due to experience; let us now examine the environmental changes that compose experiences.

Stimulus Events

All organisms live in changing environments, but some changes are more important than others. We are exposed daily to ultraviolet light, radio waves, radon gas, neutrinos, and all sorts of other physical events. Some of these events have important effects upon our bodies, yet they do not noticeably affect behavior, at least not directly. For our purposes, then, the term *experience* refers only to events that affect, or are capable of affecting, behavior. Such events may be said to stimulate behavior, so they are called **stimulus events,** or, more simply, **stimuli.**

It is impossible to determine whether a particular event is a stimulus for a particular individual without determining its effect upon that individual. The sonic boom of a jet plane flying overhead may seem a clear example of a stimulus, but it may not be a stimulus for snakes, which are deaf, or for a person who has suffered a hearing loss. Similarly, a mouse hiding in the grass a thousand yards away may not be a stimulus for a person, but it may be for a hawk. And exposure to low levels of X-radiation may have no effect upon a rat's behavior, in which case it is not a stimulus; but a slightly higher dose of X-radiation that induces the rat to vomit is a stimulus.

Various characteristics determine the power stimuli are capable of exerting over behavior. Two characteristics are particularly important. Intensity refers to the amount of energy expended in the appearance of the stimulus. In ordinary terms, intensity refers to strength: loudness, brightness, heaviness, and so on. In general, the more intense a stimulus, the more likely it is to evoke some sort of response. Often, it is not the absolute intensity of a stimulus that matters so much as its relative intensity—the intensity of that stimulus compared to other stimuli. For instance, you may answer when someone calls your name on a quiet street, but on a noisy subway car, the same greeting may go unheard.

A second important stimulus characteristic is duration. The power of a stimulus to affect behavior is related to how long the stimulus lasts. If its duration is very short, say, a very brief flash of light, the organism may behave as if the event never occurred; if, on the other hand, it continues indefinitely, as in the case of the background hum of an air conditioner, it may lose its ability to affect behavior.

Although it is proper to analyze individual stimuli in this way, adaptation ordinarily is not a response to a single stimulus event, but to a recurring *pattern* of events. In studying learning, we will be concerned chiefly with the characteristics of these patterns and the ways in which they affect behavior.

Stimulus Patterns   One characteristic of stimulus patterns is **contiguity,** or nearness, which can refer either to time or to space. **Temporal contiguity** refers to the extent to which events occur near each other in time. A bird's song, for example, consists of a series of notes that follow one another in close succession. Similarly, the dinner bell and the appearance of food on the table occur close together, if not simultaneously. Temporal contiguity has long been an important topic in the study of learning, and when psychologists use the term *contiguity,* they generally mean temporal contiguity. It is clear, however, that **spatial contiguity,** or the nearness of events in space, also is important to learning. A world in which a bird's song came from a bush behind us even while the bird was perched in a tree before us might be a difficult world in which to learn.

Another important characteristic of stimulus patterns is **contingency.** A contingency is said to exist between events when one depends upon the other. It is a kind of if-then statement about the environment: *If* the bell sounds, *then* dinner will soon be served; *if* I study hard tonight, *then* I will do well on the test tomorrow. An event that is **stimulus contingent** is one that occurs *if and only if* a particular stimulus occurs; in this case, the event is contingent upon the stimulus. For instance, a traffic light turns red if and only if the yellow light has been on. In the laboratory, a psychologist may arrange a rat's environment so that food appears in a tray if and only if a buzzer is sounding. An event that is **response contingent** is one that occurs *if and only if* a particular response occurs; in this case, the event is contingent upon the response. For example, a traffic ticket is written after a person goes through an intersection if and only if the light is red as he enters the intersection. In the laboratory, a psychologist may arrange a rat's environment so that food will appear in a tray if and only if the rat has pressed a lever.

MEASURING LEARNING

One sort of behavior change is a change in the topography of a response, which refers to the form a response takes. In the laboratory, we look for changes in the topography of simple responses. When a rat learns to press a lever, the topography of its behavior with respect to the lever changes. At first, it may press the lever in a variety of ways: standing on it with both front legs; sitting on it; depressing it with its nose; and so on. But typically, after a while, we see changes in the character of its lever pressing. The rat's behavior becomes simpler, smoother, more efficient, less variable. Eventually, the rat sits before the lever and presses it with one paw. This transformation is what is meant by a change in the topography of a response (see Figure 2-1).

We can observe the same phenomenon outside the laboratory. One difference between a novice ice skater and an expert is the form their behavior takes. Both may move across the ice without incident, but while the expert glides with ease and grace, the novice's movements are halting and clumsy. As the novice becomes more graceful and efficient, we say that he or she has learned. It is, in large part, to

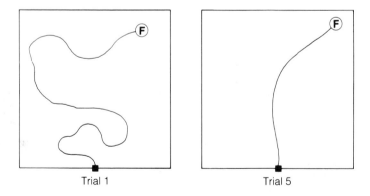

Trial 1   Trial 5

Figure 2-1   Topography as a measure of learning. On the first trial, a cat wanders around the cage until it finally discovers the food (F); by the fifth trial, the cat goes immediately to the food. (Hypothetical data.)

these changes in the topography of behavior that we refer when we speak of learning to skate.

Another measure of learning is a change in the number of errors (see Figure 2-2). A rat is said to have learned to run a maze to the extent that the rat goes from start to finish without taking a wrong turn. Similarly, a student is said to have learned a spelling list when he can spell all the words correctly, that is, without errors. A reduction in the number of errors is therefore a good measure of learning.

We can also measure learning by noting changes in the amplitude, or strength, of a response. For example, in the laboratory, rats will learn to press a lever for food. If the resistance of the lever is then increased, so that greater force is required to depress the lever, the rat will learn to increase the pressure it exerts. The increase in the pres-

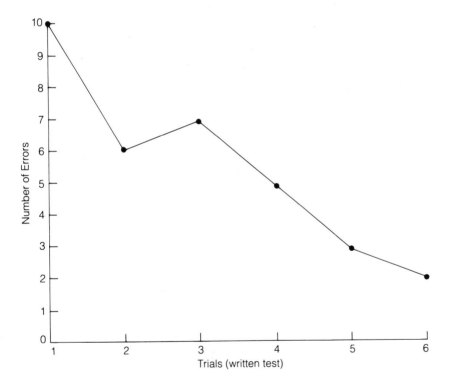

Figure 2-2   Errors as a measure of learning. The first time a driver takes the written test, he or she makes a number of errors. On succeeding tests, the driver makes fewer and fewer errors. The reduction in errors reflects learning. (Hypothetical data.)

sure exerted is a change in the amplitude of the lever press response and is one measure of learning (see Figure 2-3). The same sort of process occurs outside of the laboratory. Having taught a dog to bark on command, we can then teach it to bark more softly. Children often learn the opposite tactic: If ignored when they ask a question softly, they learn to ask questions loudly.

A change in the speed with which a response is made also indicates learning. The rat that has learned to run a maze reaches the goal faster than an untrained rat (see Figure 2-4). Likewise, the novice typist takes a long time to type a sentence, while the expert does it quickly.

A similar measure of learning is a change in response latency, which refers to the time that passes before a response begins to occur. We will see in the next chapter that a dog can be taught to salivate at the sound of a bell. As the training proceeds, the interval between the

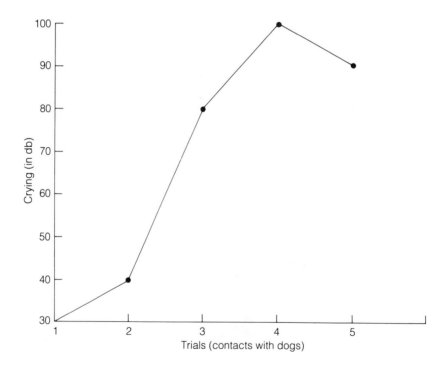

Figure 2-3   Response strength as a measure of learning. The increase in the strength of a child's cries (expressed in decibels, db) indicates that the child has acquired a fear of dogs. (Hypothetical data.)

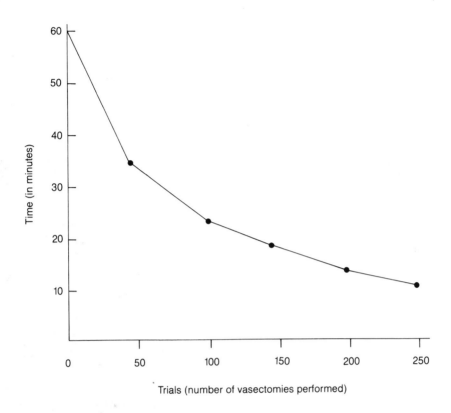

Figure 2-4   Speed as a measure of learning. The decrease in the time it takes a surgeon to perform an operation reflects (we all hope) learning. (Hypothetical data.)

bell and the first drop of saliva gets shorter, thus indicating that learning has occurred (see Figure 2-5).

Often, learning is measured as a change in the rate at which a response occurs. In the laboratory, a pigeon may be trained to peck a colored disk at a steady rate; the experimenter may then attempt to increase or decrease the rate of disk pecking. The change in response rate is a measure of learning. Similarly, a student who wants to break the habit of biting fingernails might keep a record of nail biting. Learning will have occurred if there is a decrease in the rate of nail biting.

The simplest way to record a change in response rate is to tally the number of times a response occurs. In the laboratory, we can do this by means of a **cumulative recorder** (see Figure 2-6). With this

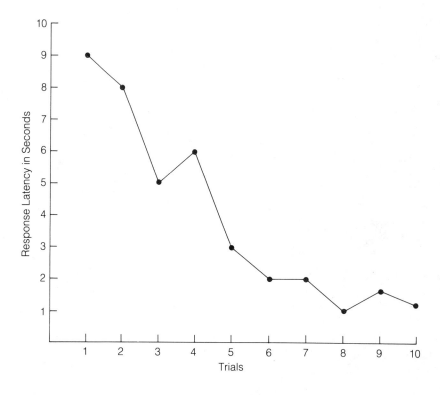

Figure 2-5   Latency as a measure of learning. The decrease in the time elapsed before a response begins indicates learning. (Hypothetical data.)

device, every occurrence of the response under study is recorded by the movement of an inked pen on a sheet of paper, which moves under the pen at a steady pace. So long as the response in question does not occur, the pen makes a straight line along the length of the paper. When a response occurs, the pen moves a short distance across the paper, providing a **cumulative record** of the response. The faster the response rate, the more pen movements and the steeper the ink line; the slower the response rate, the more nearly level the line.

Outside of the laboratory, recording response rate often is more difficult. Suppose, for instance, that we want to determine the effect of a teacher's efforts to reduce the number of times students leave their seats. We might sit in a classroom and keep a running count of the number of times the students get out of their seats, but with 30 students in a class, it may be difficult to make accurate observations.

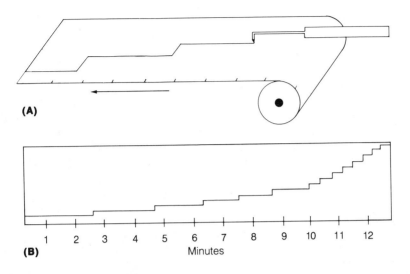

Figure 2-6   Rate as a measure of learning. If a sheet of paper moves under a needle at a steady rate, and if the needle moves at a right angle to the direction of movement each time an organism responds (A), the sheet will provide a cumulative record of the responses (B). A change in the rate at which a behavior occurs suggests learning.

One solution is to observe the behavior of a few randomly selected students for periods of, say, 20 minutes at a time, three times a day. This procedure is called response sampling. Assuming that the students and the time intervals selected are representative of the behavior of the entire class throughout the day, such sampling should yield results very similar to those that would be obtained by recording the responses of all the students.

Yet another measure of learning is a change in response probability, or the likelihood that a response will occur. There is a close connection between response probability and response rate. Assume that a pigeon pecks a disk at the rate of 12 times a minute, or an average of once every 5 seconds. Now, suppose that the pigeon increases its rate of pecking to 60 times a minute, an average of once every second. Clearly, there has been a marked increase in the rate of response, but if the bird responds at a steady pace, there also has been a corresponding increase in the probability that a response will occur in any 5-second interval. Here probability is expressed by its relationship to a time period; other times, probability is expressed by its relationship to another response. For instance, suppose a pigeon may peck either a red disk or a green disk. Initially, it pecks the red disk 8 times for every time it pecks the green disk, so the probability of the red disk being pecked is 8 to 1. But if we train the pigeon to prefer the green disk, we have changed the relative probabilities of the two responses.

The use of various kinds of behavior change as measures of learning rests on the simple fact that until an organism's behavior changes, there is no evidence of learning. But is it fair to state that, simply because an organism's behavior has not changed, it has not learned? This question gets at the distinction between learning and performance.

LEARNING AND PERFORMANCE

The fact that a rat does not run a maze does not mean that it has not learned how to do so. Nor can we assume that a child is unable to read merely because she fails to do so when asked. There is a difference between what an organism *can* do and what it *does*, between learning a response and performing it. Because of this, Gregory Kimble (1961) has argued that learning really means acquiring the *potential* to behave a certain way rather than an actual change in behavior.

The problem with this definition is that there is no way of measuring potential. We cannot open up a rat's head and determine from a study of its brain whether it has learned to press a lever. We can ask a person whether he or she has learned how to read, but until the person actually *does* read, we cannot be sure that the answer given is accurate. We must therefore define learning in terms of observable changes in behavior.

We have seen that it is possible to define behavior and experience in terms of specific responses and stimuli. Once this is done, it is possible to investigate learning in a systematic way. Let us now examine some of the research designs used to study learning.

RESEARCH DESIGNS

Group Design

One way to study learning is through **group design** experiments. In group designs, the researcher provides some subjects (the experimental group) with a particular experience and compares their behavior with that of similar subjects (the control group) that have not had that experience. Suppose that we wished to study the effects of response-contingent shocks on scratching. We might put a rat into a cage and deliver a shock through the cage floor each time the rat scratched itself. For comparison purposes, we might put another rat into a similar cage but deliver no shocks. We would repeat this procedure with all of the rats in the experimental and control groups and then compare the number of times the rats in each group scratched themselves under these different conditions (see Figure 2-7).

To rule out the possibility that any shock would modify the rate of scratching, we might give the control rats noncontingent shocks—shocks that are not dependent upon scratching. One way to do this would be to connect the floors of the two cages so that whenever the experimental rat was contingently shocked, the control rat would also receive a shock, regardless of what it was doing. This use of a **yoked control** would allow us to distinguish between the effects of contingent and noncontingent events.

The essential element of a group design is that subjects that have been exposed to some experience are compared to other subjects that have not had that experience. Any differences in their behavior are then attributed to differences in their respective experiences. Group

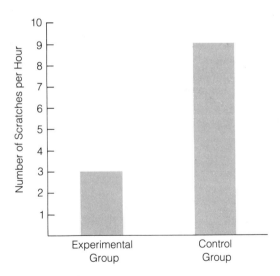

Figure 2-7   Typical presentation of group design data. Mean number of responses (scratches) per hour in experimental (response-contingent shocks) group, and in control (no shocks) group. (Hypothetical data.)

designs rest upon the assumption that the subjects being compared are very similar and that any differences in their behavior are therefore attributable to the experimental treatment. It would not do, for example, to compare bright rats with dull ones, healthy rats with ill ones, old rats with young ones, or aggressive rats with passive ones. To minimize such differences, each subject is randomly assigned to one of the two groups. Through such **random assignment,** any pretreatment differences among the animals should be distributed more or less equally between the two groups. With small groups, even random assignment leaves open the possibility of intergroup differences, so group design studies usually include at least 10 subjects in each group.

One way to keep the number of subjects down (which is desirable because it saves both time and money) is to systematically reduce the differences among the subjects through a procedure known as **matched sampling.** Rats may be matched for age, sex, and weight quite easily. Human subjects can be matched for these variables, and also for IQ, educational level, and socioeconomic background. Genetic differences may be reduced by using littermates (in the case of rats) and identical twins (in the case of humans).

Once the results of a group experiment are in, they must be submitted to statistical analysis to determine how much of the difference between the groups is attributable to the treatment rather than to extraneous differences among the subjects. Statistical analysis depends upon the assumption that the two groups of subjects are the same in all essentials other than the experimental treatment. If this assumption is in error (if, for example, the experimental group subjects happen to be, on average, faster learners), then the results will be spurious. The only sure-fire way of verifying that the results of a group design experiment are not spurious is to repeat the experiment with new subjects.

Single Subject Design

An alternative to the group design is the **single subject design.** In this case, a single subject's behavior is observed before the experimental treatment, and then during or after it. To study the effects of response-contingent shocks on scratching, we might put a rat into a cage and record the number of times it scratched itself in a given period. Then we might administer shocks contingent upon scratching and note the number of times the rat scratched itself. By comparing the rat's behavior during the two periods, we could see whether the experimental treatment had any effect. Further, we could verify the findings of such an experiment by discontinuing the response-contingent shocks and observing the rat's behavior to see if it reverted to its original level.

The pretreatment observation period is known as the **baseline period,** since it provides a baseline for comparison. It is usually labeled A, and the treatment period that follows it is usually labeled B. If the A and B periods yield different results, we can attribute those results to the experimental treatment. Because the same organism is used in both conditions, the results cannot be due to differences in subjects. However, it is conceivable that some extraneous variable coincidental to the experimental manipulation is responsible for the results. A rat could become ill during the experiment, for reasons having nothing to do with the treatment. The illness might reduce the rat's overall rate of responding, giving the illusion that shocks were reducing the rate of scratching. To rule out such possibilities, the experimenter reinstates the baseline (A) condition, in what is known as an **ABA design.** If the behavior returns to the previous baseline pattern, then the results have been replicated within the same experiment. The researcher can provide clear evidence that the behavior is under the control of the experimental treatment by repeatedly alternating between A and B conditions (see Figure 2-8).

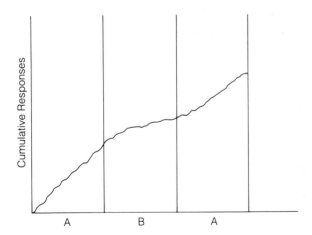

Figure 2-8   Typical presentation of single subject design data. The cumulative record shows a high rate of scratching (steep slope) when no shocks are given (A); a sharp reduction in scratching (shallow slope) when response-contingent shocks are given (B); and an increase in scratching when shocks are discontinued again (A). (Hypothetical data.)

The ABA design is especially useful for determining the effects of stimulus-contingent and response-contingent events on behavior since it allows us to see almost immediately whether a change in such contingencies will change behavior. Using the ABA design is a little like turning an electrical switch on and off to see whether it controls a given light. By switching back and forth between A and B conditions, researchers are able to demonstrate to what extent a response is controlled by the environmental manipulations under study.

Although other research designs may be used to study learning and behavior, the group and single subject experimental designs just described are the most common. Both group and single subject designs can be conducted with human or animal subjects. It is worth considering how psychologists go about deciding which subjects to use.

ANIMAL OR HUMAN SUBJECTS?

If psychologists are interested primarily in understanding how *people* adapt to changes in the environment (and most of them are), then people would seem to be the logical choice of subjects for their experiments. Why, then, do psychologists so often study animals? One reason is that some psychologists are interested specifically in animal behavior in and of itself, but the principle reason is that animals have certain important advantages over humans as research subjects.

First, since experimental animals usually are purchased from research supply companies, their genetic histories are fairly well known. It is, of course, impossible to obtain the same sort of control over genetic variability in humans. This means that experimental findings from animal subjects are less likely to be by-products of hereditary differences than are similar findings from human subjects.

Second, animals can be housed in environments that are far less complex and more uniform than their natural environments, thus essentially ruling out the influence of unintended learning experiences. Once again, this sort of control cannot be achieved with human subjects.

Third, it is possible to do research with animals that it would be unethical to do with human beings. It might be interesting to know whether a certain kind of experience would make people depressed, give them ulcers, or cause them to strike their neighbors; but psychologists are understandably unwilling to perform such experiments on people for ethical reasons. Ethical problems exist in the use of animals (see Animal Rights and Human Suffering box), but most psycholo-

ANIMAL RIGHTS AND HUMAN SUFFERING

Autism is a devastating disease of uncertain origin that strikes at or soon after birth. Its symptoms include all sorts of bizarre behavior: endless rocking back and forth, hand flapping, avoidance of eye contact, severe tantrums, little or no normal speech, and, in about 10 percent of cases, self-mutilation. The treatment of such children used to consist of little more than warehousing them in institutions. Those who tried to injure themselves or others were often tied spread-eagle to their beds; that way they couldn't hurt themselves or anyone else. It wasn't that no one cared; the problem was that no one knew what else to do. There is still no known cure for autism, but today most autistic children can be helped, and many can reach normal or near-normal levels of functioning (see Lovaas, 1987).

The treatment techniques that have proved most effective are those based on the principles of learning and behavior you will read about in this book. Those principles were discovered largely through research with animals. Some of that research involved exposing animals to shocks or other unpleasant experiences. The American Psychological Association provides guidelines for animal research to ensure that animals do not suffer unnecessarily. Nevertheless, some animal rights advocates have been critical of animal research by psychologists, arguing that this research produces no results of practical value to human beings. But it is in large part this research that has enabled psychologists to help those who suffer from autism, phobias, hypertension, ulcers, depression, schizophrenia, and countless other disorders. (For more on this, see Miller, 1985.)

We could, of course, abandon animal research. And we could go back to tying autistic children spread-eagle to their beds.

gists believe that it is reasonable to induce depression, ulcers, or violent behavior in pigeons or rats if doing so may lead to discoveries that will prevent or alleviate analogous problems in human beings. (For an excellent discussion of this issue, see Miller, 1985).

Because of these, and other, advantages, many researchers rely upon animals for their subjects. In experiments on learning, by far the most popular subjects are rats and pigeons. This preference has largely to do with economics and convenience: Rats and pigeons are inexpensive to purchase and maintain, and they take up little space. Many lower species, such as worms, sponges, and fish, share these advantages but are less desirable because they are less adept at learning. Higher animals, particularly monkeys and apes, would be preferable to rats and pigeons because they more closely resemble humans in learning ability, but they are more expensive and more difficult to care for properly.

Despite their advantages over humans as research subjects, the use of animals has been criticized. One complaint is that the results obtained with animals may not provide information that is relevant to people (see, especially, Schwartz, 1984; Schwartz & Lacey, 1982). People, after all, are not rats. The standard reply to this criticism is that we cannot assume that a finding does *not* apply to humans merely because the subjects studied are lower animals. This is a question that must be submitted to empirical test. As you will see in the chapters that follow, many experiments conducted with both animals and humans have yielded nearly identical results. Since study after study has produced comparable results for humans and lower species, we have little reason to believe that "rat psychology" is irrelevant to human behavior. Where differences do appear, they provide valuable insight into the differential roles of genetic evolution and learning in the adaptation of various species (see Chapter 10 for further discussion of this topic).

Thus, the choice of subjects is dependent upon a number of considerations. It is less a matter of which subject is the best than of which is the best in a given situation. In general, animals are used when the goal is to study the effects of a particular kind of environment on behavior in the most rigorous manner possible. Human subjects are used when the goal is to verify that a principle that has emerged from animal studies applies as well to humans, when the goal is to apply an established principle to solve a practical problem, or when the problem to be studied is best suited to humans (as, for example, in the case of speech).

This brief discussion of how learning is studied leaves much unsaid, but it should help you to understand the research that will be reported in the remaining chapters.

QUESTIONS ABOUT LEARNING

The study of learning and behavior may be viewed as an effort to answer certain key questions. The remaining chapters introduce these questions and summarize the answers that researchers have thus far been able to provide. It may be helpful to review these questions here, so that you will better understand the course upon which we are set.

Procedures   The first, and most important, question to be considered is, What kinds of experiences (i.e., changes in the environment) produce changes in behavior? As you have seen, learning researchers define experience in terms of stimulus-contingent and response-contingent events in an organism's environment. In the natural environment, these contingencies occur as the result of physical or biological forces; in the laboratory, they are arranged by the researcher. For research purposes, then, experience refers to specific *procedures* carried out by an experimenter. Thus, our question may be rephrased as follows: What kinds of experimental procedures will change behavior, and why?

Three major procedures have been identified—Pavlovian, instrumental, and vicarious—which will be dealt with in Chapters 3, 4, and 5, respectively. Although the term *procedure* refers to an artificial manipulation of the environment, the procedures studied are thought to be analogous to naturally occurring experiences. In fact, we will see that it is often possible to identify similarities between an experimental procedure and changes that occur naturally in an organism's surroundings.

Generalization and Discrimination   Another important question for learning researchers is, How does a procedure that changes behavior in one environment affect behavior in another environment? Suppose that a rat is placed into an experimental cage and is given an electric shock each time it scratches itself, and that this procedure reduces the frequency of scratching responses. What will happen if the rat is now put into another environment, such as a cage with a wooden floor? Will the rat continue to scratch at a low rate, or will it, in its new surroundings, revert to its previous rate of scratching? To put it another way: assuming that an organism adapts to a situation, will that adaptation carry over to a somewhat different situation? If the experimental procedure carries over to the new environment, we say that generalization has occurred; if the rat reverts to its pretraining pattern of responding, we say that discrimination has occurred. Since adaptation often depends upon generalizing or discriminating appropriately, understanding what determines which the organism will do following an experience is important to an understanding of behavior. We will take up this issue in Chapter 6.

Schedules of Reinforcement   One measure of learning is a change in the rate of responding. The rate of responding varies with the pattern of response consequences, called a reinforcement schedule. Basically, this has to do with how often a response is rewarded. In addition to changing response rates, reinforcement schedules also produce other changes in behavior. Schedules and their effects will be discussed in Chapter 7.

Extinction and Forgetting   Although extinction and forgetting are *not* synonymous terms, both have to do with a decline in the strength, frequency, or probability of a response. Once a change in behavior has occurred, it is appropriate to ask, Under what circumstances will it tend to disappear? Chapter 8 will attempt to answer this question.

Cognition   Throughout most of this book, we will be examining the effects of experience on overt behavior. But psychologists are increasingly inclined to ask, What is the role of experience in covert (private) behavior? Many people assume that thoughts are fundamentally different from overt (public) behavior. Remembering, insightful problem solving, psychotic delusions and hallucinations, and other forms of covert behavior are usually said to be products of mysterious brain events or, more often, products of the "mind." In Chapter 9, we will examine the extent to which thoughts, like overt behavior, are products of interactions with the environment.

Limits of Learning   What are the limits of learning as an adaptive mechanism? Researchers who focus on this question acknowledge that learning is a marvelous invention for coping with environmental change, but they also recognize that there is only so much that can be accomplished through learning; they seek to understand these limits. We will discuss their work in Chapter 10.

These, then, are the principal questions that fascinate learning researchers. The chapters that follow will attempt to offer some insight into their answers, and into the process of adaptation called learning.

SUMMARY

Before beginning the study of learning, it is necessary to have a clear understanding of certain key terms. Learning is defined as a change in behavior due to experience. A response is the action of muscles or glands. Changes in behavior can be measured in terms of changes in topography, number of errors, or changes in the amplitude, speed, rate (often recorded on a cumulative recorder), or probability of a response.

To say that learning is *due to experience* means that it is brought about by changes in the environment called stimuli. The intensity and duration of a stimulus, as well as the pattern of stimulus events, are important determinants of its effects. In particular, temporal and spatial contiguity are important, as is the degree to which stimuli are stimulus-contingent or response-contingent.

Learning usually is studied by means of one of two research designs. Group designs involve relatively large numbers of subjects. Some of these subjects are given an experience, and others are not; the effects of the experience are judged by statistical comparison of the behavior of the two groups. Extraneous differences between groups may be reduced through random assignment or by matching. The use of yoked controls helps to determine whether the contingent nature of an event is important.

Single subject designs involve relatively small numbers of subjects. Their behavior is observed before and after some change in the environment, and the effects of this experience are judged by noting changes in the subject's behavior. Sometimes the original condition is reinstated, in which case it becomes an ABA design.

Both animals and people may serve as subjects for experiments on learning. Both have certain limitations. Animals make greater control possible but leave open the possibility that the results do not apply to humans. Often, basic research is done on animals, and the principles derived from this research are tested on humans in applied settings.

The remainder of this book will attempt to provide some insight into the answers now available to certain fundamental questions about learning and behavior. These questions involve the procedures that have been found to change behavior; the circumstances under which learning in one situation carries over to another situation; the effects of different patterns of stimulus events; the durability of learned behavior; the role of learning in thinking; and the limitations of learning.

If you are typical of students taking a first course in learning, much of the material in this chapter is new to you. Be sure you understand what you have read before going on to the following chapters. An understanding of the methods of studying behavior described in this chapter is assumed in each subsequent chapter. The natural science approach to behavior that these methods represent is very different from the commonsense approach to behavior used by most students. Learning this new approach will give you a new perspective on animal and human behavior.

REVIEW QUESTIONS

1. Define the following terms in your own words. Give an example or illustration of each that is *not* provided in the text.

stimulus	random assignment
response	baseline
cumulative recorder	topography
response sampling	response rate

2. In what sense can an organism's interactions with its environment be said to constitute a kind of communication?

3. What are the principle *similarities* between single subject and group designs?

4. When would it *not* be possible to use an ABA design in the study of behavior?

5. Consider two worlds. In one world, related events (such as the movement of a woman's lips and the sound of her voice) are temporally contiguous but not spatially contiguous. In the second world, the opposite condition prevails. In which world would it be more difficult to learn? Why?

6. Explain why psychologists often speak of "responses" rather than "behavior."

7. Give an example of the use of a yoked control in a single subject design.

8. A psychologist studies maze learning in rats by running 50 rats through a maze, one at a time. He does this 10 times. Then he computes the average time for all rats on each run and plots this on a graph. Is this a group or single subject design?

9. A hawk appears outside my window (a very unusual event), and within seconds, the phone rings. Is there a contingency between the appearance of the bird and the ringing of the phone?

10. Explain how response rate is reflected on a cumulative recorder.

11. What is the chief virtue of response sampling?

12. Whether an event is defined as a stimulus or not depends upon its effects on an organism's behavior. Explain why.

13. A person says that he has a toothache. Does the term *toothache* refer to a stimulus? If so, what is it?

14. What is wrong with defining learning as the acquisition of new behavior?

15. Why does our definition of learning imply that control of the environment means control of behavior?

16. Someone insults you. You get angry and reply in kind. Is your behavior operant or respondent?

17. You are attempting to discover learning principles by studying the effects of experience on the eye blink. A friend says that eye blinking is a trivial kind of behavior, not worth studying. How do you defend your work against this criticism?

18. A friend says that psychology relies too much upon animal studies and adds that "You can't tell anything about people from research on rats." How could you defend "rat psychology" against this criticism?

19. Explain the distinction between learning and performance.

20. Some psychologists argue that learning is a change in the potential for behavior. Discuss the virtues and weaknesses of this definition.

SUGGESTED READINGS

An interesting and highly readable little book on research methods is *Psychological Research: An Introduction* (1962) by Arthur Bachrach. The author provides an insider's view of behavioral research. B. F. Skinner's 1956 article "A Case History in Scientific Method" is also well worth reading.

THREE

■

Pavlovian Procedures

BEGINNINGS

Around the beginning of this century, a Russian scientist reached a turning point in his career. He had spent several years doing research on the physiology of digestion, important research that would one day win him a Nobel prize. But at middle age, still relatively unknown, he wrestled with one of the most difficult choices of his career: Should he continue his present line of research or take up a new problem, one that might lead nowhere and that some of his colleagues might regard as an unfit subject for a respectable scientist? The safe thing to do, the easy thing to do, would have been to continue the work he had started. But if he had, psychology would have suffered an immeasurable loss, and the chances are that neither you nor I would ever have heard of Ivan Petrovich Pavlov.

The problem Pavlov decided to study was called the *psychic reflex*. But to understand why he found this phenomenon so intriguing, we have to backtrack a bit and look at his earlier work. Pavlov started his career with research on the circulatory system and then moved on to the physiology of digestion. He developed special surgical procedures that enabled him to study the digestive processes of animals over long periods of time by redirecting an animal's digestive juices to the surface of the body, where they could be measured. He used this technique to study the salivary glands, stomach, liver, pancreas, and parts of the intestine. In the case of the salivary glands, the procedure was a relatively simple operation. The salivary duct of an animal, often a dog, was detached from its usual place inside the mouth and directed through an incision in the cheek to the outside of the body. When the dog salivated, the saliva would flow through the duct to the outside of the dog's cheek, where it could be collected in a small glass tube. With animals prepared in this way, Pavlov could make precise observations of the actions of the glands under various conditions (see Figure 3-1).

Pavlov's goal was to understand how the body breaks down food into chemicals that can be absorbed into the blood. This process starts with the salivary reflex: When food is taken into the mouth, it triggers the flow of saliva. The saliva dilutes the food and produces substances that start breaking it down chemically. In a typical experiment on the salivary reflex, Pavlov would bring a dog into the laboratory, strap it into a stand, put food into its mouth, and observe the result. Pavlov was fascinated by the adaptability of the glands. He found, for instance, that if he gave a dog dry, hard food, there was a heavy flow of saliva; if he gave the animal watery food, there was very little saliva. And if he put an inedible substance into the dog's mouth, the amount of saliva produced depended upon the amount needed to eject the substance: A marble evoked very little saliva, while sand resulted in a great supply. So the reflex action of the gland depended upon the nature of the stimulus. Each time, the gland responded according to the need. "It is as if," said Pavlov, "the glands possessed a 'kind of intelligence'" (quoted in Cuny, 1962, p. 26).

Figure 3-1   Surgical preparation for studying the salivary reflex. When the dog salivated, the saliva would collect in a glass tube attached to the dog's cheek. This way the strength of the salivary response could be precisely measured.

IVAN PAVLOV: AN EXPERIMENTER FROM HEAD TO FOOT

George Bernard Shaw said he was the biggest fool he knew. H. G. Wells thought he was one of the greatest geniuses of all time. But Ivan Pavlov described himself as "an experimenter from head to foot" (in Wells, 1956, p. 38). Of the three characterizations, Pavlov's was probably the most accurate. His discoveries were much more important, and much less commonsensical, than Shaw believed, but they also failed to bring the utopia that Wells anticipated. There is, however, no denying that Pavlov was a brilliant experimenter, a zealot fiercely committed to the religion of Science.

Pavlov was born in Ryazan, a small peasant village in Russia, in September, 1849, 10 years before the publication of Darwin's *Origin of Species*. His father was a poor priest who had to keep a garden to ensure that his family would eat. As a boy, Pavlov showed little promise of later greatness. His academic performance was mediocre, and probably few people in his community expected him to become a famous scientist—or a famous anything else, for that matter.

He grew up to be slim, agile, athletic, and incredibly energetic, with blue eyes, curly hair, a long beard, and the fire of genius. As Professor Pavlov, he was sometimes an impatient, stubborn, and eccentric man who waved his hands excitedly when he spoke to others. If one of his assistants botched an experiment, he might explode in a rage; half an hour later, he would have forgotten all about it. But of all the things that one might say about Pavlov, surely the most important is this: He was an experimenter. Nothing was so important, nothing so precious, as his experiments. "Remember," he once wrote, "science requires your whole life. And even if you had two lives they would not be enough. Science demands . . . the utmost effort and supreme passion" (quoted in Cuny, 1962, p. 160).

Pavlov's passion for science stayed with him throughout his long life. Age slowed him, of course, but not the way it slows others. Ever the experimenter, he observed the toll that time had taken and noted it with objective interest. On his deathbed, he was the observer, as well as the subject, of a final experiment. As life slowly left him, he described his sensations to a neuropathologist so that these data might be recorded for the benefit of science. Somehow he kept this up almost until the end. One report of Pavlov's death (in Gantt, 1941) relates that in those last moments he slept a bit, then awoke, raised himself on his elbows, and said, "It is time to get up! Help me, I must get dressed!" (p. 35). Then it was over; he was dead.

The effort was understandable. He had been away from his laboratory, from his science, for nearly six whole days.

The cleverness of the glands did not end there, however. When an animal had been fed a number of times, it began to salivate *before* anything was put into its mouth. In fact, it might start salivating as soon as it entered the laboratory. Pavlov, like others of his day, assumed that these "psychic secretions" were caused by the thoughts, memories, or wishes of the animal. The ancient Greeks had noticed that merely talking about food often made a person's mouth water. What fascinated Pavlov was that such psychic reflexes did not occur when the animals were first brought into the laboratory, but only after they had been fed there repeatedly. How could this be? How could experience alter the action of a gland?

This question preoccupied Pavlov to the point of making him shift his attention to psychic reflexes. It was not an easy decision. It was extremely important to him that he retain his identity as a physiologist. And if psychic reflexes really were the products of the mind, of the inner life of the animal, then they were not a fit subject for a physiologist. On the other hand, if psychic reflexes involved glands, and those glands were involved in digestion, then why should a physiologist not study them? Pavlov argued with himself along these lines, back and forth; finally, he could no longer resist the challenge. He had to understand these psychic reflexes.

BASIC PROCEDURES

Pavlov (1927) began by observing: "I started to record all the external stimuli falling on the animal at the time its reflex reaction was manifested . . . at the same time recording all changes in the reaction of the animal" (p. 6). At first, the only reaction was the ordinary salivary reflex: When food was put into a dog's mouth, it salivated. But after a while, the animal would salivate before receiving food. By observing the "external stimuli falling on the animal," Pavlov was able to see what triggered these psychic secretions (see Figure 3-2). He noticed, for instance, that the sight or smell of food would cause the dog to salivate. In addition, other things besides the food itself could elicit salivation. "Even the vessel from which the food has been given is sufficient . . . and, further, the secretions may be provoked even by the sight of the person who brought the vessel, or by the sound of his footsteps" (1927, p. 13).

There are, Pavlov concluded, two distinct kinds of reflexes. One kind is the inborn, unlearned, and usually permanent reflex, described in Chapter 1, that is found in virtually all members of a

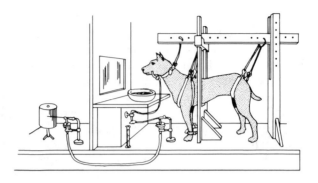

Figure 3-2   Pavlov's conditioning stand. Once a dog was strapped into a stand as shown, an experimenter could begin testing the effects of various stimuli on the salivary response. Saliva could be collected in a glass tube at the fistula (as shown in Figure 3-1) or it could be directed by a tube to a graduated vial. In addition, a cumulative record of the total amount of saliva could be recorded by the movement of a needle on a revolving drum. See Pavlov, 1927, pp. 18–19. (From Yerkes & Morgulis, 1909.)

species and that varies little from individual to individual. The dog that salivates when food is put into its mouth manifests this type of reflex. Pavlov called these **unconditional reflexes,** since they occur more or less unconditionally. The second type of reflex is not present at birth but must be acquired through experience and is relatively impermanent. Because these psychic reflexes depend upon experience, they vary considerably from species to species and from individual to individual. The dog that salivates to the sound of a particular person's footsteps manifests this type of reflex. Pavlov called these **conditional reflexes,** since they "actually do depend on very many conditions" (Pavlov, 1927, p. 25). Pavlov admitted that other terms would have served as well: Unconditional reflexes might have been referred to as inborn, unlearned, or species reflexes; conditional reflexes could have been called acquired, learned, or individual reflexes. But the terms *conditional* and *unconditional* caught on and are still used today.*

An unconditional reflex consists of an **unconditional stimulus (US)** and the response that it evokes, the **unconditional response**

* *Many authors use the terms* conditioned *and* unconditioned. *The words* conditional *and* unconditional *are, however, closer to Pavlov's meaning (Gantt, 1966; Thorndike, 1931/1968), so these terms will be used here.*

(UR). Meat powder is an unconditional stimulus that reliably evokes the unconditional response of salivation:

$$US \longrightarrow UR$$

meat powder $\longrightarrow$ salivation

A conditional reflex consists of a **conditional stimulus (CS)** and the response it reliably evokes, the **conditional response (CR)**. When the sight of a food dish regularly evokes salivation, the food dish is a CS and salivating is a CR:

$$CS \longrightarrow CR$$

food dish $\longrightarrow$ salivation

Pavlov's next question was, How does a neutral stimulus—one that does not naturally evoke a reflex response—come to do so? How, for example, does the sight of a food dish become a CS for salivating? Pavlov had noticed that stimuli that were connected with food, such as the food dish and the handler who fed the dog, became conditional stimuli for salivating. He began conducting experiments to better understand the connection. In some experiments, he paired food with the sound of a metronome. At first, the ticking had no effect on salivation; but after the sound of the metronome had been repeatedly associated with food, the ticking began to elicit the salivary reflex. Pavlov found that virtually any stimulus could become a conditional stimulus if it were regularly paired with an unconditional stimulus. A rather bizarre example will illustrate the point. If you brush or scratch a dog, it may make a number of responses, but salivating is not likely to be one of them. As far as the salivary reflex is concerned, scratching is definitely a neutral stimulus. But a few bread crumbs placed on the tongue is an unconditional stimulus that elicits salivation:

$$US \longrightarrow UR$$

bread crumbs $\longrightarrow$ salivation

Now scratch the dog and immediately put bread crumbs into its mouth:

$$CS \longrightarrow US \longrightarrow UR$$

scratch $\longrightarrow$ bread crumbs $\longrightarrow$ salivation

Repeat this procedure several times and the dog will begin salivating when you scratch it:

$$CS \longrightarrow CR$$
$$scratch \longrightarrow salivation$$

Each pairing of CS* and US is one **trial,** and the procedure is known as **Pavlovian,** or **classical, conditioning.** It is important to note two things about the Pavlovian procedure. First, the presentation of the two stimuli is independent of the behavior of the organism; the CS and US are presented *regardless* of what the animal does. Second, the behavior involved is nearly always respondent (involuntary, reflexive) behavior, not operant (voluntary) behavior (see Chapter 2).

Pairing CS and US

Pavlovian conditioning involves the pairing of two stimuli, the CS and the US. But what exactly does *pairing* mean? There are four ways in which conditional and unconditional stimuli can be paired; in a sense, each procedure represents a different kind of Pavlovian conditioning.

In **trace conditioning,** the CS begins and ends before the US is presented (see Figure 3-3). In the laboratory, trace conditioning is often used to study eyelid conditioning in the rabbit. Typically, a buzzer sounds for, say 5 seconds, and then, perhaps a half second later, a puff of air is blown into the animal's eye, causing it to blink. After several such pairings of the buzzer and air, the rabbit blinks at the sound of the buzzer. Trace conditioning also occurs outside the laboratory: We see the flash of the lightning and, a moment later, we hear the crash of thunder; the dog barks and then lunges at our leg; the mother talks to her baby before offering the nipple. The identifying feature of trace conditioning is that the CS begins and ends before the US appears.

Delayed conditioning is similar to the trace procedure in that the CS begins before the US; the difference is that in delayed conditioning, the two stimuli overlap. That is, the US appears before the CS has disappeared. To apply the delayed procedure to eyelid conditioning, we might sound a buzzer for 5 seconds and, sometime during the

---

* Technically, the stimulus that is paired with the US is not a CS until it is capable of eliciting a CR, but it is customary to refer to such a stimulus as a CS from the first pairing with a US.

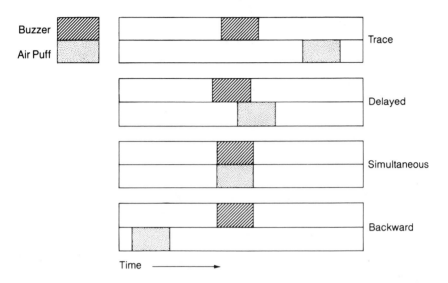

Time ⟶

Figure 3-3   Pairing CS and US. A CS (such as the sound of a buzzer) may precede, overlap with, occur simultaneously with, or follow a US (such as a puff of air). (See text for explanation.)

last 2 seconds that the buzzer is sounding, we might fire a puff of air into the rabbit's eye. Like trace conditioning, delayed conditioning often occurs outside the laboratory: We often hear the thunder before the lightning has faded from the sky; the dog may continue to snarl even as it bites; the mother may continue to talk softly as she nurses her baby. The defining characteristic of delayed conditioning is that the CS and US overlap.

Some psychologists distinguish between short-delay procedures and long-delay procedures. The difference refers to the length of time the CS is present before the US appears. In the short-delay procedure, the CS may be present for anywhere from a few milliseconds (thousandths of a second) to a few seconds before the US appears. A light may come on a tenth of a second before an electric current is applied to the grid floor of a rat's cage; both the light and the shock may continue for a few seconds. In the long-delay procedure, the CS may persist for several seconds or minutes before the US appears. A light may come on and remain on for 5 minutes before the current is applied to the cage floor; then both stimuli may continue for a second or two. Initially, short- and long-delay procedures produce similar results: A conditional response (such as an increase in heart rate) begins to appear soon after the CS appears. But in the case of long-delay conditioning, the CR latency (the interval between the CS and the CR) gradually *increases* until the CR appears just before the onset of the US. Apparently, what happens in long-delay conditioning is that the CS is not the stimulus presented by the experimenter (i.e., the light) but the combination of that stimulus and a given time interval. The animal learns to respond after the light has appeared *and* a given amount of time has elapsed.

Trace and delay procedures are the most effective, and therefore the most often used procedures in research. Two other arrangements are, however, possible.

In **simultaneous conditioning,** the CS and US coincide exactly. A sound and a puff of air can begin and end at precisely the same instant. The simultaneous appearance of CS and US also takes place in the natural environment: Thunder and lightning occur together if the storm is nearby. Simultaneous conditioning is a weak procedure for establishing a CR; in fact, if lightning always accompanied thunder but never preceded it, it is unlikely that a sudden flash of lightning would make us flinch in the least.

Finally, it is possible to arrange a situation so that the CS *follows* the US, a procedure called **backward conditioning.** For instance, a puff of air directed at a rabbit's eye could be followed by the sound of a buzzer. The US-CS sequence also can occur outside of the laboratory, as when a person sits on a splinter and *then* (having jumped up from the uncomfortable resting spot) sees the offending object. Moreover, such conditioning could have survival value, since an attack by a hidden predator is often followed by the sight, sound, and odor of the predator when it attacks (Keith-Lucas & Guttman, 1975).

Though such experiences might have survival value, there is some debate about whether the procedure actually produces conditional responses. Pavlov (1927) described some of the attempts made at backward conditioning in his laboratory. In one experiment, one of his assistants exposed a dog to the odor of vanilla after putting a mild acid into the dog's mouth. (The acid was a US that elicited salivation.) Acid and vanilla were paired 427 times, but the odor of vanilla did not become a CS for salivating. However, when another odor was presented *before* the acid, it became a CS after only 20 pairings. These results are typical of those obtained by others who have attempted backward conditioning. Nevertheless, some researchers, including Pavlov, have argued that backward conditioning is sometimes effective in establishing a CR.

For instance, T. Keith-Lucas and Norman Guttman (1975) obtained some evidence for backward conditioning in the rat. The researchers used a toy hedgehog as a CS, presenting it to the rat anywhere from 1 to 40 seconds following the onset of an electric shock. The US lasted just under 1 second and was presented while the animal ate; the CS remained present for 1 minute. The animals were given one US-CS pairing and were tested on the following day by presenting the toy hedgehog near the animal's food. (The assumption was that if conditioning had taken place, the animals would fear the CS and therefore avoid it.) The data revealed that presentation of the hedgehog 1, 5, or 10 seconds after shock onset resulted in greater avoidance of the hedgehog than in control animals.

The efficacy of backward conditioning is still debated. Some psychologists argue that experiments that purport to show backward conditioning either fail to control important variables (Cautela, 1965) or are really another form of conditioning entirely (Hall, 1976), while others (Spetch et al., 1981) conclude that backward conditioning works. In any case, backward conditioning is an inefficient procedure for producing a conditional response.

Measuring Pavlovian Learning

In most studies of Pavlovian conditioning, the CS and US are presented very close together. Since the US is by definition capable of evoking the UR, how is it possible to tell when conditioning has occurred? Suppose, for example, that you sound a tone for 2 seconds and then, 1 second after the tone stops, you put food into a dog's mouth. How can you tell when the dog is salivating to the tone as well as to the food? One way is to note when salivation begins. If the dog begins salivating after the CS but *before* the presentation of the US, conditioning has occurred. In this case, the amount of learning can be measured in terms of the latency of the response—the interval between the onset of the CS and the first appearance of saliva. As the number of CS-US pairings increases, the latency diminishes; the dog may begin salivating even before the tone has stopped sounding.

In some conditioning studies, the interval between CS onset and the appearance of the US is so short that it is very difficult to use response latency as a measure of learning. One way to test for conditioning in these situations is to use **test trials**. This involves presenting the CS alone (i.e., without the US) every now and then, perhaps on every 5th trial. If the dog salivates even when it gets no food, the salivation is a CR to the tone. Sometimes, test trials are presented at random intervals, with the CS presented alone perhaps on the 3rd trial, then on the 7th, the 12th, the 13th, the 20th, and so on. This procedure has the advantage that the subject cannot predict when the CS will appear alone (Rescorla, 1967). When test trials are used, the number of CRs in a block of, say, 10 test trials is plotted on a curve. Learning is thus represented as an increase in the probability of a CR.

Another way to measure Pavlovian learning is to measure the strength or amplitude of the CR. Pavlov noticed, for example, that the first CRs were apt to be very weak—a drop or two of saliva. But with repeated trials, the saliva flow in response to the CS increased rapidly.

Pseudoconditioning

One problem in studying Pavlovian conditioning is a phenomenon known as **pseudoconditioning** (Grether, 1938). Under certain circumstances, a stimulus may elicit a CR-like response for reasons that have nothing to do with the pairing of CS and US. Suppose that a nurse does a bad job of giving you an injection—a painful US—and then coughs loudly. Very likely you will jump, just as you did when you received the injection. Presumably, you jump in this situation because the painful injection has sensitized you to new stimuli. But note that the cough acts like a CS, even though it cannot be one. This is pseudoconditioning.

Pseudoconditioning is important because it can lead to the conclusion that conditioning has occurred when it has not. In the example just given, had a cough preceded as well as followed the injection, you might have concluded that the cough had become a CS by virtue of its single pairing with the injection. Thus, pseudoconditioning is a nuisance to psychologists studying Pavlovian conditioning. Pseudoconditioning can be ruled out, however, by presenting the CS and US to control group subjects in a random manner so that the stimuli sometimes appear alone and sometimes appear together (Rescorla, 1967). The performance of these subjects is then compared with experimental subjects for which the CS and US always (or at least often) appear together. If subjects in the experimental group perform differently than subjects in the control group, the difference in behavior may be attributed to conditioning.

HIGHER-ORDER CONDITIONING

The basic Pavlovian procedure, as you have seen, consists of pairing a neutral stimulus with an unconditional stimulus. It is easy to see how such a procedure might modify reflexive behavior in the natural environment. Anyone who has owned a dog has seen how stimuli regularly associated with food come to elicit salivation. But the pairing of neutral and unconditional stimuli is not the only Pavlovian procedure that is effective.

If a stimulus is paired with a well-established CS, the effect is much the same as if the stimulus had been paired with a US. This was demonstrated in Pavlov's laboratory by G. P. Frolov (in Pavlov, 1927). Frolov trained a dog to salivate at the sound of a ticking metronome. When the metronome was well established as a CS for salivating, Frolov paired it with another stimulus, the sight of a black square. Frolov would hold up the black square where the animal could see it and then start the metronome to ticking:

$$\text{CS} \longrightarrow \text{CS} \longrightarrow \text{CR}$$
$$\text{black square} \longrightarrow \text{metronome} \longrightarrow \text{salivation}$$

At first, the dog salivated at the sound of the metronome, but not at the sight of the black square. After several pairings of the black square and the metronome, however, the dog began salivating when it saw the square. The black square had become a CS for salivating even though it had never been associated with food:

$$\text{CS} \longrightarrow \text{CR}$$
$$\text{black square} \longrightarrow \text{salivation}$$

This procedure of pairing a stimulus with a well-established CS is called **higher-order conditioning.** Some researchers (e.g., Foursikov, in Pavlov, 1927) have attempted to carry this idea one step further by pairing a stimulus with a CS that has never been paired with a US. For example, if the pairing of the black square and the metronome results in the black square becoming an effective CS, we might then pair a bright light with the square. Note that in this case, we are attempting to establish a CS (the bright light) by pairing it with a CS (the black square) that has never been paired with food. Such efforts usually meet with limited success. Nevertheless, it is clear that Pavlovian conditioning can be achieved by pairing stimuli with well-established conditional stimuli. This greatly increases the importance of Pavlovian conditioning, because it means that many more stimuli can be effective in establishing conditional responses.

Pavlovian conditioning is not, of course, merely a procedure for training dogs to salivate. It has been found to be effective in modifying all sorts of reflexive behavior in all sorts of animals. Conditional responses—eye blinking, sneezing, knee jerking, infant sucking, leg flexion, sweating, and so on—have been developed in dozens of species, including cats, rats, mice, pigeons, monkeys, pigs, and humans. Although thousands of studies of Pavlovian conditioning have been carried out since Pavlov's early work, it remains a rich lode that psychologists continue to mine for insights into learning and behavior. Many of these studies have shed light on the role Pavlovian learning plays in the adaptation (and sometimes maladaptation) of organisms to their environments. Let us now consider research in three areas of particular interest: taste aversion, emotions, and psychosomatic illness.

TASTE AVERSION

The importance of food to survival is obvious, but the role of taste preferences in survival is a bit more subtle. One laboratory rat may prefer brand X food pellets while another prefers brand Y; and wild animals may have analogous preferences, but the importance of such preferences to survival is not as clear-cut. The fact is that while eating is essential to survival, it is also dangerous. Some tasty substances are quite toxic. It would be very helpful if animals had an innate tendency to avoid dangerous substances, but it appears that, for the most part, such behavior is learned. But how?

Much of the research on taste aversion has been done by John Garcia and his colleagues. In one of the early studies, Garcia and others (1955) gave rats a choice between ordinary tap water and saccharin-flavored water. The rats preferred the sweet-tasting water. Then the researchers exposed some of the rats to gamma radiation while they drank saccharin-flavored water. Several minutes later, the irradiated rats became nauseated. These rats later preferred tap water to saccharin-flavored water. Moreover, the higher the radiation level the rats were exposed to, the stronger their aversion to sweet water (see Figure 3-4). Presumably, sweet water had become a CS for nausea; in other words, it made the animals sick.

Garcia's study differs from Pavlov's work, and from most other research on Pavlovian conditioning, in two important ways. First, the CS and US were paired only once, whereas most studies of Pavlovian conditioning involve several, sometimes dozens, of pairings. Second, the interval between the CS and US was several minutes, whereas in most studies conditioning requires an interval of no more than a few

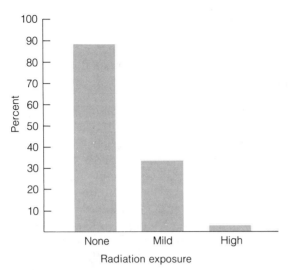

Figure 3-4   Taste aversion. Saccharin-flavored water consumed as a percentage of total water consumption. Exposure to radiation while drinking saccharin-flavored water produced an aversion for sweet-tasting water. (Compiled from data in Garcia et al., 1955.)

seconds. The fact that Garcia's effort produced conditioning under these circumstances has important implications if you consider the importance of conditioned taste aversion in the natural environment. Foods that can make an animal ill might also kill it or make it vulnerable to attack or disease, so one-trial learning can mean the difference between life and death. The animal that has a narrow escape and thereafter avoids eating that food is more likely to survive than one that must have 10 or 15 narrow escapes before it learns the lesson. Further, the efforts of poisonous foods often are delayed, sometimes for several hours. The animal that acquires an aversion for a toxic food despite such long delays has a distinct advantage over an animal that learns only if it becomes ill immediately after eating. Thus, the ability to acquire taste aversions quickly and in spite of long delays between eating and illness would seem to have considerable survival value.

Numerous studies support this view. Lincoln Brower (1971) has studied taste aversion in the blue jay, which feeds on all sorts of insects, including butterflies. In the larval stage, the monarch butterfly sometimes feeds upon a kind of milkweed that is harmless to the monarch but that renders it poisonous to other animals; it retains its poison in the butterfly stage. Wild blue jays generally refuse to eat monarch butterflies, but this tendency is not innate. If deprived of food for some time, the blue jay will eat a monarch, and if the insect is not poisonous, the bird will continue eating them. The jay quickly recovers its aversion, however, as soon as it eats a poisonous monarch. Sometimes, such jays later vomit at the mere sight of a monarch butterfly.

The survival value of such **conditioned taste aversions,** acquired through Pavlovian conditioning, is quite clear, and it is easy to see why the ability to learn from one experience despite a long interval between the CS and US would have evolved: Such learning ability is the next best thing to a natural immunity to the toxins involved. But conditioned taste aversion also works to the advantage of prey animals. For every poisonous monarch butterfly that succumbs to the attack of a jay, hundreds of others go unharmed because that bird thereafter avoids eating monarchs. Even monarchs that have not eaten the milkweed plant benefit as do butterflies that closely resemble the monarch.

There have long been reports of taste aversions in humans. The English philosopher John Locke (1690/1975; cited in Garcia, 1981) noted that a person who eats too much honey can feel ill merely at the mention of the word. Contemporary authors have reported that many people avoid eating certain foods that make them ill and are able to recall the incident that led to this aversion (Logue et al., 1981; Logue et al., 1983). As with other creatures, such aversions are particularly likely to be connected with illness (Garb & Stunkard, 1974). Martin Seligman (Seligman & Hager, 1972b) reports one such experience: He and his wife went out for a night at the opera. At dinner, Seligman had one of his favorite dishes, filet mignon with béarnaise sauce, and some time later, he became violently ill. His distress was due to flu, not the sauce (his wife had eaten the sauce without suffering), yet the next time he tried béarnaise sauce, he felt ill.

In modern societies, with their built-in protections against food poisoning, taste aversions are more likely to reflect coincidental pairings of particular foods and illness (as in Seligman's case) than poisoned foods that must be avoided. However, conditioned taste aversion has become a problem as the by-product of certain types of medical treatment. Many forms of cancer are treated with radiation or chemotherapy, each of which often causes nausea or vomiting (Burish & Carey, 1986). Ilene Bernstein (1978) wondered whether such experiences produced conditioned taste aversions. To find out, she conducted an experiment involving children under treatment for cancer. She divided the children into three groups. One group ate a novel-flavored ice cream, a combination of maple and black walnut flavors, before their regular chemotherapy treatment. The second group had chemotherapy without first having ice cream. The third group had ice cream but no chemotherapy. Two to 4 weeks later, the children were given a choice between eating the maple-walnut ice cream and playing a game. Of those in the first group, only 21 percent chose the ice cream, whereas 67 percent in the second group and 73 percent in the third group chose the dessert. Bernstein also asked the children about their diets and found that those who were undergoing chemotherapy were more likely to report aversions to specific foods than were those not undergoing chemotherapy.

Since good nutrition is especially important for cancer patients, taste aversions may pose a serious problem for patients undergoing chemotherapy. Thus, the conditioning that is so beneficial under ordinary circumstances is a hindrance under these special circumstances. However, an understanding of the role of conditioning in taste aversions may help reduce the problem. It might be wise, for example, for people who are undergoing chemotherapy to eat something with a distinct taste, a food that does not make up an important part of the patient's diet, shortly before each treatment. An aversion to that particular food would develop, but the patient's appetite for other foods might not be affected.

CONDITIONED EMOTIONAL RESPONSES

The first person to study **conditioned emotional responses (CERs)** systematically was the famous behaviorist John B. Watson. Watson and his colleagues observed the behavior of babies and discovered that a relatively small number of stimuli would evoke emotional reactions. Stroking a baby's skin, for example, is an unconditional stimulus for smiling, cooing, gurgling, and so on. This behavior can be referred to by the terms *joy, happiness, contentment,* or, more generally, *love.* We say that the baby is contented, or that he or she *loves* being stroked. Similarly, Watson found that a sudden loud noise is an unconditional stimulus for crying and other reactions commonly termed *fear.*

But adults react emotionally to many stimuli that have little or no effect on the infant. For example, babies will put nearly anything into their mouths, including objects that adults do not willingly touch, such as feces. How is it that previously neutral stimuli come to elicit disgust, fear, love, and anger? Watson's answer: through conditioning. Emotional reactions are acquired in the same way that Pavlov's dogs learned to salivate at the sound of a ticking metronome. To test this idea, Watson and graduate student Rosalie Rayner (Watson & Rayner, 1920) conducted a series of experiments. First, they tested a number of infants to see their reactions to fire, dogs, cats, laboratory rats, and other stimuli. It was then commonly thought that infants were "instinctively" afraid of such items, but the experimenters found no evidence of any such instincts. Next, the researchers attempted to establish a fear reaction through classical conditioning. Their subject was Albert B., a healthy, 11-month-old boy who showed no signs of fearing a white rat, a pigeon, a rabbit, a dog, a monkey, cotton wool, or a burning newspaper. He appeared to be a happy, normal baby, and he rarely cried. The researchers established that a loud noise was a US for fear. When a steel bar was struck with a hammer behind Albert's head, he would jump suddenly. Using this loud noise as an unconditional stimulus, it took little time to establish a conditional fear response to a white rat. Watson and Rayner presented Albert with the rat, and one of the experimenters then hit the steel bar with a hammer. This frightened Albert. After a few pairings of this sort, Albert began to cry and show other signs of fear as soon as he saw the rat. He had learned, through Pavlovian conditioning, to fear white rats.

We can readily come up with examples of fearful reactions that very likely were established in the same way that Little Albert learned to fear white rats. Most people, for example, are made uneasy (at the least) by visits to the dentist. This is hardly surprising when one considers that dental visits frequently entail some discomfort. The whine of the dentist's drill is all too often associated with pain, so the sound of the drill soon arouses our anxiety. We may even come to fear anything associated with the painful drill, such as the dentist and the dentist's assistant (Ost & Hugdahl, 1985).

Very likely, the same sort of process is involved in the acquisition of fearful reactions brought on by visits to a doctor, the school principal or dean of students, the classroom in which one is scheduled to take an important test or give a talk, and the stage upon which an actor is to perform.

Watson suggested that the same sort of experiences account not only for fear but for other emotional reactions. Babies enjoy being stroked, he argued, so any stimulus that is regularly paired with stroking will come to be enjoyable. Thus, the mother or father who fondles a baby becomes a conditional stimulus for the emotional response of love, and we say that the baby loves his or her parents.

Hostility is another reaction that can be established through Pavlovian conditioning. Leonard Berkowitz (1964) found that people who received electric shocks in the company of another person later showed hostility toward that person, even though that person had not delivered the shocks (see also Berkowitz, 1983; Riordan & Tedeschi, 1983).

Such research shows that through Pavlovian conditioning, stimuli can become conditional stimuli for positive and negative emotions. But how is it that stimuli that seem to be naturally unpleasant sometimes arouse positive emotional reactions? Consider, for example, the masochist—a person who, by definition, actually enjoys being treated in what others would consider aversive ways. Under certain circumstances, such people enjoy being humiliated. Some even enjoy being beaten. One masochistic man wrote in his diary, "Debbie spanked me so hard I was burning. My skin was blistered in certain parts . . . *I need Debbie*" (Pipitone, 1985; emphasis added).

How does a person come to *like* pain? Pavlov's work seems to provide an answer. In one experiment, he paired an electric current with food. Incredibly, the dog soon salivated in response to the shock, just as it might have salivated in response to a bell. In other words, the shock (normally a fear-eliciting US) became a CS for salivating. Other dogs learned to salivate in response to other painful stimuli, such as pin pricks. What is even more astonishing is that these stimuli seemed to lose their aversive qualities. Pavlov (1927) wrote that "not even the tiniest and most subtle objective phenomenon usually exhibited by animals under the influence of strong injurious stimuli can be observed in these dogs. No appreciable changes in the pulse or in the respiration occur in these animals, whereas such changes are always most prominent when the noxious stimulus has not been converted into [a CS for salivating]" (p. 30). Pavlov's dogs actually behaved as if they enjoyed being shocked! After witnessing one of these demonstrations, the famous British physiologist Sir Charles Sherrington remarked, "At last I understand the psychology of the martyrs!" (in Cuny, 1962, p. 75).

In the same way, stimuli that are ordinarily conditional stimuli for fear responses may come to arouse other emotions. This is nicely illustrated by the story of the young socialite who began using drugs in boarding and finishing schools and eventually developed a $300-a-day habit that forced her into the kinds of neighborhoods generally associated with violent crime. "At first," she reported, "I was scared. But then it became a part of it that I really liked, going into a really bad neighborhood" (quoted in Anderson, 1983, p. 27). Evidently, what had been frightening stimuli (i.e., a dangerous neighborhood) came to elicit good feelings because those sights and sounds were associated with acquiring the drugs that had become so important to her.

The pairing of stimuli (even, as we have just seen, aversive stimuli) with emotion-arousing unconditional stimuli establishes conditional stimuli for emotions. But not everything we react to emotionally has been paired with unconditional stimuli. Consider the strong emotional reactions that people sometimes have at the mention of certain foods. Finding chocolate-covered crickets, fried grasshoppers, roasted rat, deep-fried mice, creamed cow eyes, boiled lamb's brain, fried pig hearts, bird's nest soup, and the like on a restaurant menu (or reading it here) is likely to make many people wrinkle their noses and express feelings of disgust. Yet in many cases, those who recoil at such foods have not eaten, or even seen, these dishes. Nor can we assume that there is an innate aversion to such foods, since everything on this "menu" is eaten in some part of the world. Why, then, do some people find the idea of eating certain foods repugnant even though they have never tasted them?

Part of the answer seems to be higher-order Pavlovian conditioning. Presumably, the names for these "disgusting" items have been paired with conditional stimuli that arouse feelings of disgust. This notion is supported by a series of experiments by Carolyn and Arthur Staats. Their basic strategy was to pair a neutral stimulus with one that was presumably a CS for some emotional response. In one experiment (Staats & Staats, 1957), the researchers had college students look at nonsense syllables such as YOF, LAJ, and QUG as they were flashed on a screen. At the same time, the students repeated words spoken by the experimenters. For some students, the syllable YOF was always paired with positive words such as *beauty*, *gift*, and *win*, while the syllable XEH was always paired with negative words such as *thief*, *sad*, and *enemy*. For other students, the associations were reversed: XEH was paired with positive words, YOF with negative ones. (Notice that no US was ever presented.) After this, the students rated each nonsense syllable on a 7-point scale ranging from unpleasant to pleasant. The results indicated that the nonsense syllables had acquired emotional meanings similar to the emotional value of the words with which they had been paired. When a nonsense syllable was regularly associated with pleasant words, it became pleasant; when it was paired with unpleasant words, it became unpleasant. In other words, YOF came to elicit good feelings in some students and bad feelings in others, depending upon the words associated with it.

Can such higher-order conditioning account for the feelings we have about people? Staats and Staats (1958) performed an experiment in which they paired the names *Tom* and *Bill* with either pleasant or unpleasant words. As in the previous experiment, the pleasantness or unpleasantness of these names depended upon the kinds of words with which they had been associated (see Figure 3-5).

Staats and Staats conducted an experiment that suggests that the same sort of higher-order conditioning may play an important role in racial and ethnic prejudices. In this study, college students watched as the words *German, Italian, French,* and so on flashed on a screen while they repeated words spoken by the experimenter. Most of the nationalities were paired with unemotional words such as *chair, with,* and *twelve;* the words *Swedish* and *Dutch,* however, were always paired with more potent words. For some students, *Dutch* was paired with *gift, sacred, happy,* and other pleasant words, while *Swedish* was paired with unpleasant words such as *bitter, ugly,* and *failure.* For other students, this procedure was reversed. Afterwards, the students rated each nationality on a scale from pleasant to unpleasant. These ratings showed that conditioning had indeed taken place: The feelings associated with the words *Swedish* and *Dutch* varied with the emotional value of the words with which they had been associated.

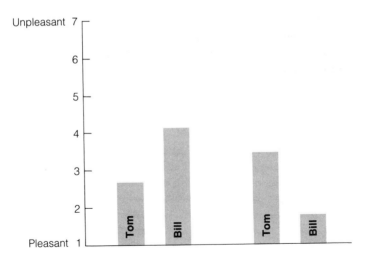

Figure 3-5 Conditioned emotional response to names. In Group I, *Tom* was paired with pleasant words and became pleasant, while *Bill* was paired with unpleasant words and became unpleasant. In Group II, the procedure was reversed, with corresponding results. (Compiled from data in Staats & Staats, 1958.)

Further support for the idea that higher-order conditioning may be involved in prejudices is offered by social psychologist Roger Brown (1965). Brown notes that adjectival forms of ethnic and national terms do not seem to arouse the same degree of emotional reaction as the noun forms of these words. *Swede, Turk,* and *Jew* sound worse than *Swedish, Turkish,* and *Jewish.* "In view of the Staats's experiment," he writes, "it seems probable that this is because the noun form has been accompanied by such disagreeable modifiers as dirty, whereas the adjective form has not" (p. 180).

It does not seem too farfetched to suppose that much of the prejudice directed toward certain ethnic, racial, and religious groups is due to the procedures that made some of the Staats's subjects dislike YOF. It can be argued, of course, that the Staatses established certain *words* as conditional stimuli, not the things those words represent. But there is evidence (e.g., Williams, 1966; Williams & Edwards, 1969) that the two are related, that if the word *Arab* is paired with words like *dirty,* this will affect how we react toward Arabs as well as toward the word *Arab.* Similarly, the words Negro, Republican, black, Irish, and communist, like YOF and XEH, are all originally neutral stimuli; they acquire emotional meaning, even without direct contact with the people they represent, apparently by means of Pavlovian conditioning. The power of Pavlovian conditioning to affect how we feel about objects has not gone unnoticed by advertisers (see Selling Pavlov box).

Before leaving the topic of emotional conditioning, it should be noted that stimuli that elicit emotional reactions have a tendency to affect other kinds of on-going behavior. The earliest psychologists to demonstrate this clearly were William Estes and B. F. Skinner (1941), who trained (through procedures to be described in the next chapter) a hungry rat to press a lever for food. When the animal was responding at a steady rate, they periodically sounded a tone; when the tone stopped, the rat received a shock. At first, the tone had no noticeable effect—the rat continued to press the lever at the same rate. But after the tone and shock had been paired several times, the rat decreased its rate of lever pressing when it heard the tone and did not resume its previous rate of activity until after it had received the shock (see Figure 3-6). Note that the rat's activity had absolutely no effect on the appearance of the tone or the delivery of the shock. Yet the tone clearly disrupted the rat's behavior. Because of the disruption of on-going behavior, this phenomenon is called **conditioned suppression.** The procedure is the same as in other studies of fear conditioning, except that the measure of learning is the suppression of some on-going behavior.

SELLING PAVLOV

It's a long way from Pavlov's lab to Madison Avenue, but people in advertising are very interested in the emotional reactions people have to objects. They are particularly interested in making objects arouse feelings of fondness, on the assumption that people are apt to buy objects they like. Though they may not always be aware that they are using Pavlovian conditioning, ad agencies regularly pair products with stimuli that reliably evoke positive emotions. In television commercials, for example, men who use a particular brand of aftershave are often accompanied by attractive women.

Can ads that associate an item with pleasant stimuli induce us to like the advertised item? Gerald Gorn (1982) conducted an experiment in which American college students listened either to a tune from the film *Grease* or to classical Indian music. (It was expected that the students would enjoy the popular American music more than the unfamiliar Eastern variety.) While listening to the music, the students viewed a slide showing either a beige or blue pen. Later, the students were allowed to have one of the pens. Of those students who had listened to the popular music, 79 percent chose a pen of the *same* color they had seen while listening to that music, while 70 percent of those who had listened to the Indian music chose a pen of a color *different* from the one they had seen on the slide. Evidently, ad agencies are correct in believing that they can induce people to feel good about, and want, a product by pairing that product with stimuli (pleasant music, attractive people, and the like) that make them feel good.

Of course, Pavlov did not invent this technique; people with something to sell have used it for centuries. What Pavlov and other psychologists have done is to help us understand the emotional side of consumer behavior. Armed with such understanding, we may be better equipped to protect ourselves.

We can see that conditioned suppression is likely to be part of any negative emotional response. Little Albert, for example, not only showed fear at the sight of the rat, he also stopped playing with blocks or whatever he happened to be up to at the moment. Charles Ferster and S. A. Culbertson (1982) extrapolate beyond these data to everyday experiences: "The same process," they write, "appears to operate when a person suddenly loses a job or when a close relative dies. One is likely to stop playing sports that one otherwise enjoys, eat less than one customarily does, and be disinclined to talk to people, except about the loss one has just experienced or about one's discomfort" (p. 115).

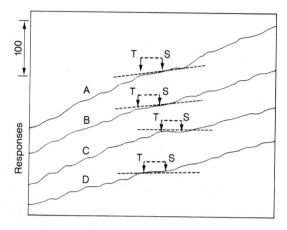

Time (each record one hour)

Figure 3-6 Conditioned suppression. When a tone (T) was paired with a shock (S), the tone suppressed the rate of an ongoing behavior. The curves show the average response rates for 6 rats on 4 consecutive days (From Estes & Skinner, 1941.)

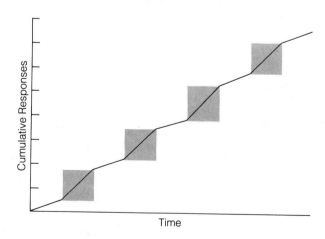

Figure 3-7 Conditioned facilitation. Shaded areas indicate the duration of a stimulus (such as a tone) that has been paired with a positive US (such as food). The tone increases the rate of an on-going behavior. (Hypothetical data.)

If a CS for fear suppresses on-going behavior, what is the effect of a CS for more positive emotions? Joseph Brady attempted to answer this question. In one experiment, Brady (1961) trained a thirsty rat to press a lever for water. Then he periodically sounded a clicker; when the clicker stopped, the rat received electrical stimulation of a pleasure center in its brain. After several such pairings, the rat began to press the lever at a faster rate whenever the clicker sounded. Lever pressing had no effect on the appearance of the clicking sound or on brain stimulation, so it seems reasonable to assume that the increased response rate reflects a change in the rat's emotional state. Because the CS increases the rate of on-going activity, the phenomenon is called **conditioned facilitation** (see Brady, 1975; see Figure 3-7). It is arguable whether the rat works faster because it "feels happy," but it is hard to escape the comparison between the rat's behavior and the attempts of factory managers to increase worker productivity by periodically piping music into the work area.

PSYCHOSOMATIC ILLNESS

The term *psychosomatic illness* means "a psychogenic (or partly psychogenic) disorder having somatic or physiological symptoms and (potentially) producing harmful structural somatic alterations" (English & English, 1958). The word *psychosomatic* is formed from the Greek words *psyche,* meaning mind or soul, and *soma,* meaning body. Hence, a psychosomatic illness is, traditionally, a disease of the body caused by the mind. This view is now largely rejected in scientific circles, though many psychiatrists and clinical psychologists of the "old school" cling to it. The more modern view replaces the concept of mind with that of experience, so that **psychosomatic illnesses** are those organic disorders or symptoms in which experience plays a significant part. Examples include allergic reactions, asthma, fainting, and hypertension (high blood pressure). There is evidence that Pavlovian conditioning is one kind of experience that is involved in these and some other psychosomatic complaints.

For the sake of illustration, let us look at an experimental demonstration of the role of Pavlovian conditioning in allergic reactions. An allergic reaction involves the release of histamines by the immune system in response to certain kinds of substances known as allergins. The histamines serve to rid the body of allergins by attacking them at the molecular level and expelling them from the body by, among other methods, sneezing and coughing.

It has long been known that allergic reactions are not entirely attributable to genetically based reactions to allergins. A hundred years ago, J. MacKinzie (reported in Russell et al., 1984) described the case of a patient who had an allergic reaction when presented with an *artificial* rose. As a result of such reports, some scientists have wondered whether some allergic reactions might be partly the result of learning. Michael Russell and his colleagues (1984) sensitized guinea pigs to the protein BSA; that is, they made the guinea pigs allergic to BSA. Next, the researchers paired BSA (now a US for an allergic response) with the odor of fish or sulfur (neutral stimuli). After several pairings, the guinea pigs were tested with the odors alone. The animals reacted with an immediate rise in blood histamine, a sure sign of allergic reaction; the odors had become conditional stimuli that elicited a conditional allergic response. In other words, the animals had become allergic to odors through Pavlovian conditioning. Russell suggests that in this same way, a person who is naturally allergic to one substance may become allergic to things naturally associated with the allergin. Thus, the person who is allergic to rose pollen may sneeze at the *sight* of a rose—even an artificial one.

It is popularly assumed that psychosomatic disorders are "all in the head." This is usually said (sometimes by physicians, unfortunately) with a certain disdain for the suffering patient. The implication is that if an illness is psychosomatic, the symptoms are less "real" than those that can be attributed to viruses, tumors, injuries, and the like. But Russell and his colleagues note that the histamine levels produced in response to conditional stimuli in their experiment were nearly as high was those elicited by BSA. Thus, the person who, as a result of Pavlovian conditioning, is sneezing continually, has an excrutiating headache, is laid low by an aching back, or has any number of other symptoms is not necessarily experiencing less misery than those whose symptoms are due to a virus or injury.

At first, it may seem that "conditioned illnesses" such as those we have considered are anything but adaptive. Certainly, anyone who has ever suffered an allergic reaction to artificial roses or acquired an ulcer on the way up the corporate ladder must find it difficult to believe that the ability to "learn to be sick" has survival value. After all, it is hard to fend off either jungle or corporate tigers if one is sneezing. But the ability to be changed by experience—to learn—usually is adaptive. The person who is so frightened at the sight of a dangerous predator that he faints may escape injury. Not only is he more likely to escape detection but, if detected, he may yet survive, because some predators spurn dead prey. Viewed in this

---

"I'M SICK OF THIS JOB"

Can your job make you sick? Can people who do not enjoy their work actually become physically ill as a result? Consider the following:

> Dear Dr. Steincrohn: Two years ago I started feeling lightheaded at work. This never occurred at home. I had a complete checkup with normal results. I have seen two doctors. Each tells me I am under stress for lack of work in the office. I feel my symptoms come on *the closer I approach the company parking lot*. Both doctors suggest I change jobs. Might this help? (From Steincrohn, 1984; emphasis added.)

How might this letter writer's complaints be due to Pavlovian conditioning? Given what you now know about Pavlovian conditioning, how would you advise him?

---

way, fainting resembles the "playing dead" tactic of opossum and certain other animals. Moreover, in some cases, the learned response makes it possible for the victim to avoid danger by avoiding cues associated with it. If one is allergic to tomatoes and regularly finds tomatoes in salads, one may avoid the tomatoes by avoiding salads.

VARIABLES AFFECTING PAVLOVIAN CONDITIONING

Many aspects of Pavlovian conditioning can vary, and the particular form that Pavlovian conditioning takes greatly affects the outcome. Indeed, whether it is possible to establish a CR at all depends upon many variables. We will consider here only the most important variables affecting Pavlovian conditioning.

Stimulus Features

It might seem that given several completely neutral stimuli, one stimulus would serve as a CS as well as another. After all, we have just seen that even as unlikely a stimulus as a painful electric shock can become a CS for salivation. But while nearly any stimulus can become an effective CS, some stimuli serve the purpose more readily than others.

This is illustrated by experiments in which the CS consists of two or more stimuli (e.g., a red light and a buzzer) presented simultaneously. Such a **compound stimulus** is paired with a US for one or more trials, after which the experimenter tests for conditioning by presenting the compound stimulus and each component of the CS alone. In one of the first studies of compound stimuli, a Dr. Palladin (in Pavlov, 1927), working in Pavlov's laboratory, simultaneously presented cold and tactile stimulation to a dog, followed by a few drops of acid in the mouth (a US for salivation). Then the dog was tested with the tactile stimulation alone, the thermal stimulation alone, and the compound stimulus. The results revealed that while both the tactile stimulus and the combination of tactile and thermal stimuli were effective conditional stimuli, the thermal stimulus alone was utterly ineffective.

Of course, this result could mean merely that thermal stimuli make poor conditional stimuli. But studies consistently reveal that neutral stimuli that are quite capable of becoming conditional stimuli when paired with a US may be ineffective when part of a compound stimulus. This phenomenon is known as **overshadowing** since, as Pavlov (1927) noted, "the effect of one [stimulus] was found very commonly to overshadow the effect of the others almost completely" (p. 141). The overshadowed stimulus does not go entirely unnoticed; it simply is not an effective CS (Rescorla, 1973).

Perhaps the chief distinguishing characteristic of an effective CS is its intensity: Strong stimuli overshadow weak ones. Leon Kamin (1969) used a compound stimulus consisting of a strong light and a weak tone, and found that the light alone produced a stronger CR than the tone. Other studies demonstrate that a loud noise makes a better CS than a soft noise, that a bright light is more effective than a soft light, that a distinct flavor or odor works better than a bland one, and so on.

The intensity of the US also is very important, with stronger stimuli producing better results, in general, than weaker ones. This was demonstrated by Kenneth Spence (1953) in a study of eyelid conditioning. The US was a puff of air exerting either 1/4 pound of pressure per square inch (psi) or 5 pounds psi. In a 20-trial test period, college students trained with the weak US gave an average of fewer than 6 conditional responses to the CS, while those trained with the stronger US gave an average of 13 CRs. In a more recent experiment, Brett Polenchar and his colleagues (1984) used four levels of mild shock (from 1 to 4 milliamps) as the US. The shock was delivered to the hindleg of a cat, causing it to flex its leg; a tone

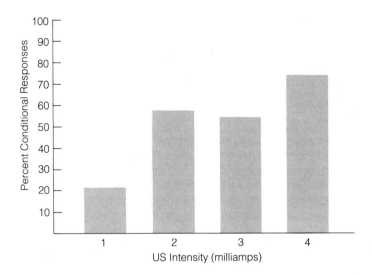

Figure 3-8   Conditioning and US intensity. Average percentage of CRs on seventh day of training for cats exposed to four levels of shock. Generally, the more intense the US, the more effective the training. (Compiled from data in Polenchar et al., 1984.)

preceded the shock. The rate of CR acquisition was found to increase steadily with the intensity of the shock (see Figure 3-8).

It is possible, however, for a CS or US to be too intense. In eyelid conditioning, a bright light may make a better CS than a dim one, but if the light is very strong, it may be an unconditional stimulus for blinking and will therefore interfere with learning. Likewise, while a very weak electric shock makes a poor US, so may a very strong one.

CS-US Contiguity

Another important variable in Pavlovian conditioning is contiguity (see Chapter 2). In Pavlovian conditioning, contiguity refers to the length of the interval between the CS and the US. In general, the shorter this **interstimulus interval, or ISI,** the more quickly a CR will appear. However, the optimum ISI depends upon a number of variables.

One important factor is the kind of response being conditioned. For instance, we saw that it was possible to obtain very good results with long ISIs in studies of taste aversion. Some researchers have produced conditioned taste aversions with CS-US intervals of several hours (Revusky & Garcia, 1970; Wallace, 1976). On the other hand, in establishing a conditioned eye-blink response in rabbits, long ISIs are unlikely to be effective. Indeed, in this case, an interval of 1/2 second may be best.

The optimum ISI also varies according to the type of conditioning procedure used, with short intervals generally being less important in delayed conditioning than in trace conditioning. However, even in trace conditioning, extremely short ISIs may not work well, as a study by Gregory Kimble (1947) demonstrates. Kimble trained college students to blink in response to a light. The gap between the light and a puff of air was short, from 1/10 second to about 1/2 second. On every 10th trial, Kimble withheld the US to see whether or not the students would blink. At the end of the experiment, he compared the response rates and found that the group with the longest ISI produced conditional responses on 95 percent of the test trials. Groups with shorter ISIs responded less frequently; the shortest ISI produced CRs on an average of only 45 percent of the test trials.

It is no longer possible to state a simple generalization about the role of contiguity in conditioning. We cannot say, for example, that short ISIs are essential to learning, or even that they are always helpful. The ideal ISI varies in complex ways from situation to situation. However, the ISI cannot be ignored, because the success of any given conditioning procedure will vary with the length of the interstimulus interval.

CS-US Contingency

You will recall from Chapter 2 that a contingency is a kind of if-then statement. A contingency exists between two events, A and B, when it can be said that B occurs *if and only if* A occurs. The case for the importance of contingency in Pavlovian conditioning has been clearly argued by Robert Rescorla (1968; Rescorla and Holland, 1982). Rescorla maintains that it is not the pairing of CS and US that produces learning, but the degree of contingency between them. It is not, he asserts, the *number* of CS-US pairings, but the *relative probabilities* of a US appearing in the presence and absence of the CS (Rescorla, 1968).

Rescorla and others have performed experiments on the power of contingency in conditioning. In one study, Rescorla (1968) exposed rats to a stimulus followed by a shock. While all of the rats were exposed to the same number of CS-US pairings, in additional trials the US sometimes appeared alone. In one group, the shock occurred in the absence of the CS in 10 percent of the additional trials; in a second group, the US appeared alone in 20 percent of the trials; and in a third group, the US appeared alone in 40 percent of the trials. The results showed that the degree of conditioning depended upon the degree to which the CS predicted shock. When the CS was nearly always followed by the US, conditioning occurred. When a shock was about as likely to occur in the absence of a CS as in its presence (the 40 percent group), little or no conditioning took place.

In the laboratory, it is a simple matter to ensure rapid learning by presenting the CS and US together on every trial. Outside the laboratory, however, the rate of learning is seldom optimal because a given stimulus will sometimes be paired with a US and other times will appear alone. Imagine that you take a job in the stockroom of a department store. A telephone in the stockroom is connected to a switchboard, and the operator has instructions that you are to receive outside calls only in cases of emergency. Thus, all the calls you receive will be either important (probably frightening or depressing) outside calls or routine calls from people within the company requesting supplies. Suppose that during your first week on the job, you get 3 outside calls: The first is from a relative who informs you that your father (to whom you were very close) has just died; the second is from the police, who tell you that your new car was stolen and wrecked; the third is from your landlord, who wants you to know that a burst water pipe has ruined all your personal belongings. The questions is, Will the ring of the telephone have become a CS for a conditioned emotional response? The answer depends upon how many times the phone rang and was *not* paired with such aversive stimuli. If those 3 calls were the only calls you received, then you will probably jump out of your skin the next time the phone rings. If, however, the 3 unpleasant calls were distributed randomly among 50 or 100 calls for supplies, so that the ringing often appeared alone (or, more accurately, with relatively neutral stimuli), then you will be far less likely to be upset by a ringing phone. In the natural environment, such variations are quite common and may account for the fact that some people dread answering the phone, while others are delighted to receive a call.

Prior Experience With CS and US

The effects of conditioning depend partly upon the organism's previous exposure to the stimuli that will serve as CS and US. Suppose, for example, that before a conditioning experiment begins, a dog hears a bell that is sounded repeatedly but is never paired with food.

If the experimenter begins pairing the bell with food, how will the dog's previous experience with the bell affect conditioning? What happens is that it takes longer for the bell to become a CS than if the dog had never heard the bell by itself. Being exposed to a stimulus in the absence of a US interferes with the ability of that stimulus to become a CS. This phenomenon is called **latent inhibition** (Lubow & Moore, 1959).

At first, it may seem odd that experience with a stimulus in isolation can interfere with that stimulus becoming a CS. But does the stimulus actually appear alone? Latent inhibition may be viewed as the result of a form of Pavlovian conditioning in which a neutral stimulus is paired with weak stimuli (the ordinary surroundings). This view is supported by a study by P. Rozin and James Kalat (1971) in which rats were exposed to a novel food 3 1/2 hours before, and again 1/2 hour before, being made ill. As you know, a single pairing of food and illness can produce conditioned taste aversion. But in this case, the animals were exposed to the food twice, the first time without ill effects. The result was that the animals acquired only a very weak CR. Rozin and Kalat reasoned that the animals had learned something from their first uneventful exposure to the new food: that it was safe to eat.

This finding suggests that the more experience an organism has with a stimulus "in isolation" from a US, the more difficult it is to establish that stimulus as a CS for a given response. This seems to be the case. Alexandra Logue and her colleagues (1983) found that many people have conditioned taste aversions (about 30 percent report them). Although such aversions usually are traced to an experience in which eating the food was followed by some sort of illness, the researchers found that these aversions generally involved foods with which the person had had relatively little experience before becoming ill. Some alcoholics, for example, had conditioned aversions to certain alcoholic beverages, but these tended to be drinks that had never formed an important part of their diet.

Such studies demonstrate that novel stimuli (stimuli with which the organism has had little experience) are more likely to become conditional stimuli than are familiar stimuli that have not been paired with the US. But what if the novel stimulus is part of a compound stimulus that includes an effective CS? Suppose, for example, that a researcher conducts an experiment on Pavlovian conditioning in rats, first by repeatedly pairing a tone and electric shock, then by repeatedly pairing a compound stimulus consisting of the tone and a novel stimulus—light—with the shock. What will happen if the researcher now presents the *light* alone? Leon Kamin (1969) performed this experiment and found that the light did not become a CS. This phenomenon, called **blocking,** resembles overshadowing in that one stimulus interferes with the ability of another stimulus to become a CS. In overshadowing, however, the effect is due to differences between the stimuli in intensity or similarity; in blocking, the effect is due to prior experience with one part of the compound stimulus.

There is another way in which experience with a neutral stimulus can affect later conditioning. Suppose that two neutral stimuli, such as a bell and a light, are repeatedly presented together but are not paired with a US. Then one of these stimuli, perhaps the bell, is paired with an unconditional stimulus so that it becomes a CS. What effect will this procedure have on the capacity of the light to become a CS? Wilfred Brogden (1939), using dogs as subjects, paired a light and a bell for 2 seconds, 20 times a day for 10 days. Then, for some of the dogs, he repeatedly paired the bell with a shock to one of the animal's front legs to elicit a reflex movement. Next, Brogden presented the light to see what would happen. He found that this stimulus often elicited a CR even though it had never been paired with the US, a phenomenon Brogden called **sensory preconditioning.** Control animals, dogs that had not been exposed to the bell-light pairing, did not respond to the light in this way. In general, then, a stimulus will become a CS more rapidly if it has been paired with another stimulus that has subsequently become a CS for that response.

Intertrial Interval

Another time interval that affects classical conditioning is the gap between successive trials. Recall that each association of the CS and US is one trial. Obviously, the rest period between trials can vary from less than a second to several years. Let's say, for example, that you want to condition a dog to flex its leg to the sound of a bell. You decide that you will pair the bell with a shock for a total of 10 trials using a trace conditioning procedure. How much time should you allow between trials?

In general, experiments comparing various **intertrial intervals,** or **ITIs,** yield results showing that longer intervals are more effective than shorter ones. Whereas the best interstimulus interval is often a second or less, the optimum intertrial interval may be 20 or 30 seconds or more (see, for example, Prokasy & Whaley, 1963).

Number of Stimulus Pairings

The essential nature of classical conditioning suggests that unless a neutral stimulus is paired with an unconditional stimulus (or a well-established CS), the neutral stimulus will not become a CS. It seems only logical, then, that the more often the neutral and unconditional stimulus appear together, and the less often either appears alone, the more efficiently learning will occur. In general, nature accepts this logic: CR latency, amplitude, and probability all demonstrate increased learning with each CS-US pairing.

However, the relationship between the number of stimulus pairings and the amount of learning is not linear; that is, the first few associations are more important than later ones (see, for example, Hovland, 1937b). Thus, measures of learning follow a decelerating curve (see Figure 3-9). We have observed this already in studies of taste aversion and emotional responses; in both cases, the first pairing of conditional and unconditional stimuli produces marked changes in behavior, while later pairings have little additional effect (Rescorla & Wagner, 1972; Wagner & Rescorla, 1972).

From a survival standpoint, this makes excellent sense. If important stimuli are reliably associated, the sooner the organism adapts, the better. If, for instance, a certain food makes an organism seriously ill, it is important that the organism "learn its lesson" after one or two pairings since it may not survive many more than that. Similarly, if the sight of the poisonous snake is associated with a painful bite, it is important that the organism acquire a healthy fear of the snake without being bitten several times.

Characteristics of the Learner

Classical conditioning does not proceed in a uniform fashion for all species, or for all members of a given species. Pavlov noticed that some dogs are highly excitable while others are much more sedate, and these "personality" differences affect conditioning. The conditionability of an organism also varies with its physiological state. Salivary conditioning proceeds more rapidly with a hungry dog than with a sated one. There is also some evidence that moderate levels of anxiety improve conditioning (see Figure 3-10). And drugs that sedate or excite an organism affect conditioning for better or worse.

As an example of the way in which learner characteristics can affect conditioning, let us consider a study by Harry Braun and

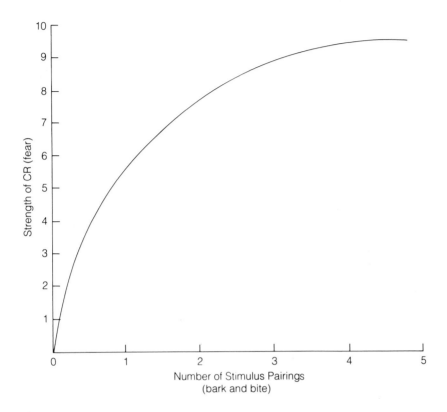

Figure 3-9 Number of stimulus pairings and conditioning. The more often a dog barks and then bites you, the stronger your fear. However, the first few stimulus pairings are more important than later pairings. (Hypothetical data.)

Richard Geiselhart (1959). These researchers investigated eyelid conditioning in people as a function of age. Their subjects were children, young adults, and senior citizens. As Figure 3-11 shows, learning was closely related to age; in fact, the procedure was not effective in establishing a conditional eye blink in the oldest subjects.

Thus, the course of conditioning varies with the organism undergoing training. One rat does not respond to conditioning in *precisely* the same manner as another, nor do rats in general respond to conditioning in *precisely* the same manner as human beings. There are differences within and between species, and these differences influence the effect that Pavlovian procedures have. (For more on this, see Chapter 10.)

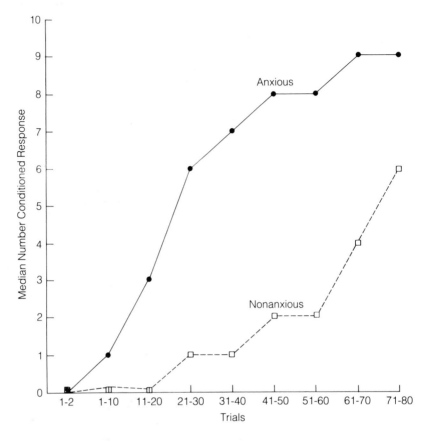

Figure 3-10   Conditioning as a function of anxiety. Eyelid conditioning proceeded more rapidly among anxious college students than among relaxed ones. (From Taylor, 1951.)

WHAT IS LEARNED IN
PAVLOVIAN CONDITIONING?

When a dog salivates at the sound of a bell or a baby cries at the sight of a rat, learning clearly has taken place, but what exactly has been learned?

Stimulus Substitution Theory

Pavlov proposed what has been called the **stimulus substitution theory.** Using the salivary reflex as a model, his thinking went some-

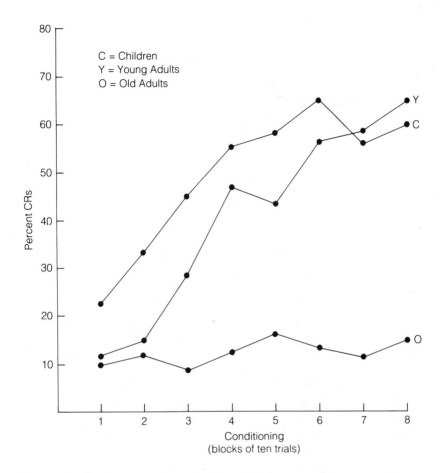

Figure 3-11 Conditioning and age. Eyelid conditioning proceeded more rapidly among younger subjects. (After Braun & Geiselhart, 1959.)

thing like this: The dog is born with an unconditional salivary response to certain stimuli, such as food placed in its mouth. The unconditional stimulus, Pavlov theorized, activates a particular area or zone in the brain, and the excitation of this zone triggers salivation. All that Pavlov or any other experimenter actually saw was the unconditional stimulus and the response it elicited. Pavlov believed, however, that some sort of neurological connection links the US and UR (see Figure 3-12).

Now, a neutral stimulus, such as a bell, is by definition one that does not elicit the salivary response. There is, in other words, no

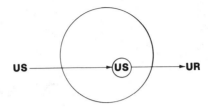

Figure 3-12

connection in the brain between the bell and the salivary response. What conditioning does, then, is establish such a connection. But how? Pavlov assumed that any stimulus must have some effect on the nervous system. The sound of a bell excites a particular area of the brain (see Figure 3-13). By presenting the CS and the US together, a new connection begins to form between their respective areas in the brain (see Figure 3-14). After several pairings of CS and US, the new link is strong enough that presenting the CS alone will cause salivation (see Figure 3-15).

Pavlov's theory assumes that a new connection is formed between the CS zone and the US zone, the zone that triggers the salivary response. Pavlov used the newly invented telephone as a convenient analogy. "My residence," he wrote, "may be connected directly with the laboratory by a private line, and I may call up the laboratory whenever it pleases me to do so; or on the other hand, a connection may have to be made through the central exchange. But the result in both cases is the same" (1927, p. 25). In other words, once conditioning has taken place, the CS merely substitutes for the US. The new stimulus (the CS) substitutes for, or takes the place of,

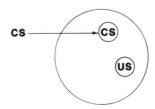

Figure 3-13

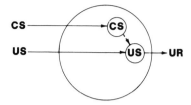

Figure 3-14

the old stimulus (the US). According to Pavlov, conditioning does not involve the acquisition of any new *behavior*, but rather the ability to respond in old ways to new *stimuli*.

This theory of stimulus substitution implies that the CR and UR are the same, but evidence has since indicated that they are not. As a rule, the conditional response is weaker than, occurs less reliably than, and appears more slowly than the UR. In addition, there are often qualitative differences between conditional and unconditional responses. For instance, Karl Zener (1937) trained dogs to salivate and then watched their spontaneous responses to food and to the conditional stimulus. Like Pavlov, Zener found that both the CS and the US elicited salivation. But Zener noticed that the two stimuli also elicited other behavior as well. When the dog received food, it made chewing movements but otherwise remained still; when the CS appeared, the dog became active but did not chew. Sometimes, the CR is even the opposite of the UR (Hilgard, 1936). The unconditional response to electric shock, for example, is an increase in heart rate, while a CS that has been paired with shock elicits a *decrease* in heart rate.

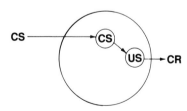

Figure 3-15

Preparatory Response Theory

The discovery of differences between CR and UR undermined Pavlov's stimulus substitution theory but led gradually to the **preparatory response theory,** the idea that what is learned during Pavlovian conditioning is a response that will prepare the organism for the appearance of the US. Sometimes, the response required is, as Pavlov believed, nearly identical to the UR. On other occasions, the CR is quite different. But in both cases, they help the organism prepare for what is about to happen.

When a dog responds to a bell by salivating, for instance, this prepares the animal for the food that is about to come. By beginning to salivate even before food arrives, the dog prepares to digest the food it will receive. Similarly, when a rat responds to a CS with a reduced heart rate, this subdues the potentially harmful effects of an increase in heart rate following shock. In the same way, responding with fear at the sight of a dog that bit us on a previous occasion prepares us to fight or flee the danger. Thus, Pavlovian conditioning involves something more complex than the substitution of the CS for the US. This complexity has been carefully examined in studies of the effects of addictive drugs (for a review, see Siegel, 1983; for a summary, see Chance, in press).

Shepard Siegel (1983) believes that when a person habitually uses an addictive drug in the presence of certain stimuli, those stimuli become conditional stimuli for a CR. In the case of addictive drugs, the CR is often the exact opposite of the UR. The unconditional response to morphine includes, for instance, decreased sensitivity to pain, but the CR to stimuli associated with morphine is *increased* sensitivity to pain (Siegel, 1975). The CS has the effect of subduing or moderating the effects of the US: The organism prepares for the drug by suppressing the body's response to it. (Siegel states that the organism "compensates" for the drug, thereby maintaining the body at near normal functioning.)

This means that when people habitually take a drug in a particular setting, their reaction to the drug is progressively reduced; that is, they develop tolerance. L. O. Lightfoot (1980) had male college students drink a substantial amount of beer (about 3 12-ounce bottles for a man of 150 pounds) in a 30-minute period on each of 5 consecutive days. The first four drinking sessions took place in the same location. On the fifth day, some students drank beer in the familiar setting, while others imbibed in a new place. All the students took tests of intellectual and perceptual-motor skills after drinking. Those who drank in the familiar setting scored higher on the tests, indicating that the stimuli previously associated with drinking had muted the effects of the alcohol. In other words, conditioning had prepared these men to respond to stimuli associated with drinking in such a way as to moderate the normal effects of the drug. When those conditional stimuli were not present, the drug hit with full force.

Sometimes, sudden death resulting from drug use may be explained in much the same way. Such deaths are commonly attributed to an accidental overdose, but often they occur following a dose that, given the person's level of tolerance, should have proved harmless (Reed, 1980; Siegel, 1984). Evidence suggests that the deaths are often due to the absence of stimuli normally present during drug use. Siegel and his colleagues (1982) gave three groups of rats, some of whom had never received heroin before, a strong dose of heroin. The heroin-experienced rats received the test dose either in the same place they had received the previous doses or in a novel setting. The results were clear-cut: The dose was lethal for 96 percent of the inexperienced rats, but for experienced rats, mortality depended upon the cues present. Of those injected in a strange environment, 64 percent died; but of those injected in a familiar environment, only 32 percent died.

The same pattern is revealed by the reports of human drug users. Siegel (1984) asked 10 former heroin addicts who had nearly died following drug use about the circumstances surrounding their close call. In 7 cases, there was something unusual about the near-fatal event. Two addicts had used different injection procedures, two had taken the drug in unusual locations, and so on. Sometimes, very subtle differences in context were enough to trigger a life-threatening reaction. A woman who usually required two or more attempts at penetrating a vein nearly died after she injected herself successfully on the first trial.

These studies are interesting in their own right, but they are also important to an understanding of what is learned during Pavlovian conditioning. When an addictive drug is the US, learning appears to be a compensatory response, a reaction of the body that subdues the effects of the US. This response prepares the organism to cope with the US. When the US is food, the CR is salivation. Again, the CR prepares the organism for the US that is about to appear.

Some psychologists have said that in Pavlovian conditioning, the organism learns to anticipate the US, that what the organism learns is that the US follows the CS (see Schwartz & Lacey, 1982). To some people this implies that thinking is involved. But Pavlovian conditioning has been demonstrated in human fetuses (see, for example, Cordes, 1984; Spelt, 1948) and in decorticate animals (Pavlov, 1927). Pavlovian learning therefore appears not to require higher brain centers. Thus, we cannot assume that Pavlovian conditioning involves acquiring knowledge about the CS-US relationship, though such knowledge may be obtained (Grant, 1973; Hilgard & Humphreys, 1938). We are safe in assuming, however, that Pavlovian conditioning means learning to respond to the CS in a manner that helps the organism prepare for the US. This preparatory response is sometimes quite different from the UR, and it has made us appreciate that Pavlovian learning is far more complex than most people, including Pavlov, thought.

SUMMARY

For centuries, we have known that people and certain animals will salivate at the sight of food. These "psychic secretions" were thought to be caused by the person's or animal's thoughts about food, but no one had given serious attention to this phenomenon until the Russian physiologist Ivan Pavlov took up the problem around the beginning of this century. By carefully controlling the environment of a dog, Pavlov was able to identify the conditions under which it would salivate.

This research convinced Pavlov that there are two kinds of reflexes, unconditional and conditional. An unconditional reflex consists of an unconditional stimulus (US) and an unconditional response (UR); a conditional reflex consists of a conditional stimulus (CS) and a conditional response (CR). Unconditional reflexes are inborn; conditional reflexes are acquired. The procedure by which a conditional reflex is acquired is called Pavlovian, or classical, conditioning.

Various techniques are used to measure the effectiveness of Pavlovian procedures. One is to continue pairing CS and US and observe whether the reflex response occurs before the presentation of the US; another is to note increases in the strength of the CR with conditioning trials. An alternative is to present the CS alone on certain trials and see whether the probability of a CR on such test trials increases. In testing for conditioning, it is important to control for the phenomenon of pseudoconditioning, in which a stimulus may elicit a CR even though it has not become an effective CS.

In most conditioning experiments, a CS is paired with a US, such as food. In higher-order conditioning, a CS is paired with a well-established CS. This procedure is less effective in establishing a CR than CS-US pairings.

Salivary conditioning is a kind of prototype for studying Pavlovian conditioning, but the same procedures have enhanced our understanding of a number of areas of human and animal behavior. Conditioned taste aversions, such as those that cause nausea, are now known to be the product of the pairing of distinctive flavors and aversive stimuli. Studies of conditioned emotional responses have demonstrated how likes and dislikes can be produced by pairing neutral objects with those that elicit positive or negative emotions. When the neutral stimuli themselves come to elicit emotional responses, their presentation will affect other on-going behavior. When the response is positive, the rate of on-going behavior tends to increase, a phenomenon called behavioral facilitation; when the response is negative, behavioral suppression occurs, that is, the rate of responding decreases. Pavlovian conditioning has provided a new understanding of psychosomatic illnesses. Through conditioning, neutral stimuli can come to elicit physiological responses that mimic disease processes.

Although Pavlovian conditioning appears to be quite simple, it is affected by a number of complicating variables. Chief among these is the manner in which CS and US are paired; these include trace, delayed, simultaneous, and backward procedures. Characteristics of the stimuli used also affect conditioning results. When a compound stimulus is used as CS, for example, one aspect of the stimulus may overshadow another. Prior experience with the CS and US can have important effects, as can the interstimulus interval, intertrial interval, number of CS-US pairings, and characteristics of the individual undergoing training. Often, these and other variables interact in complex ways, thus complicating this "simple" form of learning even further.

Pavlov believed that what an organism learned during conditioning was to respond to the CS in the same way as to the US. He believed the CR and UR were the same and that the CS merely substituted for the US. Subsequent research showed that the CR and UR are often quite different, and this led to the idea that Pavlovian learning involves the formation of a response that prepares the organism for the US. This implies that Pavlovian learning is more complex than Pavlov thought.

It is to be hoped that by now that the reader appreciates not only the complexity of Pavlovian conditioning but its richness as a source of understanding behavior. For if Pavlovian procedures were not effective in modifying behavior, few higher species, and certainly not human beings, could survive. "The inborn reflexes by themselves," wrote Pavlov (1927), "are inadequate to ensure the continued existence of the organism, especially of the more highly organized animals. . . . The complex conditions of everyday existence require a much more detailed and specialized correlation between the animal and its environment than is afforded by the inborn reflexes alone" (p. 16). As a result of Pavlovian conditioning, people withdraw their hands before they are burned by the fire; they become frightened when they see the oncoming truck, not just when it hits them. "It is pretty evident," wrote Pavlov (1927), "that under natural conditions the normal animal must respond not only to stimuli which themselves bring immediate benefit or harm, but also to other [stimuli] which in themselves only *signal* the approach of these stimuli; though it is not the sight and sound of the beast of prey which is in itself harmful . . . but its teeth and claws" (p. 14).

Of course, there is a price for everything, and our conditionability can cost us plenty. It's important to keep in mind that learning can mean acquiring inappropriate and undesirable reactions as well as appropriate and desirable ones. Thus, a person may not only acquire adaptive reactions, such as the fear of fire, but maladaptive ones, such as the fear of harmless animals. Yet our ability to be modified by the pairing of stimuli adds greatly to the richness of our lives. Do you, for example, prefer jazz to classical music? Are you more comfortable alone than in large crowds? Does your blood boil when you see Ku Klux Klansmen marching in a parade? Does the very thought of eating filet mignon make you mouth water, while thoughts of tripe make you ill? All such reactions, and thousands of others that we think of as embedded in the very fiber of our personalities, are at least partly attributable to Pavlovian learning.

Pavlov's discoveries are significant for still other reasons. What Pavlov and his successors have done is to suggest a new image of human nature: Little Albert was not afraid of the white rat because he was timid; he was timid because of the experiences he had had with the rat. Thus, Pavlov's work began to move the causes of human behavior from inside the person (where they had existed in the form of qualities such as cowardice, bravery, honesty) to outside the person, where they existed in the form of specific kinds of observable experiences.

There are, of course, many kinds of behavior that are not due to Pavlovian conditioning. But it cannot be denied that such conditioning plays a profound role in determining many of our most basic and common acts. Pavlov, like Darwin, helped change our definition of what it means to be a human being.

REVIEW QUESTIONS

1. Define the following terms:

psychic reflex	conditional response
pseudoconditioning	conditioned suppression
compound stimulus	latent inhibition
stimulus substitution	contiguity

2. What did Pavlov mean when he said that glands seemed to possess intelligence?

3. Why was Pavlov so reluctant to study psychic reflexes?

4. One of Pavlov's most important discoveries was that salivation could be attributed to events occurring in the dog's environment. Why might this discovery be considered important?

5. In what sense is a CR "conditional?"

6. Why do you suppose Pavlovian conditioning is also called classical conditioning?

7. Why do you suppose higher-order conditioning gets less satisfactory results than pairing a neutral stimulus with a US?

8. Suppose that your doctor advises you to eat liver because of its high iron content and that you have a conditioned aversion to the taste of liver. Assuming that you wish to follow your doctor's advice, how might you deal with the problem this taste aversion presents?

9. A man of about 70 named Albert walks into a psychologist's office asking for help in overcoming an irrational fear of laboratory rats and other white, furry creatures. What can the psychologist do to help him?

10. Explain Sherrington's remark, "At last I understand the psychology of the martyrs!" What do salivating dogs have to do with martyrs?

11. It has been said that people who have amorous encounters under clandestine conditions are later unable to enjoy amorous experiences under more ordinary "safe" conditions. Why might this be the case?

12. What is the significance of the Staats and Staats research for an understanding of international politics?

13. In what sense are psychosomatic illnesses caused by events outside the patient's body? What would be a better term for psychosomatic illnesses?

14. In what sense is Pavlovian conditioning a simple form of learning? In what sense is Pavlovian conditioning complex?

15. Explain the differences among trace, delay, simultaneous, and backward conditioning procedures. Illustrate each procedure with an example not given in the text.

16. Joe tells you that in Pavlovian conditioning, the organism learns that the CS predicts the US. What evidence can you muster in opposition to this view?

17. What is the principle flaw in Pavlov's stimulus substitution theory?

18. In what sense is a CR a preparatory response?

19. Give an example of an instance in which it can be said that Pavlovian learning backfired as an adaptive mechanism.

20. How has the discovery of Pavlovian conditioning altered our view of human nature?

SUGGESTED READINGS

Pavlov's *Conditioned Reflexes* (1927) is unquestionably the most important text on this subject from a historical point of view, but it is also well worth reading as a study in scientific method. Modern texts leave out much of the *process* of scientific discovery; Pavlov lets us look over his shoulder as he works. Fortunately, he writes well enough that we can enjoy the view.

Other works by Pavlov are also well worth perusing. In his later years, his interests turned to the analysis of psychiatric problems. *Conditioned Reflexes and Psychiatry* (1941) (vol. 2 of his *Lectures on Conditioned Reflexes*) describes his views on this subject. His article *Reply of a*

Physiologist to Psychologists (1932) is seldom read today, but it discusses fundamental, and still relevant, issues on the nature of behavioral science.

Some people make the mistake of thinking that everything that anyone could want to know about Pavlovian conditioning has been discovered. Glance through some recent issues of the *Pavlovian Journal of Biological Science* or the *Journal of Behavior Therapy* and you will see that Pavlovian conditioning is as rich a soil for scientific discoveries today as it ever was.

FOUR

■

Instrumental Procedures

BEGINNINGS

At about the same time that Pavlov was trying to solve the riddle of the psychic reflex, a young American graduate student named Edward Lee Thorndike was tackling another problem, animal intelligence.

In the late 19th century, most people believed that higher animals learned through reasoning. Anyone who owned a dog or cat could "see" the animal think through a problem and come to a logical conclusion, and stories of the incredible talents of animals abounded. Taken together, these stories painted a picture of animal abilities that made some pets little less than mute Albert Einsteins. Thorndike recognized the impossibility of estimating animal abilities from this sort of anecdotal evidence: "Such testimony is by no means on a par with testimony about the size of a fish or the migration of birds," he wrote, "for here one has to deal not merely with ignorant or inaccurate testimony, but also with prejudiced testimony. Human folk are as a matter of fact eager to find intelligence in animals" (1898, p. 4).

This bias led people to report remarkable feats, but not more ordinary, unintelligent acts. "Dogs get lost hundreds of times and no one ever notices it or sends an account of it to a scientific magazine," wrote Thorndike (1898), "but let one find his way from Brooklyn to Yonkers and the fact immediately becomes a circulating anecdote.

Thousands of cats on thousands of occasions sit helplessly yowling, and no one takes thought of it or writes to his friend, the professor; but let one cat claw at the knob of a door supposedly as a signal to be let out, and straightway this cat becomes the representative of the cat-mind in all the books. . . . In short, the anecdotes give really the . . . *supernormal* psychology of animals" (pp. 4–5).

But how could one go about studying the *normal*, or ordinary, psychology of animals? How could one study animal intelligence sci-entifically? Thorndike's answer was to test an animal's performance at solving a problem. Then he would give the animal the problem again and see if its performance improved, test it again, and so on. He would, in other words, study animal intelligence by studying animal learning.

In one series of experiments, Thorndike put a chick into a maze (see Figure 4-1). If the chick took the correct route, it would find its way to a pen containing food and other chicks. When Thorndike first put the animal into the maze, it tried to jump out of the enclosure and then wandered down one blind alley after another, peeping loudly all the while, until it finally found its way out. With succeeding trials, the chick became more and more efficient; finally, when placed in the maze, it would go directly down the appropriate path. Thorndike recorded the time it took the chick to reach its destination on each succeeding trial and plotted the time to produce a learning curve (see Figure 4-2).

Thorndike's most famous experiments were done with cats. He would place a hungry cat in a box (see Figure 4-3) and put food in plain view but out of reach. The box had a door that could be opened by some simple act such as pulling a wire loop or stepping on a

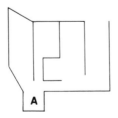

Figure 4-1   One of the mazes used by Thorndike. A chick was placed at A and would find other chicks and food in another pen when it reached the exit. The walls of this maze were made of books stood up on end. Thorndike referred to these structures as pens, but they were probably the first mazes ever used to study learn-ing. (From Thorndike, 1898.)

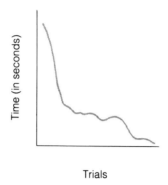

Trials

Figure 4-2   Learning curve showing the decrease in time one chick took to escape a maze similar to the one shown in Figure 4-1. (After Thorndike, 1898.)

treadle. Like the chicks, the cat began by making a number of ineffective responses. Thorndike (1898) wrote that the cat typically "tries to squeeze through any opening; it claws and bites at the bars or wire; it thrusts its paws out through any opening and claws at everything it reaches; it continues its efforts when it strikes anything loose and shakey; it may claw at things within the box" (p. 13). Eventually, the cat would happen to pull on the loop or step on the treadle, the door would fall open, and the cat would make its way to the food. When the cat was returned to the box for another trial, it went through the same sort of random activity until it again made the correct response.

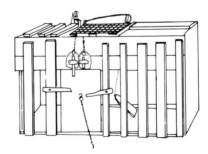

Figure 4-3   This is box K, typical of the boxes Thorndike used in his experiments with cats. Stepping on the treadle released the door bolt. A weight attached to the door then pulled open the door and allowed the cat to escape. (From Thorndike, 1898.)

With succeeding trials, the animal made fewer and fewer random movements "until, after many trials, the cat will, when put in the box, immediately claw . . . the loop in a definite way" (1898, p. 13; see Figure 4-4).

In experiment after experiment, with chicks, cats, dogs, and, later on, with fish and monkeys, Thorndike saw little evidence of the kind of reasoning that seemed to proliferate in the literature on animal intelligence. Instead, he observed a great deal of more or less random activity that eventually included the appropriate behavior. Over a series of trials, this response became more and more likely to occur, while other, useless acts tended to disappear. Animal learning seemed to result not from abstract intellectual activity but from "trial and accidental success" (1911, p. 174).

When an animal is placed in a particular situation, such as a maze or a box, it reacts by making a number of responses. A given response may have either of two kinds of consequences or effects. Thorndike called one kind of consequence a "satisfying state of affairs," the other an "annoying state of affairs." If, for instance, a chick goes down a wrong alley, this response is followed by continued hunger and separation from other chicks—an annoying state of affairs. If the chick goes down the correct alley, this response leads to food and contact with other chicks—a satisfying state of affairs. When a hungry cat tries to squeeze through the bars of its cage, it stays hungry—an annoying consequence; when it pulls at a wire loop, the door opens and it gets food—a satisfying consequence. Thorndike found that when a response is followed by a satisfying state of affairs, it

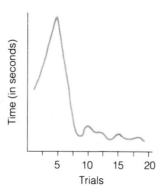

Figure 4-4 Learning curve showing how the time one cat took to escape from a puzzle box decreased. (After Thorndike, 1898.)

tends to be repeated; when a response is followed by an annoying state of affairs, it tends to disappear (see Figure 4-5). In other words, the probability of a response depends upon its effect on the environment, a principle that Thorndike called the **Law of Effect.**

Later on, Thorndike (1931/1968) studied the Law of Effect as it applied to human learning. In one experiment, he asked college students to learn the meanings of a number of uncommon English words. Students would read one of the strange words, then examine a series of possible synonyms and make a guess as to which was the right one. Thorndike would tell the students whether they had guessed correctly, then give them the next item. By going through the list of words in this way, the students eventually learned their meanings. Once again, learning depended upon the effects of behavior: Answers that produced desirable effects (hearing that the answer was correct) tended to be repeated, while those that produced unfavorable effects (being told the answer was wrong) tended to die out.

Building on the foundation laid by Thorndike, B. F. Skinner (1938) began a series of studies in the 1930s that would greatly advance our understanding of learning and behavior. Skinner designed an experimental chamber now commonly known as a Skinner box (see Figure 4-6). The box, now a standard feature of behavioral laboratories, was designed so that from time to time a magazine could automatically drop a few pellets of food into a tray. After a rat became accustomed to the noise of the action of the food magazine and readily ate from the tray, Skinner installed a lever and observed the animal's behavior. As the hungry rat explored its environment, it would occasionally depress the lever. Skinner's next step was to connect the lever to the food magazine so that, when the rat pressed the lever,

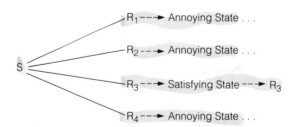

Figure 4-5   Faced with a given stimulus, S, an animal makes a number of responses, R_1, R_2, R_3, R_4, and so on. Those responses that are followed by annoying states tend to disappear; those that are followed by satisfying states tend to be repeated.

E. L. THORNDIKE: WHAT THE
OCCASION DEMANDED

E. L. Thorndike started life on the 31st of August 1874, the son of an itinerant Methodist minister. His parents, who were bright and idealistic, ran a tight ship—so tight, in fact, that someone once said of the family, "There is no music in the Thorndikes." Thorndike's biographer, Geraldine Joncich (1968), wrote that there was "a smothering of lightheartedness and carefree gaiety . . . with Victorian culture and fundamentalist religion" (p. 39). This homelife produced a boy who was well mannered, industrious, and studious, but also shy, serious, and moderate to excess. Thorndike himself hinted that he lacked spontaneity and humor when he said, "I think I was always grown-up" (in Joncich, 1968, p. 31).

In 1893, the young grown-up went off to Wesleyan University, where he developed an interest in literature. As a graduate student at Harvard, he shifted from English to psychology and took up the problem of animal intelligence. There being no laboratory space for his subjects, he kept the animals in his room and conducted the experiments there "until the landlady's protests were imperative" (Thorndike, 1936, p. 264). Finally, William James (one of the founders of modern psychology) offered him the use of his cellar, and this became Thorndike's new laboratory. The work in James's basement went well, but Thorndike had little money, and when the offer of a fellowship at Columbia University came along, Thorndike packed up his "two most educated chickens" and moved to New York. It was at Columbia that Thorndike wrote the dissertation on animal intelligence that started him off on a brilliant career.

Toward the end of that career, Thorndike must have thought about these and other events in his life as he prepared a short autobiographical article. In it, he argued that his accomplishments were not the result of any deliberate plan or "inner needs." Instead, he seemed to compare his own behavior with the trial-and-error activity of his experimental animals. "I did," he explained, "what the occasion seemed to demand" (1936, p. 266).

The occasions seemed to have demanded a great deal. Thorndike's bibliography lists over 500 items, including 78 books. In addition to his work in learning, he made important contributions to educational psychology (a field he practically invented) and to psychological testing. If, as Thorndike seemed to suggest, his behavior was simply the product of a fortuitous environment, then psychology is lucky indeed that Thorndike had such a splendid environment.

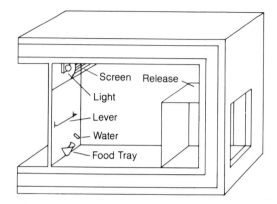

Figure 4-6   One of Skinner's original experimental boxes, now generally referred to as a Skinner box. One wall has been cut away to show the inside of the box. The food magazine and other apparatus were contained in the space outside of the left panel. Each time a rat pressed the lever, it activated the food magazine which dropped a few pellets of food into the tray. (From B. F. Skinner, *The Behavior of Organisms: An Experimental Analysis,* © 1938, Renewed 1966, p. 49. Reprinted by permission of B. F. Skinner.)

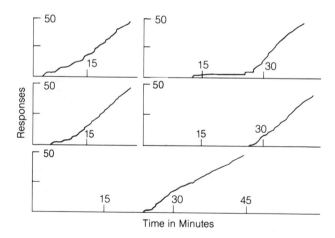

Figure 4-7   Lever pressing. In addition to operating the food magazine, a lever press also causes a needle to inscribe a moving roll of paper, thus providing a permanent record of the total number of lever presses in a given period (see Figure 2-6). The cumulative records above show that when each lever press is reinforced with food, the rate of pressing increases rapidly. (From B. F. Skinner, *The Behavior of Organisms: An Experimental Analysis,* © 1938, Renewed 1966, p. 68. Reprinted by permission of B. F. Skinner.)

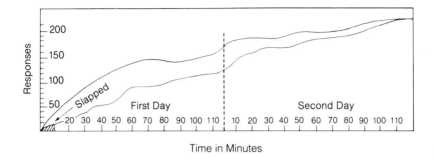

Time in Minutes

Figure 4-8 Punishment. After reinforcing lever pressing with food, all reinforcement was withheld. In addition, for some rats (lower curve) all lever presses were punished for ten minutes. This suppressed the rate of lever pressing for some time afterward. (From B. F. Skinner, *The Behavior of Organisms: An Experimental Analysis*, © 1938, Renewed 1966, p. 154. Reprinted by permission of B. F. Skinner.)

food would fall into the tray. In other words, if the rat pressed the lever, this response would have a positive effect. Under these conditions, the rate of lever pressing increased dramatically (see Figure 4-7).

After a rat had learned to press the lever, Skinner modified the experimental chamber. Now lever pressing no longer produced food; instead, each time the rat pressed the lever, a mechanism slapped its paw; that is, if the rat pressed the lever, an aversive (painful, unpleasant) effect would result. Under these conditions, the rate of lever pressing (which had been high) declined dramatically (see Figure 4-8).

These procedures, whereby behavior is either strengthened or weakened by its consequences, became known as **instrumental conditioning** since the behavior is instrumental in determining what those consequences will be. (Notice that, in contrast to Pavlovian conditioning, the behavior that is modified is operant, not respondent, behavior. Hence, these procedures are also often called **operant conditioning**.)

BASIC PROCEDURES

Skinner (1938, 1953) identified four basic procedures, two of which strengthen (increase the rate of) behavior and two of which weaken (decrease the rate of) behavior. He called procedures that strengthen behavior **reinforcement,** those that weaken behavior **punishment.**

There are two kinds of reinforcement procedures. In **positive reinforcement,** a response is followed by the appearance of, or an increase in the intensity of, a stimulus. This stimulus, called a **positive reinforcer,** is ordinarily something the organism seeks out, such as food. The effect of the procedure is to increase the frequency of the response that precedes the positive reinforcer. For instance, a dog may happen to bark when it is hungry. If someone then gives it a bit of food, the dog is likely to bark again. In positive reinforcement, the occurrence of a response (R) is followed by a reinforcing stimulus (S^R):

$$R \longrightarrow S^R$$
$$\text{bark} \longrightarrow \text{receive food}$$

In **negative reinforcement,** a response is followed by the removal of, or a decrease in the intensity of, a stimulus. This stimulus, called a **negative reinforcer,** is ordinarily something the organism tries to avoid, such as an electric shock. The effect of the procedure is to increase the frequency of the response that precedes the negative reinforcer. For instance, a person with a headache may take an aspirin. If the headache goes away, the person is likely to take aspirin the next time a headache occurs. In negative reinforcement, as in positive reinforcement, a response is followed by a reinforcing event:

$$R \longrightarrow S^R$$
$$\text{take aspirin} \longrightarrow \text{pain stops}$$

Punishment procedures weaken (reduce the rate of) behavior. There are two kinds of punishment procedures. In one, a response is followed by the appearance of an aversive (painful, unpleasant) stimulus. For instance, when you remove your sunglasses on a very bright day, the sunlight hurts your eyes. The response (R) is followed by an aversive event (S^P):

$$R \longrightarrow S^P$$
$$\text{remove sunglasses} \longrightarrow \text{blinding sunlight}$$

In another kind of punishment, sometimes called **response cost,** the response is followed by the removal of a positive reinforcer. In this case, something desirable is taken away. A 6-year-old who throws food across the dinner table may be sent to bed without supper. The misbehavior is followed by removal of food:

$$R \longrightarrow S^P$$

throw food $\longrightarrow$ food taken away

Students have a good deal of difficulty keeping the four instrumental procedures straight; negative reinforcement is especially likely to cause difficulty. In distinguishing between negative reinforcement and punishment, try to remember that reinforcement procedures, including negative reinforcement, *increase* the frequency of a response, while punishment procedures *decrease* the frequency of a response.

These four basic procedures have been used in hundreds of experiments with children and adults, as well as with many kinds of animals, to strengthen or weaken dozens of kinds of behavior. The procedures clearly account for changes in the frequency of existing behavior, but how do they account for the appearance of new forms of behavior? Dogs learn not only to bark when hungry, but to "beg," "shake hands," and perform numerous tricks they rarely do spontaneously. And people learn to read, drive automobiles, and do all sorts of other things they never did before. How is this possible? The answer is a pair of procedures first described by Skinner, shaping and chaining.

SHAPING

Suppose that, through reinforcement, you have trained a rat to press a lever. You notice, however, that the rat exerts the minimum amount of effort necessary to depress the lever, a force of about 35–40 grams. How could you train the rat to use greater force, say 60 grams, when pressing the lever? Skinner's (1938) answer was to reinforce lever pressing only when a force of *at least* 40 grams was applied. In response, the rat began applying more pressure to the lever, perhaps 40–45 grams instead of 35–40 grams. At this point, Skinner reinforced lever pressing only when the rat exerted at least 45 grams of pressure. This produced an additional increase in the average effort exerted, so that the rat typically applied a force of 45–50 grams. Skinner continued increasing the amount of force required for reinforcement until the rat reached the desired level. Thus, Skinner was able to train the rat to make a response it had never made before, pressing the lever with a force of 60 grams. Instead of waiting for the desired behavior to occur spontaneously (which might never have happened), Skinner reinforced any behavior that approximated the desired act. In this way, an entirely new response, one that had never occurred before, was made to appear. The process of building new responses by systematically reinforcing successive approximations to the desired response is called **shaping.**

Skinner "shaped" all sorts of behavior in rats and in pigeons. In one experiment, he trained a pigeon to make clockwise turns. He began by reinforcing any slight clockwise movement. When the bird regularly turned slightly in the desired direction, Skinner withheld reinforcement until the animal turned further than it had before, perhaps a quarter turn. When the bird regularly made quarter turns, Skinner demanded half turns. When half turns were forthcoming, Skinner reinforced only complete clockwise turns. Although this procedure may seem slow and tedious, in fact learning proceeds very rapidly; Skinner found it possible to teach a hungry pigeon to make clockwise turns in a few minutes. (This does not necessarily mean that it is easy to do, as many students have discovered. They often take hours to accomplish what Skinner or another experienced "behavior shaper" could do in minutes. Often, the difference is that the student resorts to techniques, such as shouting at the animal or pounding on its cage, intended to "supplement" the instrumental procedure. These techniques usually delay learning.)

Shaping is not merely a laboratory procedure. We often witness shaping taking place in human society, especially as adults interact with children and animals. Some people I know, for example, inadvertently shaped up persistent barking in their dog. Normally, they kept the dog in their house or tied in the back yard, but sometimes they put the dog in a pen. When they first did so, the dog began to bark. After a few minutes of this noise, the dog's owners released it "to shut it up." The next time they put the dog into the pen, it barked again, but its owners ignored it for several minutes before giving in, thereby reinforcing the dog for prolonged barking (though clearly this was not their intention). The owners continued to try to outwait the dog, but always ended by reinforcing prolonged barking until finally the dog would bark unceasingly for several hours. Barking was, of course, not a new kind of behavior in this dog. What was shaped up was not barking, per se, but prolonged, persistent barking. We may say that the dog's owners taught it (albeit unintentionally) to be persistently noisy.

SHAPING UP TEACHER

Eye contact is a powerful reinforcer that can be used to shape behavior. There is an anecdote about the use of eye contact to shape the behavior of a famous university professor, an expert on instrumental conditioning. The story has it that some students decided to train the professor to lecture from one corner of the classroom. They used eye contact as a reinforcer and began reinforcing successive approximations to the desired response: Each time the instructor moved toward the appropriate corner, the students would look at him; if he moved in another direction, they looked away. By gradually reinforcing successive approximations to the desired response, the students were able to get the instructor to deliver his lecture while huddled in one corner of the room.

Whether this experiment was actually performed is uncertain. Nevertheless, the story offers a plausible illustration of how reinforcers can be used to shape behavior in ordinary situations. They may even work on an instructor you happen to know.

You may observe parents shaping up inappropriate behavior in their children in much the same way. It is normal for young children to be unhappy when denied something they wish to have. It is not, however, inevitable that under such circumstances children should throw themselves upon the floor, attack it with hands and feet, and scream like rock stars. Rather, such behavior is usually shaped by parental reinforcement. A tired parent may give in to a child's demands so as to "shut him up," just as the dog owners did. Often, parents succumb to avoid a scene in a restaurant or at home when guests are present, in which case the child may succeed merely by repeatedly requesting something. On the next occasion, simple entreaties may not suffice, and the parent may become annoyed and tell the child harshly that the request is denied. This change in the rules is apt to induce crying, which often will make the parent yield. On a subsequent occasion, the parent may refuse to comply when the child cries and may, instead, strike the child. This, of course, does not stem the crying but rather brings forth a torrent of tears accompanied by bugle-like wails. Ultimately, the parent gives in. And so it goes: The parent gradually "demands" more outrageous behavior for reinforcement and the child obliges, eventually engaging in full-fledged tantrums. Needless to say, the parents involved typically have little insight into their role in the problem, though their children sometimes are able to state the rules involved (e.g., see Thorndike, 1931/1968, p. 169f.).

It is reasonable to suppose that the same sort of process takes place in the animal world and contributes in important ways to survival. The goats of the Serengeti Plain normally graze upon grass, but during prolonged droughts they must turn to the leaves of trees. As the lower leaves are devoured, the goats are forced to go after those higher up. Presumably, it was this shaping of behavior that resulted in goats actually climbing into trees to feed during the drought of 1984.

Some adult animals seem to use a kind of shaping procedure in the training of their young. Otters, for example, first feed their young on prey that they have killed; their young have only to tear the prey apart and eat. As the otters mature, their parents bring animals that are dying; the young otters find the prey easy to kill. After this, the parents bring injured prey; their young must finish the job in order to eat. Finally, the adults take their young to the hunting area and bring them uninjured prey. Thus, the young otters build upon past skills until they master the art of hunting and killing prey on their own.

CHAINING

Shaping does much to explain how new forms of behavior may be acquired: They are, in a sense, "constructed" out of old behavior. But some kinds of behavior consist of long series of acts. Many of these series are so complex that it is hard to see how they could be shaped up in this way. Such behavior usually can be accounted for by a procedure called **chaining,** which involves establishing a sequence, or chain, of responses, the last of which is followed by a reinforcer. The procedure usually begins with shaping, in the manner just described, the last response in a sequence of acts. When this response is well established, the response that is to precede it is shaped up, and so on. Thus, we might train a pigeon to peck an illuminated red disk by making food available when it has pecked the disk three times. When the bird is pecking the red disk steadily, the light behind the disk may be turned off and the light behind a green disk turned on. If the pigeon pecks the red disk, nothing happens. But if it pecks the green disk three times, the green disk goes off and the red disk goes on. Now if the bird pecks the red disk, it is rewarded. The reinforcer for pecking the green disk is access to a lighted red disk. In this way, the pigeon might learn to peck a series of five disks in sequence.

Skinner (1938) used shaping and chaining to build a complex sequence of responses in a rat. The rat would pull a string that would release a marble from a rack, pick up the marble with its forepaws, carry it to a tube projecting 2 inches above the floor of its cage, lift the marble to the top of the tube, and drop it inside. To establish this behavior, "every step in the process had to be worked out through a series of approximations, since the component responses were not in the original repertoire of the rat" (p. 340). In other words, the rat's behavior had to be viewed as a complex response chain; each response in the chain was shaped through the reinforcement of successive approximations.

Other psychologists have since trained laboratory animals to perform even more complex behavior chains. Carl Cheney (1978) used shaping and chaining to build the long chain of complex activities shown in Figure 4-9. The chain began when the rat was placed at the

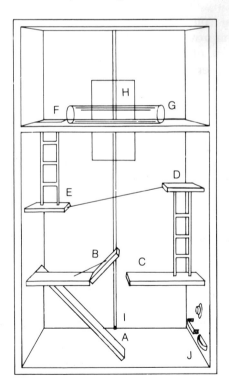

Figure 4-9   Chaining. Starting at A, rat climbs ramp to B, crosses drawbridge to C, climbs ladder to D, crosses tightrope to E, climbs ladder to F, crawls through tunnel to G, enters elevator at H, descends to I, presses lever at J, receives food.

foot of a ramp. The rat climbed the ramp, crossed a drawbridge, climbed a ladder, walked across a tightrope, climbed another ladder, crawled through a tunnel, stepped into an elevator that carried it back down to its starting point, pressed a lever, and received a few pellets of food. It may seem hard to believe that any animal would do so much for a few pellets of food. But remember that the chain was built up gradually; initially, the rat had only to press the lever, then to run from the elevator and press the lever, and so on.

The same sort of response chains occur in humans. Students learn to do long division, which consists of a series of multiplication and subtraction operations performed in a particular order. And when the students fix themselves a snack, they perform a sequence of acts: going to the refrigerator, taking out the milk, getting a glass from the cupboard, and so on. In these and other instances, reinforcement is normally available only upon completion of the last response in the chain.

Instrumental conditioning procedures, including shaping and chaining, have improved our understanding of many kinds of behavior in many kinds of organisms. To illustrate, we will consider in some detail a problem that has been analyzed in terms of instrumental conditioning: superstition.

SUPERSTITIOUS BEHAVIOR

In the experiments cited so far, the behavior causes, or at least is reliably followed by, a reinforcer or punisher. But it sometimes happens that the occurrence of an important event following a particular response is merely coincidental. This raises an interesting question: What is the effect of a reinforcer or punisher if its appearance following a response is only accidental? Suppose that you put a pigeon into a Skinner box and modified the feeding mechanism so that grain became available at intervals of, say, 15 seconds, *regardless* of what the animal happened to be doing. Would the delivery of food in this way affect the pigeon's behavior?

B. F. Skinner (1948a) performed an experiment very much like this. He found that out of 8 pigeons, 6 acquired some clear-cut response: One bird turned in counterclockwise circles, another raised its head toward one of the corners of the cage, 1 pigeon bobbed its head up and down, 2 birds swung their heads to and fro, and the 6th pigeon made brushing movements toward the floor, as if trying to peck it. The animals appeared to have learned to perform strange rituals, in spite of the fact that the reinforcer came *whether or not* the birds made those responses. Skinner called these acts **superstitious behavior** since the birds behaved as if their rituals produced reinforcement, when in fact they did not.

Skinner's explanation of this phenomenon is quite simple. When the first reinforcer arrived, the animal had to be doing *something*. If the bird happened to be bobbing its head up and down (something that pigeons are inclined to do occasionally), then head bobbing was accidentally reinforced; that is, **adventitious reinforcement** has occurred. A response that is followed by food is likely to be repeated, so the animal was probably bobbing its head the next time food came. This, in turn, meant that head bobbing was likely to occur again, which meant it was still more likely to be reinforced, and so on.

Supertitious behavior is not restricted to pigeons. In one study, Alfred Bruner and Samuel Revusky (1961) used adventitious reinforcement to establish superstitious behavior in 4 high school students. Each student sat in front of four telegraph keys. If the student pressed the right key, a bell would sound, a red light would go on, and a counter would record the response. Each time this happened, the student would have earned 5 cents, which could be collected later on. The correct response consisted of depressing the third key from the student's left, but this response was reinforced only when it occurred after an interval of several seconds. What happened was that the students began plunking the other keys during these periods of nonreinforcement. Eventually, the nonreinforcement period would end, the student would happen to hit key 3 again, and this act would be reinforced. However, the responses that immediately preceded hitting key 3 also were reinforced, even though they had nothing to do with producing the reinforcers. Eventually, each student worked out a pattern of key presses, such as 1, 2, 3, 4, 1, 2, 3. Interestingly, the experimenters report that none of the students suspected that any part of their behavior was superstitious.

Richard Herrnstein (1966) has argued that superstitious behavior can occur as a kind of by-product of training. He notes that in many instances, a particular feature of a response is essential for reinforcement, but other features are not. If the essential feature produces reinforcement, the other features are adventitiously reinforced. He cites handwriting as an example. In making the various letters of the alphabet, reinforcement is contingent upon producing certain features of the letters. However, there is a good deal of latitude in how the letters may be formed. For example, in making a cursive, lowercase *t*, it is necessary to produce a nearly vertical straight line and to cross that line with a horizontal line. But the vertical line may, in fact, be a loop (like the cursive letter *l*), and it can be short or long; likewise, the horizontal line can be short or long, perfectly horizontal or angled up or down, and it can appear near the top of the vertical line or near the bottom. If an essential feature is performed in such a way as to gain reinforcement, other nonessential features of handwriting are adventitiously reinforced. The implication is that the wide differences in handwriting, among other idiosyncracies, are kinds of superstitious behavior.

Skinner suggests that a good deal of everyday human activity may be superstitious behavior established through adventitious reinforcement. He cites as a likely candidate "the bowler who has released a ball down the alley but continues to behave as if he were controlling it by twisting and turning his arm and shoulder. . . . These behaviors have, of course, no real effect upon . . . a ball halfway down an alley" (1948a, p. 171). Other examples include a professional basketball player who insists on wearing the same pair of "lucky" socks during games, the baseball player who flaps one arm as he awaits the pitch, the stockbroker who never buys or sells on Tuesdays, the woman who never dates men named Bruce, and the student who always takes the aisle seat in the next-to-last row.

But many human superstitions seem too complex and too widespread to be attributed to adventitious reinforcement. People sprinkle salt over their shoulders, carry amulets, and, in some societies, have engaged in rain dances and human sacrifice. Can such complex and improbable behavior be attributed to adventitious reinforcement? Herrnstein (1966) argues that it is unlikely that such behavior is shaped by adventitious reinforcement, but that it may be *maintained* by such reinforcement. In examining Skinner's original pigeon experiment, Herrnstein notes that the superstitious behavior that appeared was "distinctly pigeon-like": Pigeons often bob their heads, turn in circles, and so on. Skinner's procedure merely increased the rate at which one of these innately dominant responses occurred. (A similar argument was made by Staddon & Simmelhag, 1971; see also Timberlake & Lucas, 1985, for a discussion of these issues.)

Herrnstein argued that any behavior, if made likely to occur, might be maintained by adventitious reinforcement. To test this idea, he trained a pigeon to peck a disk by reinforcing each disk peck that occurred after an 11-second interval. (In other words, the bird received no reinforcement for disk pecks during the interval.) When disk pecking was well established, Herrnstein stopped reinforcing this behavior and began providing food every 11 seconds *regardless* of what the animal did, that is, he switched to Skinner's superstition procedure. Note that though the reinforcement contingencies had changed, the animal was expected to show a relatively high frequency of disk pecking, at least initially. Thus, the now ineffectual behavior of disk pecking could easily be adventitiously reinforced. Under these conditions, the rate of disk pecking declined somewhat but did not die out. Apparently, the adventitious reinforcement was sufficient to maintain the behavior.

The significance of Herrnstein's experiment is that it suggests that any behavior, however complex and improbable, can be maintained through adventitious reinforcement *if the organism can be induced to perform it at least once.* He notes further that the most common human superstitions arise "in a social context." We hear about rabbits' feet, about the dangers of black cats, about Friday the 13th, about spilling salt; further, we are prompted to perform superstitious acts. Children, for example, may be required by a parent to throw a bit of salt over one shoulder after spilling salt on the dinner table. Once performed, there is the chance that such behavior will be adventitiously reinforced, so that children are likely to perform the act the next time they spill salt.

Of course, it should be noted the "social context" to which Herrnstein refers often provides ample reinforcement for the maintenance of superstitious behavior. Not only are we advised of the wisdom of "knocking on wood," but following this advice is reinforced by the approval of those who recommend it. This kind of reinforcement is by no means adventitious since it depends upon the performance of the superstitious behavior. Superstitious behavior in humans is therefore likely to be maintained both by adventitious and contingent reinforcement.

It is perhaps for this reason that superstitious behavior persists in spite of its apparent lack of adaptive value. Herrnstein (1966) notes that behavior may be expected to "drift" toward the minimal essential features. If no feature is essential for reinforcement (as is the case in superstitious behavior), then we may expect that it will disappear. However, if adventitious reinforcement occurs occasionally, superstitious behavior may be maintained indefinitely (see Schwartz & Reilly, 1985).

Although superstitious behavior is, by definition, not effective in producing the reinforcers that maintain it, this is not to say that it is utterly useless. Individual superstitions, such as that of the gyrating bowler, give the person the illusion of control over uncontrollable events. This may be why superstitions are particularly common among those engaged in hazardous occupations such as sailing (Malinowski, 1922). Even group superstitions, such as the rain dance or the chanting of shamans over the ill, may serve to give the individuals involved the illusion of control and, in addition, may help the group to remain together in trying times. These are certainly reinforcing events, so superstitions may be more functional than they seem.

VARIABLES AFFECTING INSTRUMENTAL CONDITIONING

R-S Contiguity

The gap between a response and its consequences (whether reinforcing or punishing) has a powerful effect upon the rate of instrumental learning. In general, the shorter this interval is, the more effective the consequences will be (see Hunter, 1913; Thomas et al., 1983). Suppose, for example, that you are learning to ride a bicycle. In this case, the consequences that lead to learning are the sensations that tell you when you are well balanced and when you are falling. Now, suppose that you have a middle ear infection that prevents you from perceiving subtle differences in balance. Theoretically, you could still learn to ride if someone were to stand nearby and shout "Good!" whenever you appeared to be distributing your weight appropriately and "Bad!" whenever you were in danger of falling. The main difference between the natural consequences and the artificial ones is that in the former case, the consequences would follow the behavior immediately, whereas in the latter case, the consequences would be delayed slightly. So far as I know, an experiment of this sort has not yet been performed, but it seems likely that learning with such delayed consequences would be quite slow.

Jeffrey Weil (1984) pointed out that most studies of delayed reinforcement are confounded by another factor, the number of times the response is reinforced. To illustrate, let us compare two conditions. In one, lever pressing is reinforced immediately with electrical stimulation of the brain's pleasure center; in the second, the response is reinforced in the same way except that there is a 5-second delay. If we run animals under both conditions for 1 hour, we are likely to find that immediate reinforcement results in a sharper increase in lever pressing. But a problem arises in interpreting the results because immediate reinforcement means that the response is reinforced more often in an hour's time than is the case with delayed reinforcement.

(With a 5-second delay, a response can be reinforced a maximum of 720 times in an hour; with immediate reinforcement, over 7,000 lever presses could be reinforced.) Weil dealt with this problem by making the number of reinforcers constant. The results showed that reinforcement delay in and of itself is an important factor in operant learning: the shorter the interval, the more rapidly learning occurs.

One reason that immediate consequences usually produce better results is because a delay allows time for other behavior to occur. This behavior, and not the appropriate response, is then reinforced. Suppose you try to increase your roommate's frequency of using curse words. Each time he or she says "Damn" or uses some other expletive in the course of a conversation, you look at your roommate, nod your head, and say "I see," "Good," or "Right!" as appropriate. The rest of the time you look down at the floor or off to the side and say nothing. But instead of reinforcing immediately, you delay the reinforcer by counting silently to yourself for 3 seconds before responding to a curse word. In this situation, by the time you look up and say "Right!," your roommate has emitted three or four words since the curse word. There may also be other changes. For example, he or she may have just spoken in a slightly louder voice, in which case you will have adventitiously reinforced an increase in speaking volume. As you know from the discussion of superstitious behavior, we may expect under these circumstances that your roommate will begin to speak louder. It matters little that you did not *intend* to modify how loudly your roommate speaks. The point is that delay of reinforcers and punishers interferes with conditioning because it results in behavior other than the target response being reinforced or punished.

R-S Contingency

The very term *instrumental conditioning* implies that a contingency of some sort exists between a response and a reinforcing or punishing event. We flip a switch and the room lights go on. The lights do not ordinarily go on when we haven't thrown the switch, nor do they usually fail to go on if we do flip the switch. Similarly, if you insert a knife or other metal object into an electrical outlet, you will get a shock, but you do not get a shock if you avoid the outlet. In each of these cases, the response causes, or is instrumental in producing, the event that follows. In the laboratory, instrumental conditioning usually means arranging the environment in such a way that a response has reliable consequences. We may arrange a rat's environment so that each time it presses a lever, it receives a bit of food, but otherwise receives nothing. A clear contingency then exists between lever pressing and food.

But there are many situations in which the relationship between a response and an important event is more ambiguous. A pianist who performs on tour may find that playing a Chopin concerto in a particular style pleases some audiences more than others. Likewise, we can arrange a rat's environment so that some lever presses produce food and others do not. The greater the degree of correspondence between a response and a reinforcer or punisher, the more rapidly the behavior will change. If, say, 80 percent of all lever presses are reinforced with food, the rate of lever pressing will climb more sharply than if only 40 percent of lever presses are reinforced. In the same way, a pianist is more likely to perfect an original rendition of a concerto if most audiences applaud enthusiastically than if they seem not to notice.

Response Features

Certain qualities of the behavior to be modified affect the course of conditioning. It is fairly obvious that learning to walk a balance beam is easier than learning to walk a tightrope. It is somewhat less obvious that behavior that depends upon smooth muscles and glands (i.e., respondent behavior) is harder to modify through instrumental conditioning than is behavior that depends upon striated muscles (i.e., operant behavior). Yet all of the instances of instrumental conditioning cited thus far have involved behavior controlled by striated muscles, behavior that we ordinarily think of as voluntary.

It used to be assumed that so-called involuntary behavior could be altered only through Pavlovian procedures. It seemed absurd, for example, to think that people might learn to regulate their heart rate or their blood pressure through instrumental conditioning. But in the 1960s, Neal Miller and Alfredo Carmona (1967) used instrumental conditioning to train a dog to salivate, something that wasn't supposed to be possible. Then Miller and Leo Di Cara (1967) took on the problem of teaching rats to control their heart rates. In order to ensure that changes in heart rate were not due to the animal learning to tense and relax certain voluntary muscles (and thereby indirectly changing heart rate), they curarized rats (that is, the rats were given a derivative of the drug curare, which temporarily paralyzed their voluntary muscles). Miller and DiCara then reinforced changes in heart rate by electrically stimulating a pleasure center in the rat's brain. At first, the researchers reinforced small changes in heart rate that were in the desired direction; then they required greater and greater deviations from the normal rate. During a 90-minute training period, the rats learned to increase or decrease their heart rates by an average of about 20 percent.

These astonishing results prompted dozens of other researchers to apply instrumental procedures to respondent behavior. Some of that research has supported the early findings of Miller and his colleagues, while other research has not. Miller himself has expressed doubts about such "visceral learning." After studies involving 2,500 rats, he and collaborator Barry Dworkin (Dworkin & Miller, 1986) conclude that "the existence of visceral learning remains unproven" (p. 299; see also Miller, 1978). Thus, the extent to which respondent behavior can be modified by instrumental procedures remains uncer-tain. The point here, however, is that instrumental conditioning proceeds much more rapidly and predictably when applied to some kinds of behavior than when applied to others. Even with the best of reinforcers, learning to lower your blood pressure is more difficult than learning to row a boat.

Consequence Characteristics

The rate of instrumental conditioning also is affected by certain characteristics of reinforcing and punishing consequences. A 2-second shock, for instance, is less punishing (i.e., is less effective in suppressing the behavior it follows) than a 5-second shock. Similarly, a slice of bread is more reinforcing to a hungry man than a few crumbs. The effectiveness of a reinforcer or punisher tends to increase, then, with its size, duration, and intensity (see Church, 1969; Logan, 1960).

O. Hobart Mowrer (1960) argued, however, that strong consequences produce emotional side effects that may interfere with learning. Positive reinforcement is a very safe procedure since it produces positive emotional side effects (Epstein, 1985b). It is possible, however, for positive emotions to interfere with the course of learning. The teacher who rewards fourth-graders for behaving well during a study period by complimenting them probably will get good results. But the teacher who rewards fourth-graders by announcing that they will be allowed to go to recess 10 minutes early may find that their joyous reaction makes it impossible for them to learn anything during the next lesson.

Negative reinforcement, said Mowrer, produces relief. The stronger the aversive stimulus that is removed, the greater the relief. But the research of Hans Selye (1976) on stress suggests that it requires considerable effort to endure strong aversive stimuli. The use of such stimuli may produce fatigue, and their removal in negative reinforcement might be accompanied by a lack of activity as the organism recovers, which can interfere with further learning.

In recent years, a good deal has been written about the possibility of adverse by-products of reinforcement. In essence, the idea is that reinforcing a response makes the response *less* likely to occur once the reinforcement contingency is withdrawn. For example, if children are reinforced for finger painting, something they normally like to do, they spend less time painting when reinforcers are no longer available for that activity. It is said that reinforcement "turns play into work" (Lepper & Greene, 1976; 1978). Recent analysis (Timberlake, 1980) implies, however, that this interpretation is mistaken. Children like to do many things, one of which is finger painting. If they have the opportunity to fingerpaint (whether under reinforcement conditions or not), they will do so, but eventually they will turn to other activities. Reinforcement maintains the behavior at a high rate, but when reinforcement is withdrawn, the children do what they would have done in the absence of reinforcement—they turn to something else. Reinforcement does not, therefore, turn play into work. It merely makes one form of play more appealing than another.

Punishment, according to Mowrer, tends to arouse anger or fear. If strongly aversive stimuli are used, the emotion may inhibit learning. The normally docile dog may attack its master if beaten harshly; a child may become overly shy and nervous if parental punishment is too severe. Punishing by withdrawing a reinforcer produces its own special form of emotional reaction: disappointment or depression. The teacher who tells his students that they may not go outside during recess is apt to be greeted with protests. Withdrawal of stronger reinforcers may produce more serious emotional reactions, the most obvious example being the death of a loved one. People who are close to us provide all sorts of powerful reinforcers; when they die, those reinforcers are suddenly withdrawn. Another example is the depression that comes from a sudden loss of income. In the stock market crash of 1929, some very wealthy people became paupers overnight, and some of those paupers jumped out of windows. Such depression is not ordinarily conducive to learning.

A word should be said about the special effects of punishment. Textbooks traditionally warn students about the dangers of punishment, and for good reason. If not properly used, punishment procedures can do more harm than good. Some writers have recently suggested, however, that we textbook authors may have overstated the case against punishment. Saul Axelrod (1983) writes that "in fact, the vast majority of studies have reported positive side effects" from punishment (p. 8; see also Newsom et al., 1983; Van Houten, 1983). There is no doubt that punishment can be extremely effective (see Figure 4-10).

Nevertheless, punishment carries with it special risks. For instance, if the punished person or animal is able to escape punishment, the problem behavior may be made worse. The dog that gets into the garbage but runs off when its owner tries to punish it has learned to "eat and run." Similarly, the child who is spanked for stealing from the cookie jar will learn to lie if lying means avoiding a spanking. One must also be careful that the behavior being punished is the behavior one wants to punish. Thousands of dog owners call a misbehaving pet to them for punishment and later wonder why the animal no longer comes when called. They fail to understand that they have punished good behavior (approaching when called) rather than misbehavior (garbage scrounging). There have also been reports of increases in punished behavior when the punishment contingency is no longer in force—a case of "When the cat's away . . ." (Newcome et al., 1983). Yet another problem is that if the punishment is

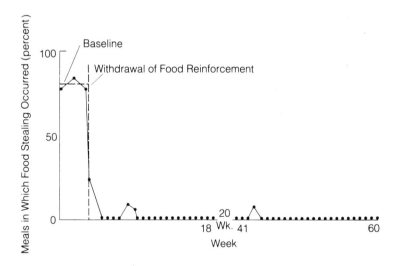

Figure 4-10 Punishment of food stealing. A psychiatric patient was stealing food at about three-fourths of the meals. When an attempt to steal resulted in loss of food, the rate of stealing dropped to zero almost immediately. (After Teodoro Ayllon, "Intensive Treatment of Psychotic Behavior by Stimulus Satiation and Food Reinforcement," *Behavior Research and Therapy*, 1963, 1, p. 55, figure 1. Reprinted with permission of Pergamon Press, Ltd. and Teodoro Ayllon.)

too weak to be effective, the person administering it may gradually increase its intensity until a much stronger punishment is required than would have been necessary had a stronger punishment been used from the start. Well-meaning teachers and parents often fall into this trap by "going easy on" a child for the first offense and gradually increasing the punishment with each subsequent offense. Our courts regularly do the same thing when they dismiss the charges or give a light punishment for a first offense. Perhaps the greatest danger of punishment comes from its association with strong emotions. Parents, for example, tend to use corporal punishment when they are angry, and the severity of punishment used has more to do with their anger than with the offense committed or the punishment necessary to suppress the misbehavior. Indeed, child abuse often occurs when parents "discipline" a child while they themselves are furious. It seems, then, that while punishment is a safe and effective procedure in the hands of an expert, those not trained in its subtleties would do well to rely upon reinforcement (especially positive reinforcement) whenever possible.

Deprivation Level

An important factor in instrumental conditioning is the level of **deprivation,** the extent to which the organism has been deprived of the reinforcer. Food is more reinforcing to a hungry animal than to a sated one. To the psychologist, a hungry animal is one that has been deprived of food. An animal may be maintained at 80 percent of its *ad lib* weight, what it weighs when allowed to eat all it wants. Another way of defining hunger is in terms of a period of food deprivation. A hungry rat is one that has had no food in, say, 12 hours. Similarly, a rat that has been deprived of water for a specified period is, by definition, thirsty.

The effectiveness of a reinforcer such as food, water, sex, and warmth varies with the degree of deprivation. In general, the greater the level of deprivation (e.g., the longer the interval since last eating), the faster learning proceeds, though learning may be inhibited if the level of deprivation is too great. A dog that has been deprived of food for many hours may behave in a very excited manner. Thus, learning proceeds more rapidly as the deprivation level increases, but after a certain point, increases in deprivation may interfere with learning.

The examples considered thus far involve reinforcers that reduce a physiological need. Water reinforces the behavior of a thirsty rat because it replaces water lost through bodily functions. This implies that as reinforcement proceeds, the reinforcer will become less effective. When the reinforcer is no longer effective (when a rat will, for example, no longer press a lever to obtain food), the animal is said to be **satiated**.

Not all reinforcers meet physiological needs, however. Money is a powerful reinforcer, but it does not alleviate a physiological condition induced by depriving an organism of money. Similarly, praise is a reinforcer, but there is no physiological state associated with deprivation of praise. Deprivation level is important, then, only when the reinforcer alters some physiological condition. (Why other kinds of stimuli are reinforcing will be discussed later on.)

Characteristics of the Learner

As with Pavlovian conditioning, the effectiveness of instrumental procedures varies with the organism involved. Most studies utilizing lower species involve changes in the rate of some very simple response. However, it is amazing what can be done even with animals as lowly as the cockroach. There have been reports of a sideshow act in which roaches swung on swings, sat in tiny chairs, opened tiny newspapers, and ate off of tiny dishes. The trainer of these diminutive stars never divulged how he got them to perform these feats, but it is fairly certain that he used instrumental procedures. Nevertheless, higher species generally respond more readily to instrumental procedures than do lower ones.

There are also individual differences within species. Peter Dews (1959) wanted to see if lever pulling could be shaped up in three octopi, Albert, Bertram, and Charles. Each animal lived in a tank filled with salt water. A lever was attached to the tank during training sessions. The basic procedure consisted of providing food when an octopus approached the lever, then when it touched the lever, and finally only when it pulled it. Conditioning proceeded by the book with both Albert and Bertram. Charles also learned to pull the lever, but things did not go as smoothly with him. Instead of pulling the lever while floating, Charles anchored himself to the sides of his tank and pulled the lever with great force, eventually breaking it. Charles's most bizarre behavior was a tendency to squirt water at people. Dews writes that "the animal spent much time with eyes above the surface of the water, directing a jet of water at any individual who approached the tank" (p. 62.) Charles's bizarre behavior may have been due to genetic influences or to previous learning experiences. The point is that individual differences affect the course of conditioning.

While the Law of Effect seems to hold for most, if not all species, and for all individuals within a species, there are limitations. One does not return Lazarus from the dead by reinforcing successive approximations to life. And while both pigeons and elephants can learn all sorts of complex response chains, it is decidedly easier to teach one to fly than it is the other. In addition, there are certain peculiarities in the readiness with which certain responses appear in various species. It is, as a result, very easy to teach a pig to dig into the ground with its snout, but it is more difficult to get a cat to do the same thing. Similarly, pigeons have a predisposition to peck, so it is very easy for them to learn to peck a disk for food. These topics will be discussed in more detail in Chapter 10. For now, it is enough to note that while instrumental conditioning procedures work in much the same way from individual to individual, and from species to species, there are individual differences that affect the rate of learning.

THEORIES OF REINFORCEMENT

It is often said that "practice makes perfect," as if merely performing some act repeatedly is all that is required to master the act. Indeed, this view is still considered by many laymen to be commonsense. Thorndike (1931/1968), however, long ago showed that the commonsense view was in error. He conducted several experiments in which he attempted to separate the influence of practice from the influence of reinforcement. In one experiment, he tried to draw a 4-inch line with his eyes closed and without any feedback concerning his performance. He drew the line over and over again for a total of 3,000 responses, yet there was no improvement. On the first day of practice, the lines varied from 4.5 to 6.2 inches; on the last day, they varied from 4.1 to 5.7 inches. The medians for each day also reveal no evidence of learning (see Figure 4-11). Thorndike concluded that practice is important only insofar as it provides the opportunity for reinforcement.

It is clear that reinforcers produce learning because they "select" certain responses. We saw this with Thorndike's cats, and we can see that Thorndike's failure to improve in drawing a line was the result of the absence of events that would reinforce appropriate responses. But *why* do reinforcers strengthen behavior? Many psychologists have attempted to solve the riddle; here, we will consider the efforts of Hull, Premack, and Timberlake.

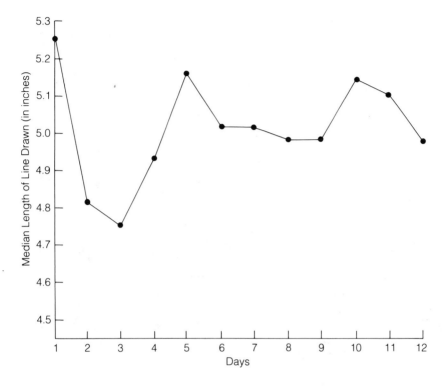

Figure 4-11 The effect of practice without reinforcement. Attempts to draw a 4-inch line while blindfolded showed little improvement. (Compiled from data in Thorndike, 1931/1968.)

Drive-Reduction Theory

One of the most devoted students of the question of why reinforcers reinforce was Clark Hull (1943, 1951, 1952). Hull believed that behavior was driven, that is, that animals and people behaved because of **drives** caused by physiological needs. An animal deprived of food is driven by the need for food. Other drives are associated with deprivation of water, sleep, oxygen, and sex. A reinforcer is a stimulus that reduces one of these (or other) physiological needs. To an animal that has been deprived of food, for example, food is an effective reinforcer because it reduces the drive known as hunger. An animal that is sated on food, in contrast, learns slowly when reinforced with food.

Hull's **drive-reduction theory** works reasonably well with reinforcers such as food and water, but there are many other reinforcers that do not seem to reduce physiological needs. Money is a very effective reinforcer for human beings, as are praise and compliments. But there is no evidence that money, praise, and compliments satisfy physiological needs.

Hull answered this criticism by suggesting that there are two kinds of reinforcers. **Primary reinforcers** reduce physiological needs found in all members of a species. Examples of primary reinforcers include food and water. **Secondary reinforcers** do not reduce physiological needs; instead, they derive their reinforcing powers from their association with primary reinforcers. Food reduces hunger, and since one needs money to buy food, money is regularly associated with food and acquires some of its reinforcing properties.

The distinction between primary and secondary reinforcers is widely used by psychologists today, but Hull's critics were not satisfied. They pointed out that some reinforcers seemed to be neither primary reinforcers nor secondary reinforcers. It has been demonstrated, for instance, that bringing an image into focus will reinforce the behavior of a baby (Siqueland & Delucia, 1969). This reinforcer does not seem to reduce any known physiological need, nor does it depend upon associations with primary reinforcers. Many other reinforcers are equally troubling. Because of this problem, most psychologists today find Hull's drive-reduction theory an unsatisfactory explanation of why reinforcers work. (However, it is not without its defenders; see Smith, 1984.)

Relative Value Theory

David Premack (1959, 1965) took an altogether different approach to the problem of reinforcement. Whereas reinforcers are ordinarily viewed as stimuli, Premack noticed that they could be thought of as behavior. Take the case of reinforcing lever pressing with food. The reinforcer is usually said to be food, but it can just as easily be taken to be eating. In this context, it becomes apparent that under certain circumstances, some kinds of behavior have a greater likelihood of occurrence than others. A rat that has been deprived of food is more likely to eat (given the opportunity to do so) than it is to press a lever. Different kinds of behavior have different relative values at any given instance, and it is their relative values that determine which will reinforce which. This theory, which may be called the **relative value theory,** makes no use of assumed physiological drives. It is strictly empirical; that is, to determine whether a given activity will reinforce another, we must be able to predict the respective values of each activity.

As a measure of the relative values of two activities, Premack suggested measuring the amount of time engaged in both activities, given a choice between them. This leads to the following generalization, known as the **Premack Principle:** "Of any two responses, the more probable response will reinforce the less probable one" (Premack, 1965, p. 132). In other words, high probability behavior reinforces low probability behavior.

We may expect that a rat that has been deprived of water will, given a choice between running in an exercise wheel or drinking, spend more time drinking than running. This, in turn, suggests that drinking can be used as a reinforcer to increase the rate of various kinds of behavior, including running. Premack (1962) demonstrated that this was so by conducting an experiment in which he made drinking contingent upon running in thirsty rats. The result was that the time spent running increased. That is, drinking reinforced running.

But Premack's theory suggests that this relationship between drinking and running could be reversed, that drinking could be reinforced by running if the relative value of running could be made greater than that of drinking. Premack tested this idea by providing rats with free access to water, but restricting their running to less than their baseline rate (the rate at which a given activity is engaged in when there are no restrictions). He then made running contingent upon drinking, so that to get to the exercise wheels, the rats had to drink. Under these circumstances, time spent drinking increased by a factor of 3 or more over the baseline rate. In other words, running reinforced drinking (see Figure 4-12).

In another experiment, Premack (1959) gave first-graders the opportunity to eat candy dispensed from a machine or to play a pinball machine. The children could stick with one activity or alternate between the two. Some children preferred (i.e., spent more time on) the pinball machine; others preferred to eat candy. After identifying these relative values, Premack made access to each child's more probable behavior contingent upon performance of that child's less probable behavior. For instance, a child who spent more time playing pinball now had to eat candy to get access to the pinball machine. The result was that the less probable behavior increased.

Premack's theory of reinforcement has the advantage of being strictly empirical; no hypothetical concepts, such as drive, are re-

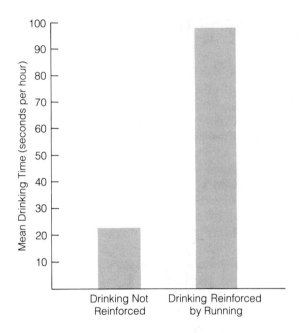

Figure 4-12   Relative value of reinforcement. In thirsty rats, water will reinforce running, but Premack showed that in rats deprived of exercise, running will reinforce drinking. (Compiled from data in Premack, 1962.)

quired. An event is reinforcing simply because it provides the opportunity to engage in preferred behavior. The theory is not, however, without its problems. Timberlake (1980) found that, contrary to Premack's theory, *low* probability behavior will reinforce *high* probability behavior if the subject has been prevented from performing the low probability behavior at its baseline rate.

Equilibrium Theory

Because of such problems, Timberlake (1980; see also Timberlake & Allison, 1974) proposed what has been called the **equilibrium theory** of reinforcement, which states that organisms strive to maintain a certain equilibrium in their activities. The equilibrium is indicated by the rates at which the activities are engaged in when there are no restrictions. If this equilibrium is disrupted, any behavior that provides opportunities to engage in the behavior below the baseline level, thereby restoring equilibrium, will be reinforced. For instance, suppose a person normally watches 3 or 4 hours of television each evening. This, then, is the person's baseline rate for this activity. Now suppose that something disrupts this pattern of behavior. With television viewing reduced to, say, 2 hours, the person is likely to engage in any activity that results in television viewing. If carrying out the garbage or performing other household chores is followed by access to a roommate's working television set, the frequency of such activities will increase.

One implication of equilibrium theory is that the time spent in a given activity is not an adequate measure of its reinforcing value. Suppose that an animal normally spends 1 hour a day running on an exercise wheel and 2 hours a day drinking. Now suppose that access to water is limited to 1-1/2 hours. The animal still spends more time drinking than running, yet drinking will reinforce running—the animal will run in order to get water.

Another implication of equilibrium theory is that if the baseline rate of a behavior differs from one time to another, or from one individual to another, then the reinforcing power of that activity will also vary. Two rats may spend the same amount of time on an exercise wheel, but one may do the bulk of its running in the morning, while the other runs more in the afternoon. It is likely that access to an exercise wheel will reinforce drinking in the first rat in the morning better than in the afternoon. We can observe the same tendency in people. If you are a slow starter, a person who moves about sluggishly in the morning, then the opportunity to engage in physical activity will have little reinforcing value for you at that time of day. On the other hand, the same activity might be very reinforcing in the early afternoon when you are "more awake." Thus, equilibrium theory would seem to account for the fact that reinforcers vary in effectiveness from one time to another and from one individual to another.

Equilibrium theory works well enough for primary reinforcers such as drinking and exercising. But what about secondary reinforcers? Words such as *yes, right,* and *correct* can be powerfully reinforcing. Had someone looked over Thorndike's shoulder as he tried to draw a 4-inch line while blindfolded and said "shorter" or "longer" after each trial, depending upon whether his line was too long or too short, it is certain that he would have improved rapidly. But how are we to fit such findings into equilibrium theory? Gordon Bower and E. R. Hilgard (1981) conclude that it is unclear how or whether such examples of reinforcement can be accounted for by this theory.

INTERACTION OF INSTRUMENTAL AND
PAVLOVIAN CONDITIONING

Instrumental and Pavlovian conditioning would appear to be two independent and distinct procedures. For one thing, Pavlovian conditioning involves respondent behavior, while instrumental conditioning involves operant behavior. For another, Pavlovian conditioning involves pairing stimuli (the CS and US), while instrumental conditioning involves pairing responses and stimuli. Both of these distinctions are real, but somewhat artificial. In fact, Pavlovian and instrumental conditioning probably always occur together.

The interaction of classical and instrumental procedures is most evident in instances of negative reinforcement. Consider the rat that receives a shock through a grid floor 5 seconds after a light goes on unless it presses a lever. At first, the light is followed by shock. This would appear to be a clear instance of Pavlovian conditioning, and the light no doubt becomes a CS for fear. But eventually the rat presses the lever, and this response is reinforced by the delay of shock, a clear instance of instrumental conditioning. It is plain that both Pavlovian and instrumental learning are involved in this situation.

The case of Little Albert, discussed in Chapter 3, also illustrates the interaction of Pavlovian and instrumental conditioning. Albert learned to fear a white rat when the rat was paired with a loud noise. This would appear to be a simple case of Pavlovian conditioning, and so it is. But Albert did not merely cry as a result of the training, he also fled the area. Fleeing was reinforced by distance from the rat, so instrumental conditioning was also involved.

In some instances, Pavlovian and instrumental procedures are so intertwined that it is hard to say where one begins and the other ends. In one experiment, J. Bruce Overmier and Martin Seligman (1967) strapped a dog into a harness and presented a tone followed by shock. The shock always followed the tone, and nothing the dog did—jumping about, barking—had any effect on the shock. Next, the experimenters put the dog into a box divided by a barrier. When a shock was delivered through the floor of the box, the dog could easily escape it by jumping the barrier to the other side. Normally, dogs learn this escape task very quickly, but the experimenters found that their dog behaved very differently. Instead of jumping the barrier, it lay down and endured the shock passively.

Seligman called this phenomenon **learned helplessness.** The pairing of tone and shock looks like a straightforward case of Pavlovian conditioning, and we can probably assume that the dog learned to fear the tone. But another way to look at the experiment is as the punishment of *all* behavior. Everything the dog did in its attempt to escape was punished. According to this interpretation, the dog later failed to escape shock because it had learned to do nothing in the presence of the shock. It had learned to be helpless.

Even positive reinforcement may involve Pavlovian conditioning. Consider the dog trainer who reinforces the appropriate responses to various commands, such as *sit, stay, come,* and *fetch.* Each appropriate response is followed by a bit of food. Described this way, this seems to be a simple case of instrumental conditioning. But notice that the commands are followed by food, and this pairing of stimuli (command and food) is the essence of Pavlovian conditioning. We may expect, therefore, that the dog will come to like the sounds of the commands given it, as well as respond appropriately to them.

The point is that the distinction between Pavlovian and instrumental conditioning that researchers make in their laboratories is actually rather arbitrary. It is likely that when one sort of conditioning occurs, so does the other. The labels allow us to focus upon one aspect of a learning experience, but they are more often a matter of convenience than a reflection of reality. (For more on this topic, see Pear & Eldridge, 1984.)

SUMMARY

The scientific study of instrumental conditioning began with the puzzle box experiments of E. L. Thorndike and his formulation of the Law of Effect. B. F. Skinner built upon this foundation with his studies of response rate change in rats and pigeons using an experimental chamber known as the Skinner box.

The term *instrumental conditioning* takes its name from the fact that the behavior is usually instrumental in producing an important effect. Of the four basic procedures, two strengthen the behavior and two weaken it. Those that strengthen, or increase the rate of, behavior are called reinforcement procedures and can be either positive or negative. Those that weaken, or decrease the rate of, behavior are called punishment procedures.

Through shaping and chaining, new complex forms of behavior can be acquired. Shaping is the process of reinforcing successive approximations of some desired behavior. Chaining is the process of sequentially shaping a series of connected responses.

Many kinds of behavior have been analyzed in terms of instrumental procedures. One important example is superstition. Skinner found that providing a reinforcer at regular intervals resulted in the adventitious reinforcement of behavior. Since the behavior was not required for reinforcement, its performance was superstitious. Herrnstein suggested that widespread complex superstitions are not actually shaped by adventitious reinforcement, but may be maintained by such reinforcement.

The apparently simple procedures of instrumental conditioning are actually quite complex, because their outcomes depend upon a number of variables. One important example is the interval between a response and the stimulus that follows it; the longer the delay, the slower learning occurs. Other variables that affect instrumental learning include the degree of R-S contingency, response features, characteristics of the stimulus, deprivation level, and characteristics of the learner.

Many theorists have wondered what it is about reinforcers that makes them reinforcing. Hull proposed the drive-reduction theory, based on the idea that reinforcers reduce a drive caused by physiological deprivation. Premack discarded the drive concept and argued that reinforcers are effective because they provide access to preferred kinds of behavior. Timberlake has recently suggested that reinforcement does not depend upon the relative value of the responses so much as upon the discrepancy between the baseline rate of a response and the present opportunity to make the response.

Although Pavlovian and instrumental conditioning are normally treated as separate and distinct procedures, they more often interact. This is true particularly in negative reinforcement and in Seligman's learned helplessness procedure.

Clearly, instrumental learning is essential to the adaptation of higher organisms to a changing environment. Many lower organisms can survive in their relatively stable environments with the minimal learning provided by Pavlovian experiences. The fundamental importance of instrumental learning to higher forms of life is reflected in the consequences of an inability to benefit from the lessons taught by the effects of behavior. Pavlovian learning is important to survival, but foraging, hunting, avoiding predators, gaining access to mates, and other forms of complex behavior all require that the animal learn from its successes and its failures.

The importance of instrumental learning to people is especially great. It is largely through instrumental conditioning that we have learned not only to find edible fruits and berries but to grow crops;

not only to find safety and comfort in caves but to build houses; not only to find warmth in the hides of animals but to fashion clothes. Indeed, most of what we think of as culture would not be possible were we unable to benefit from the consequences of our behavior. The fact that humans live in homes with hot and cold running water, and gorillas do not, has little to do with our respective fixed action patterns or with differences in our ability to benefit from Pavlovian experiences. It has a great deal to do with differences in our ability to benefit from the consequences of behavior.

REVIEW QUESTIONS

1. Define the following terms in your own words:

   Law of Effect   reinforcement
   punishment   reinforcer
   chaining   shaping
   hunger   Premack Principle

2. Why was Thorndike not impressed by reports of remarkable animal intelligence? Relate Thorndike's reasoning about animal anecdotes to anecdotes about other remarkable phenomena such as telepathy and dreams that "predict" the future.

3. One of Skinner's chief contributions to psychology is said to be the use of response rate as a dependent variable. How does this approach differ from Thorndike's timed studies of chicks running mazes?

4. Instrumental conditioning is often referred to as "trial-and-error" learning, but Thorndike preferred the term "trial-and-success." Why do you suppose he did so?

5. How was the Skinner box an improvement over Thorndike's puzzle boxes?

6. Explain the difference between negative and positive reinforcement.

7. Describe the procedure you would use to train a dog to retrieve the morning newspaper from your front porch. (Hint: A chain has many links.)

8. In a superstition experiment, what do you think would be the effect of reducing the interval between reinforcers? What would be the effect of increasing the interval?

9. What is the crucial difference between the superstition experiment and the more usual form of instrumental conditioning?

10. How are shaping and chaining related?

11. What is the R-S interval? What is its counterpart in Pavlovian conditioning?

12. What do you think would be the likely effect of adventitious punishment? Design an experiment that would answer the question.

13. Express the relationship between the intensity of a stimulus and its reinforcement value in terms of a line graph.

14. How do psychologists define a hungry rat? How might a psychologist define a cold rat?

15. A pigeon receives food when it makes two clockwise turns with no more than 2 seconds pause between the turns in the presence of a red light. What has the pigeon learned?

16. Design an experiment to determine the importance of the contingency between a response and its consequence.

17. What are the problems with the drive-reduction theory?

18. What is the chief difference between Premack's relative value theory and Timberlake's equilibrium theory?

19. What are the essential differences between Pavlovian and instrumental conditioning?

20. Why do you suppose some religious and political leaders are upset by suggestions that instrumental conditioning accounts for much of human behavior? What would your reply to their concerns be?

SUGGESTED READINGS

The two classics in instrumental conditioning are Thorndike's *Animal Intelligence* (1911) and Skinner's *The Behavior of Organisms* (1938). These two works, as with classics in general, are talked about more often than they are read. This is unfortunate, because both of them are quite readable and will entertain anyone with a modicum of interest in behavior.

Most of Skinner's books are both fascinating and easy to read. *Science and Human Behavior* (1953) is particularly recommended for its discussion of the role that instrumental conditioning plays in determining human behavior. Skinner's controversial utopian novel, *Walden Two* (1948b), illustrates how the principles of instrumental conditioning could be applied to the design of a society.

Skinner is one of the most influential psychologists who ever lived and one of the most important contributors to the development of a science of behavior. His three-volume autobiography—*Particulars of My Life* (1976), *The Shaping of a Behaviorist* (1977), and *A Matter of Consequences* (1983a)—makes fascinating reading.

FIVE

■

Vicarious Procedures

BEGINNINGS

Sometimes the history of science is the story of a steady progression, rather like the ride on an up escalator. Or perhaps a better metaphor would be the climb up a winding staircase. Progress requires effort, and occasionally the scientist finds himself panting on a landing, but movement is always forward and usually upward. The study of classical conditioning, for example, began with the brilliant experiments of Pavlov and his co-workers and progressed more or less steadily until today our understanding of this phenomenon is fairly sophisticated. Instrumental conditioning followed a similar course. But sometimes the history of science is more like a roller coaster ride than the climb up a staircase: One moment we're plummeting toward ruin, the next we seem to be headed for the stars. Vicarious learning is a case in point.

The problem posed by vicarious learning seems simple enough: Can one organism learn from the experience of another? The search for an answer to this question began with Thorndike. In Thorndike's day, animals were thought to learn either by reasoning things out or by imitating the acts of others. The house cat that opens a cabinet door with its paw has either thought through the problem and come up with a solution or it has watched others open the door and is imitating their behavior. As you saw in Chapter 4, Thorndike pretty much ruled out the first possibility by showing that the cat's progress is more likely the result of "trial-and-success" learning (i.e., instrumental conditioning). But what about the second possibility? Could cats and other animals learn by observing and imitating the behavior of others? According to both common sense and casual observation, the answer was yes.

Nevertheless, Thorndike treated this assumption with the same skepticism that he had treated animal intelligence: He submitted it to experimental test. His subjects were, once again, chicks, cats, and dogs. In a typical experiment, Thorndike (1898) put one cat in a puzzle box and another cat in a nearby cage. The first cat had already learned how to escape the box, and the second had only to observe its neighbor to learn the trick. But when Thorndike put this cat into the box, he found that it did not imitate its more learned fellow. Instead, it went through the same sort of trial-and-success process any other cat went through in learning to solve a problem. No matter how often one cat watched another escape, it seemed to learn nothing. Thorndike found that there was not the slightest difference between the behavior of cats that had observed a successful model and those that had not. He got similar results with chicks and dogs and concluded that "we should give up imitation as an a priori explanation of any novel intelligent performance" (p. 62). In other words, until someone demonstrates that animals learn by observing others, we ought not to assume that they do.

These experiments on vicarious learning, perhaps the first ever done, were published in 1898 as part of Thorndike's classic treatise on animal intelligence. Shortly thereafter, Thorndike (1901) conducted similar experiments with monkeys, but despite the popular belief that "monkey see, monkey do," Thorndike concluded that "nothing in my experience with these animals . . . favors the hypothesis that they have any general ability to learn to do things from seeing others do them" (p. 42). A few years after this, John B. Watson (1908) performed a similar series of experiments on monkeys with nearly identical results.

These negative findings seem to have had a devastating effect on research on vicarious learning. There was, in fact, almost no experimental investigation of this problem for a generation. Then, in the 1930s, Carl Warden and his colleagues at Columbia University conducted a number of carefully controlled experiments and clearly demonstrated that monkeys can learn by observing others. In one experiment (Warden & Jackson, 1935), one monkey observed as another pulled a chain that opened a door and revealed a raisin that the model quickly retrieved and ate. After watching the model perform this act five times, the observer got a chance to perform. According to the early work of Thorndike and Watson, this procedure should not have resulted in much learning; the observing monkeys should have spent their time exactly as if they had never seen the model.

They did not. In fact, the observers made it quite clear that they had benefited substantially from watching the model, often responding correctly on the first trial. Furthermore, when an animal succeeded, it often did so in so little time that the solution could not possibly have been due to instrumental learning. In many cases, the observers performed the necessary act almost as quickly as the model had.

Warden and his co-workers performed other, similar experiments with equally encouraging results. For instance, in one study (Warden et al., 1940), observer monkeys made the correct response on 76 percent of 144 trials, and about half of the solutions occurred within 10 seconds. These results should have prompted an upswing in research on vicarious learning, but instead there followed another long period during which it received little attention.

Then, in the 1960s, research on vicarious learning began to take off. Much of the impetus for this change was the brilliant work of Albert Bandura and his colleagues at Stanford University. In several of these studies, a child observed a model whose aggressive acts were reinforced either by another person or by the natural consequences of the behavior. These studies (to be described later in this chapter) made it fairly clear that children, at least, can learn simply by observing others. This research renewed interest in vicarious learning, and many psychologists now believe that this subject deserves the same sort of attention that classical and instrumental procedures have received.

BASIC PROCEDURES

Learning is a change in behavior brought about by experience. In the case of Pavlovian and instrumental conditioning, the experience consists of exposure to an arrangement of stimuli. In **vicarious conditioning,** experience consists of exposure to a model undergoing Pavlovian or instrumental conditioning.

In **vicarious classical conditioning,** a dog (the observer, designated O) might look on as another dog (the model, M) is exposed to the pairing of a CS and a US:

$$O \begin{bmatrix} CS & \longrightarrow & US \\ bell & \longrightarrow & food \end{bmatrix}$$

The model, of course, responds to this procedure by learning to salivate to the sound of the bell. If, upon being exposed to the bell, the observer salivates, or if the observer comes to salivate after fewer CS-US pairings than the model required, then we may say that the observer has learned vicariously.

A similar procedure can be carried out with an aversive US. If a dog is touched by its handler and then shocked, we may expect the dog to be fearful when approached by the handler. If another dog *observes* as this conditioning takes place, and if the observer shows signs of fear when touched by the handler, then vicarious learning has occurred.

In **vicarious instrumental conditioning,** an observer looks on as a model undergoes instrumental conditioning. For example, a monkey (the observer) might look on as one of its peers (the model) lifts a cup, under which it finds a raisin:

$$O \begin{bmatrix} R & \longrightarrow & S^R \\ lift\ cup & \longrightarrow & find\ raisin \end{bmatrix}$$

Clearly, the model will learn to lift the cup. But will the observer do likewise when given the opportunity? If it does, or if it learns to do so more quickly than the model did, then vicarious learning has taken place.

The same sort of vicarious learning occurs if the observer benefits from a punishment procedure. For instance, a monkey that receives a rap on its knuckles each time it attempts to retrieve a raisin from a bowl will soon desist in its efforts to obtain the fruit. If another monkey observes this sequence of events and is then given the opportunity to take a raisin from the bowl but declines to do so, it is clear that the observer benefited from the model's training.

In the examples just given, the model undergoes a conditioning procedure as the observer looks on. In some studies, however, a previously trained animal or person acts as the model (e.g., Epstein, 1984). In these studies, the model provides an expert demonstration of the act to be performed. Another variation of the basic procedures involves the use of "verbal modeling." As Bandura (1971a) points out:

People are aided in assembling and operating complicated mechanical equipment, in acquiring social, vocational, and recreational skills, and in learning appropriate behavior for almost any situation by consulting the written descriptions in instructional manuals. Verbal forms of modeling are used extensively because one can transmit through words an almost infinite variety of behavioral patterns that would be exceedingly difficult and time-consuming to portray behaviorally. (p. 41)

Although such verbal modeling is important, it is a subject that falls beyond the scope of this text.

Attempts have been made to examine the role of vicarious learning in the modification of many kinds of behavior. For illustrative purposes, we will consider three areas in which vicarious learning seems to be important: fears, foraging, and social aggression.

FEARS

The best evidence for vicarious classical conditioning is in the acquisition of fear. Many people fear things with which they have had little or no direct experience. These unreasonable fears, or phobias, may be partly attributable to vicarious Pavlovian conditioning. R. A. Kleinknecht (1982) found, for example, that half of the members of the American Tarantula Society admitted to having been afraid of tarantulas, yet none attributed their fear to direct experience with tarantulas. Similarly, Bandura and F. L. Menlove (1968) found that children who were afraid of dogs were not particularly likely to have had traumatic experiences with dogs, but they were likely to have dog-fearing parents. A survey of blood and dental phobics (Ost & Hugdahl, 1985) found that while direct conditioning was important in establishing many of these fears, many others were attributable to vicarious experiences.

There is also some experimental evidence to support the view that fears may be acquired from observing others. Patricia Barnett and David Benedetti (1960) conducted a study in which a model (a confederate of the experimenter) *appeared* to receive shocks shortly after a buzzer sounded. The observer, who was never shocked, watched as the model underwent training. The experimenters did not expect the observers to withdraw their hands; after all, *they* were not touching the shock apparatus. But the researchers reasoned that if vicarious conditioning did take place, it would be revealed in a change in the observer's galvanic skin response (GSR), since the GSR is an indicator of emotional response. Barnett and Benedetti were not disappointed: The buzzer did come to elicit a GSR change in observers.

One problem with the study just described, and others like it, is that they leave open the possibility that the observer's reactions are due to a kind of pseudoconditioning (see Chapter 3). There is, after all, no proof that the conditional response was due to observing the pairing of CS and US. It is possible, for example, that the observers in the Barnett and Benedetti study would have shown the same GSR if they had been led to believe that the model was merely moving his hand voluntarily. Seymour Berger (1962) conducted a series of experiments to try to rule out this possibility.

In one experiment, Berger took GSR readings of observers as they watched a model under one of four conditions. In all cases, the model sat at a table and rested a finger on a shock apparatus. Periodically, a buzzer sounded, followed closely by the dimming of a light. Berger told one group of observers that the model would periodically receive a shock; in this condition, each time the light dimmed, the model quickly withdrew her hand from the apparatus. Berger gave a second group of subjects the same instructions, but in this case, the model did not move her hand when the light dimmed. A third group of subjects was told that the model would not be shocked, but the model moved her hand as in the first condition. Subjects in the fourth group were told that the model would not be shocked, and in this case, the model did not move her hand.

Berger was interested in observing the extent to which these different instructions would affect the formation of a conditional response, as measured by the GSR, in the observer. The results revealed that the likelihood of a conditional response depended upon the apparent pairing of CS (buzzer and light dimming) and US (shock) (see Figure 5-1). Observers in the Shock-Movement condition gave GSRs on far more of the trials than did those in the No Shock-No Movement condition. When observers were told that the model would be shocked but the model did not move her arm (Shock-No Movement), there were markedly fewer CRs than in the Shock-Movement condition. Many of these subjects later said that they believed the model was not being shocked, or that the shocks were extremely mild.

Fearfulness is often a very appropriate response to events in the environment. As a rule, feared objects are those that cause injury and are therefore well avoided. Obviously, the animal that is injured by a predator and thereafter fears that species has a better chance of sur-

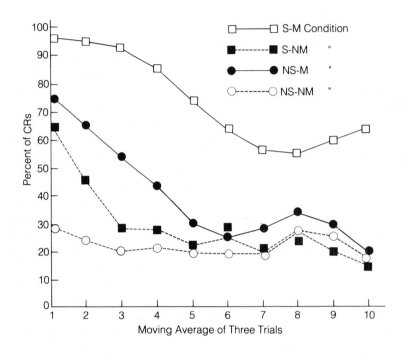

Figure 5-1   Vicarious Pavlovian conditioning. Percentage of observers giving CRs during apparent conditioning of models. (After Seymour Berger, "Conditioning Through Vicarious Instigation," *Psychological Review*, 1962, *69*, p. 458, figure 2. Copyright 1962 by the American Psychological Association. Reprinted by permission of Seymour Berger.)

viving than one that does not learn from the experience. Just as obviously, the animal that acquires such a fear from observing another individual receive an injury also has a better chance of surviving. The role of vicarious fear learning seems to be particularly important in human beings. As Mary Cover Jones (1924a) wrote long ago, although direct Pavlovian conditioning is an important source of fears, especially sensible fears, vicarious learning is "perhaps the most common source of maladjustive fear" (p. 390).

FORAGING

Surviving also means finding food, and experiments have shown how vicarious instrumental conditioning may aid in the search for food.

In one experiment, Connie Gaudet and M. Brock Fenton (1984) studied vicarious learning in three species of bats. They began by training one member of each species to find a bit of mealworm from a target fastened to a wall. The bats would fly to the target, remove the food, return to their starting point about 2 yards away, and eat the meal. A bat of the same species was allowed to observe the model up to 20 times a day for 5 days. (Contrary to popular belief, most bats are *not* blind.) There were two control groups. In one group, the bats were simply put into the experimental chamber alone; in the other, the bats were individually trained, through instrumental conditioning, to find the food. The result was that the bats that were allowed to observe a model learned faster than those that were trained through instrumental conditioning. Bats that were placed in the chamber without benefit of a model or instrumental training did not find the food.

Field studies also support the view that vicarious learning is important in the search for food. One fascinating study involves British songbirds. J. Fisher and R. A. Hinde (1949; Hinde & Fisher, 1972) reported that songbirds made a regular practice of opening and drinking from milk bottles left on porches. It appeared that a few birds learned the trick on their own and were imitated by other birds.

The significance of Britain's milk-drinking birds is a subject of some debate. David Sherry and B. G. Galef (1984) point out that the fact that many birds are drinking from bottles does not necessarily mean that many birds have learned to open the bottles, let alone that they have learned to open them through observation. They note that the presence of a bottle opened by 1 bird would provide the opportunity for many birds to feed without their having vicariously learned anything about bottle opening. To test this notion, Sherry and Galef captured 16 black-capped chickadees on the campus of the University of Toronto and presented each with a foil-covered plastic cream tub of the sort restaurants serve with coffee. Four of the birds spontaneously pecked through the foil top and fed upon the cream. These 4 birds then served as models for 4 birds that had not opened the tubs. Each model demonstrated the technique for an observer on five trials. Four more birds were given five training trials in which they were exposed to an open tub containing a peanut and a seed. The remaining 4 birds were given five trials with a sealed tub. After this, all of the birds were presented individually with a sealed tub. The researchers found that birds in the vicarious learning group learned to open the tubs, as did those that had merely been given opened tubs, but none of those presented with a sealed tub learned to find food. The researchers concluded that some birds probably learn to take advantage of previously opened bottles, but that others may learn to open milk bottles by observing others do so.

Less ambiguous evidence of the role of vicarious learning in foraging is provided by a study by Syumzo Kawamura (1963). In order to make naturalistic observations of macaque monkeys, Kawamura placed sweet potatoes (a monkey treat) near a lake, thus attracting the animals to the lakeshore so that they tended to congregate and could be easily observed interacting. Since the potatoes were placed on the beach, they tended to get sand on them. One of the monkeys learned that the sand could be removed by dipping the potatoes into the water. Soon, other macaques followed this monkey's lead, and eventually, all but the oldest animals regularly washed their potatoes before eating them. Here was a very clear instance of social transmission, that is, of vicarious learning (see Eaton, 1976, for another example).

SOCIAL AGGRESSION

Social aggression plays a major role not only in individual survival but in the survival of the species. An understanding of the origins of human aggression is especially important in this age of nuclear weapons, when an aggressive act can mean the destruction of millions of people. Numerous studies have shown how vicarious learning influences the aggressive tendencies of people toward one another.

In one study (Bandura et al., 1963), some nursery school children watched a 5-minute videotape of two men, Rocky and Johnny, interacting in a playroom. Johnny plays with toy cars, plastic farm animals, and various other appealing toys. When Rocky asks Johnny to share the toys and Johnny refuses, Rocky hits Johnny several times with a rubber ball, overpowers him when he tries to defend his property, hits him with a baton, and otherwise gives poor Johnny a rough time. Rocky's aggressive behavior is reinforced, since he ends up having all the fun. The researchers write that:

> the final scene shows Johnny seated dejectedly in the corner while Rocky is playing with the toys, serving himself generous helpings of 7-Up and cookies, and riding a large bouncing hobby horse with gusto. As the scene closes, Rocky packs the playthings in a sack and sings a merry tune, "Hi, ho, hi, ho, it's off to play I go," as he departs with the hobby horse under his arm and the bulging sack of loot over his shoulder. A commentator's voice announces that Rocky is the victor (p. 602)

After watching the videotape, each child went to a playroom that contained a number of toys, including those shown in the film and several others. Each child spent 20 minutes in the room while judges watched through a one-way mirror and noted how often the child hit a Bobo doll (a large, inflated doll) or performed other aggressive acts. The data indicated that children were far more likely to commit a given aggressive act if they had seen a model reinforced for the same behavior. The similarity of the children's behavior to that of the model was sometimes striking. At the end of one session, a little girl who had imitated a good deal of Rocky's behavior looked at the experimenter and asked, "Do you have a sack here?" (p. 605).

If aggressive behavior is punished in a model, this tends to make imitation of aggressive acts less likely in observers. Mary Rosekrans and Willard Hartup (1967) had nursery school children watch an adult model as she played with some toys, at times beating a Bobo doll on the head with a mallet and poking a clay figure with a fork. As she played, the model made such comments as "Wham, bam, I'll knock your head off" and "Punch him, punch him, punch his legs full of holes." In one condition, these aggressive acts were reinforced by an adult who made such remarks as "Good for you! I guess you really fixed him that time." In another condition, the model's behavior was repeatedly punished by an adult who said such things as "Now look what you've done, you've ruined it." After watching the model play and seeing her behavior either reinforced or punished, the observer then got a chance to play with the same toys. The results showed that children were much more likely to play as the model had when the model's behavior was reinforced than when her behavior was punished (see Figure 5-2).

One particularly undesirable form of aggressive behavior is crime. Bandura (1973) has analyzed this problem and provides a great deal of evidence that criminal behavior is powerfully influenced by observation. He finds, for instance, that both children and adults have unlimited opportunities to learn "the whole gamut of felonious behavior within the comfort of their homes" (p. 101). As Bandura points out, people often put such learning to use: "Children have been apprehended for writing bad checks to obtain money for candy, for sniping at strangers with BB guns, for sending threatening letters to teachers and for injurious switchblade fights after witnessing similar performances on television" (p. 101f.).

The studies reported in this chapter suggest that people are unlikely to imitate criminal acts they observe unless those acts are reinforced. So witnessing criminal acts on television should lead to criminal behavior only if the modeled behavior is reinforced. But often

PIE IN THE SKY

On Wednesday, December 1, 1971, a passenger on Northwest Airlines flight 305 handed a stewardess a note demanding that the airline give him $200,000. Then he opened his briefcase and revealed what looked very much like a bomb.

The passenger, registered under the name D. B. Cooper, had thought things out carefully. The airline would have the cash, and four parachutes, ready when the plane touched down at Seattle-Tacoma International Airport in Washington, or the airline would lose one Boeing 727, 36 passengers, and a crew. The airline came up with the money and the parachutes. Cooper let everyone deplane in Tacoma except the cockpit crew and one stewardess; then he ordered the pilot to head for Mexico. Once aloft, however, Cooper made his escape 10,000 feet above the forested countryside of southwestern Washington. He was never captured.

Naturally, Cooper's very clever crime got a lot of coverage in the news media, so much so that anyone who cared to follow his lead had access to all the pertinent details. And follow his lead they did. Bandura (1973) later wrote that "within the next few months . . . a number of hijackers, emboldened by the successful example, copied the specific tactics, including threats of bombing unless passengers were exchanged for ransom money and parachutes" (p. 107).

This incident demonstrates very nicely the role vicarious learning plays in crime. When you think about it, it becomes clear that it would be very difficult for the novice criminal to learn his trade strictly through trial-and-error. It is only through vicarious learning that people can efficiently acquire the sophisticated skills necessary for pulling off a successful burglary, extortion scheme, bank robbery, or bookie operation. This raises intriguing questions: If people were not so adept at learning from models, would crime cease to be an important social problem? And if so, would we gain more than we would lose?

Questions like these are not easily answered. Except, perhaps, by the likes of Mr. D. B. Cooper.

television crime *is* reinforced. Otto Larsen and his co-workers (1968) found that in television programs intended for children, socially approved goals were achieved by violent or illegal acts 56 percent of the time. The study of vicariously acquired social aggression illustrates one of the paradoxes of behavior: What is adaptive for the individual may not be adaptive for the group.

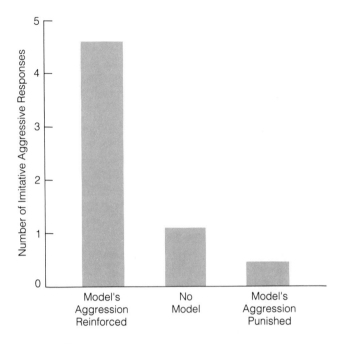

Figure 5-2 Average number of imitative aggressive responses by observers who saw the aggressive acts reinforced or punished or who saw no model. (Compiled from data in Rosekrans & Hartup, 1967.)

VARIABLES AFFECTING VICARIOUS CONDITIONING

Less is known about the factors affecting vicarious conditioning than about those affecting Pavlovian and instrumental procedures, though factors that are important in direct conditioning apparently affect vicarious conditioning in a similar manner. For example, it is well established that the course of instrumental conditioning varies with the degree of contingency between a response and a reinforcer. The same seems to hold true for vicarious instrumental conditioning. When a model's behavior is consistently reinforced, the observer tends to adopt it; when it is consistently punished, the observer tends to avoid making it; and when the model's behavior is sometimes reinforced and sometimes punished, the observer's tendency to imitate the model falls between the other two conditions (e.g., Rosekrans & Hartup, 1967; see Figure 5-3). The variables that have received the most systematic attention, however, are the characteristics of the

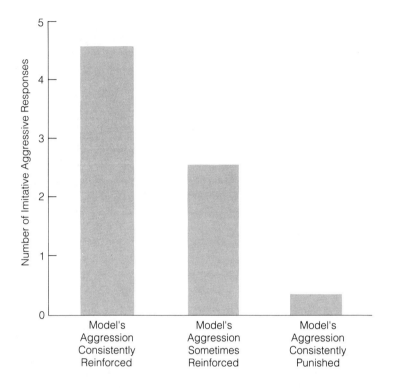

Figure 5-3   Average number of imitative aggressive responses by observers who saw aggressive acts consistently reinforced; sometimes reinforced and sometimes punished; or consistently punished. (Compiled from data in Rosekrans & Hartup, 1967.)

model and of the observer as they affect vicarious instrumental conditioning.

Characteristics of the Model

Numerous studies have demonstrated that observers tend to learn more from a model when the model is competent, attractive, likeable, and prestigious than when he or she does not have these characteristics. A study by Berger (1971), in which college students participated in what was ostensibly an investigation of ESP, will serve as an example. The model was introduced to the observer as either a fellow subject or as an assistant to the experimenter. Later on, when the observers were tested for the strength of the learned response, those who thought they had watched a fellow student showed less evidence of imitation than did those who thought they had observed an assistant. Since the model was actually the same person in each case and behaved in the same way, the difference in the observer's behavior must have been due to the model's status. Studies of this sort raise an interesting question: Why should model characteristics such as status, attractiveness, competence, and so on have any effect on what an observer learns?

Research by Judith Fisher and Mary Harris (1976) provides a plausible answer. Fisher and Harris approached people in a shopping center or on a college campus and asked them to guess the prices of certain items. An experimenter would appear to approach two subjects simultaneously, but one of the persons was actually a confederate who acted as a model. In one experiment, the model sometimes wore an eyepatch. The model would guess at the price of an item and then the observer would make a guess. Later on, when the observers tried to remember the answers the model had given, it turned out that people were generally more accurate in recalling responses when the model wore an eyepatch.

In another experiment, the researchers manipulated the mood of the model. In one condition, the model smiled and nodded her head as the experimenter asked her questions. In another condition, the model frowned and shook her head. In a third condition, the model behaved in a neutral manner. In other respects, the experiment was similar to the first. The observers who had witnessed one of the more expressive models recalled her behavior better than did observers who saw an impassive model. It made no difference whether the model's mood was positive or negative, so long as it was not neutral.

According to Fisher and Harris, these model characteristics (eyepatch and moodiness) affected the observer's learning because they attracted the observer's attention. Status, likeability, age, sex, competence, and other model characteristics affect vicarious learning because they influence how carefully the observer studies the model. The more attentive an observer is to a model, the more likely he or she is to learn from the model's behavior.

Characteristics of the Observer

The success of vicarious procedures varies greatly with the learner. Whereas classical and instrumental conditioning occur readily in hundreds of species, vicarious learning seems to be restricted to a handful. Humans and other primates often learn vicariously with little trouble, but dogs and cats appear to learn vicariously only with

THE VENUS EFFECT, OR HOW CAN I LEARN ANYTHING WHEN YOU LOOK AT ME WITH THOSE BIG BROWN EYES?

There's no doubt about it, emotional arousal can have a profound effect on learning. It's not always clear why this should be so, but sometimes the reason is fairly obvious.

Warden and Jackson, you will recall, trained a monkey to solve a problem and gave other monkeys the opportunity to profit by the model's experience. Several observing monkeys did just that, but some paid little or no attention to the problem or how the model went about solving it. These wayward animals seemed interested in another sort of problem. The researchers noted that animal H, for example, "showed sex interest in [model]; 'presented' to him and ignored the problem; sat at screen near [model]." About another miscreant they wrote simply, "sex excitement marked," and they noted that another "masturbated frequently and ignored the problem."

That the emotional state of the observers put them at a severe disadvantage becomes immediately clear when their performance is compared to that of the less distracted animals. Only 1 of the 6 sexually aroused monkeys solved problem 1 on the first trial, while a third of the other monkeys did so. And the difference between aroused and unaroused monkeys increased with succeeding problems, as Figure 5-4 shows.

It may have already occurred to you that monkeys are not the only creatures affected by the Venus Effect. In fact, it seems likely that this phenomenon is at work (in somewhat milder form, of course) in high school and college classrooms around the world.

(continued on next page)

difficulty, and most lower species seem to be incapable of learning vicariously.

There is also tremendous variability within a given species in the ability to profit from the experience of others. This variability seems to be due to a number of characteristics, one of which is the age of the learner. In general, adults learn better than children from observation, and older children learn better than younger ones. Those advanced in years, however, often are slower to benefit from the experiences of others than are the young. You may recall that Kawamura (1963) found that young monkeys readily imitated the washing of sweet potatoes, whereas older ones did not.

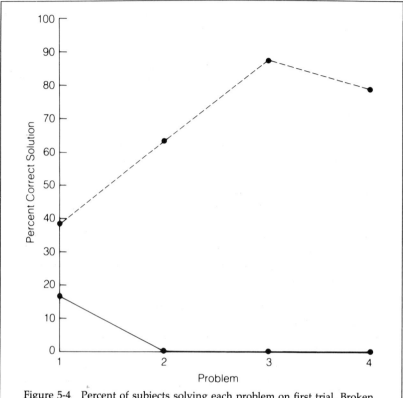

Figure 5-4   Percent of subjects solving each problem on first trial. Broken line shows performance of observers who attended to the problem; solid line shows performance of observers who were sexually aroused and attended to other matters. (Compiled from data in Warden & Jackson, 1935.)

Another important characteristic is the learning history of the observer. John Wolfe (1936) taught chimpanzees how to use a poker chip or brass slug to get fruit from a kind of vending machine. Wolfe would pick up a token, show it to the animal, and then put the token into a slot, thereby tripping a mechanism in the machine and causing a grape to fall into a food tray. Wolfe found that the animals could learn to use tokens in this way, but that some chimps learned the task much more readily than others. A chimp named Moos learned the trick after only 1 demonstration, while others required as many as 237 demonstrations. Apparently, one factor that contributed to this wide range of learning abilities was the learning histories of the various animals: Moos had participated in other experiments and may have learned that it is sometimes a good idea to pay attention to what humans do.

The emotional state of the learner while observing the model is also important. One study of vicarious classical conditioning found that people who were anxious showed more evidence of learning than did those who were more relaxed (Haner & Whitney, 1960). Similarly, Bandura and Theodore Rosenthal (1966) found that learners were more likely to acquire a conditional response if they had received a stimulant before the vicarious classical conditioning procedure. And Warden and Jackson (1935) found that some of their monkeys became sexually excited by the model and that this arousal severely interfered with learning.

THEORIES OF VICARIOUS CONDITIONING

Most theories of vicarious learning focus upon vicarious instrumental conditioning, so this discussion will be limited to that topic. (For a theoretical discussion of vicarious classical conditioning, see Green & Osborne, 1985). The two main competing theories are the Miller-Dollard theory and the theory of Bandura.

Miller-Dollard Theory

It is possible to treat vicarious instrumental conditioning as merely a variation of instrumental conditioning. According to this view, set forth by Neal Miller and John Dollard (1941), the changes in an observer's behavior are due to the consequences of *the observer's* behavior, not those of the model (see Skinner, 1969, for a similar analysis). Suppose, for example, that a model is presented with a table covered with brightly colored boxes. The model selects one of the red boxes, finds a bit of candy, and eats it. After observing this behavior, a second person is given access to the table. This person selects a green box but finds it empty. The model is given another turn, selects a red box, and eats the candy it contains. When given another turn, the observer selects a red box and finds candy. The imitative response is thus reinforced. It is, argue Miller and Dollard, the reinforcement of the *observer's* imitative responses that changes the observer's behavior, not the reinforcement of the model's behavior.

One apparent contradiction of this interpretation is the fact that people often imitate in the absence of reinforcement. For example, a 14-year-old boy may throw a basketball through a hoop, thus providing a model for his 10-year-old brother. The younger boy may never make a basket or receive words of praise for his efforts, yet may persist in the attempt to shoot a basket. The same phenomenon has been observed in animals. Robert Epstein (1984a) trained a pigeon to peck a ping pong ball or pull on a rope. Once trained, this bird served as a model for pigeons that previously had shown no particular inclination to perform these acts. The performance of the model sharply increased the tendency of the observers to peck the ball or pull the string. Yet the observer's imitative acts were not reinforced. The Miller-Dollard theory attributes such imitative responding to previous learning. The reason the 10-year-old keeps tossing the basketball in the absence of reinforcement is because previous imitative acts have been reinforced.

Some psychologists have asked why, if a model's behavior is a cue for imitative acts, such acts occur even when the model is no longer present. In one experiment, pigeons pecked a ping pong ball 24 hours after observing a model do so, even though the observer had no opportunity to perform the act in the presence of the model (Epstein, 1984a). But this phenomenon would seem to pose no special problem for Miller and Dollard. We often continue to be influenced by a stimulus that is no longer present. You may, for example, see an ad for a movie on one day and go to the theater the next. The ad is long since gone, yet it still affects behavior. Stimuli generally have their most powerful effects immediately, but they may continue to affect behavior long after they have disappeared.

One potential criticism of this theory stems from the fact that the number of times the model is observed to perform a response is strongly related to the observer's performance. In one study, Marvin Herbert and Charles Harsh (1944) designed a structure (see Figure 5-5) that would allow as many as 4 cats at a time to watch a model as it worked at one of five problems. In the Turn Table problem (see Figures 5-6), a circular platform rotated on a bicycle axle. By grasping the black cleats on the turntable, a cat could spin the platform so that a food dish came into its cage. On any given problem, the cat that served as model would have 30 trials while observer cats looked on. Some observers watched all 30 of a model's trials; others watched only the last 15 trials. By comparing the performances of the observers with those of the models, the experimenters could determine how much vicarious learning had taken place.

The results showed that, overall, the observer cats were markedly superior to the models (see Figure 5-7). Miller and Dollard can account for this finding by arguing that the cats had previously learned, through instrumental conditioning, to imitate other cats. The rein-

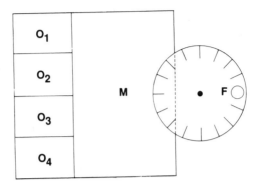

Figure 5-5   View from above the Herbert and Harsh cage, showing the Turn Table problem installed. Observers sat in chambers at O_1, O_2, O_3 and O_4 and watched as a model, at M, worked on the problem of getting the food at F. (After Herbert & Harsh, 1944.)

forcement of the model is of no importance, except as a cue to imitate. But Herbert and Harsh found that the results depended upon the number of trials the observers witnessed. On the Turn Table problem, for instance, cats that had observed 15 trials took an average of 57 seconds to solve the problem, while those that had observed 30 trials took an average of only 16 seconds. If reinforcement of the model is unimportant, why should more observations have such a powerful effect?

Albert Bandura (1971b) has criticized the Miller-Dollard theory for a number of reasons. His most telling criticism, however, is that it does not account for the sudden acquisition of novel behavior. How is it, for instance, that Wolfe's (1936) clever chimpanzee, Moos, was able to use a token appropriately after only one demonstration? The Miller-Dollard theory accounts for the fact that Moos made an effort

Figure 5-6   Miss White working at the Turn Table problem. (After Herbert & Harsh, 1944.)

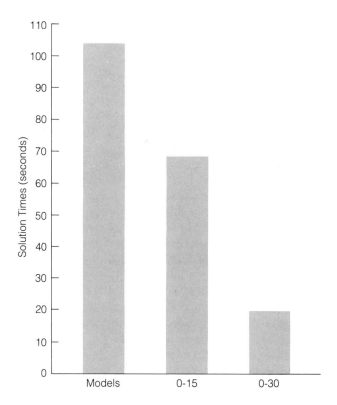

Figure 5-7   Average solution times on first trial of four problems by models and observers. Observers watched model perform on last 15 trials (0–15) or on all 30 trials (0–30). Data from one problem, failed by 4 observers, are *not* included. (Compiled from data in Herbert & Harsh, 1944.)

to imitate the model's use of a token, since imitative behavior may have been reinforced previously. But how is it that Moos was *able* to imitate the model? Moos's behavior did not require shaping; it was quite effective on the first try. Similarly, E. Roy John and his colleagues (1968) noticed that their observer cats often "performed correctly at the first opportunity and committed few or no errors while reaching criterion" (p. 1491). In vicarious conditioning, in other words, a good deal of learning has taken place *before* the observer begins to imitate the model.

Miller and Dollard might argue that this apparently sudden acquisition of behavior is due to the similarity of the new behavior to behavior that is already in the observer's repertoire. It is hard to dismiss this explanation entirely, since it is impossible to prove that an organism has never learned a response that is similar to the modeled behavior. However, the previous learning explanation does not account for the improvement one sees in an observer with repeated demonstrations by a model. Recall that in the Herbert and Harsh (1944) study described earlier, cats that observed a model solve a problem 30 times did far better than did cats that observed only 15 demonstrations. It seems unlikely that this difference was due to differences in the previous learning of the two groups of observers. Because of these difficulties with the Miller-Dollard theory, many (but by no means all) psychologists prefer Bandura's theory.

Bandura's Theory

Albert Bandura (1965, 1971a, b, c, 1977) argues that vicarious instrumental learning takes place during the process of observing the model, that is, *before* the observer makes any imitative act. To Bandura this means that vicarious learning must involve acts performed by the observer during the observation stage of learning. Often these acts are performed covertly (that is, they involve thinking). Bandura believes that two types of covert behavior are especially important to vicarious learning: **attentional processes** and **retentional processes.**

Attentional processes have to do with the organism observing the relevant aspects of the model's behavior and its consequences. Various studies have demonstrated that if the observer does not attend to the model, or attends to irrelevant aspects of the model's behavior, little learning will take place. As we saw earlier, a number of variables affect the extent to which an observer attends to the appropriate aspects of a model's behavior.

Once an organism is attending to the relevant aspects of the model's behavior, Bandura reasons, retentional processes come into play. These are acts the observer performs to aid recall of the model's behavior. One important retentional process is something Bandura calls **symbolic coding,** which consists of representing the model's behavior in some way, often in words. With the acquisition of language, it is often possible to reduce complex behavior to a few words.

Another important retentional activity is **covert rehearsal,** which consists of repeatedly performing the model's behavior, or a verbal representation of that behavior, in some covert way. After seeing a tennis pro demonstrate the perfect backhand, for example, you may covertly imitate that behavior without making any perceptible movement of your arm. Or you might silently repeat some verbal representation of the model's behavior, such as, "Keep the wrist straight."

Attentional and retentional activities can be easily illustrated. Suppose that your rich aunt points to a wall safe and says, "I'm going to open that safe and then lock it again. I will then give you one chance to open it; if you succeed, you can keep whatever you find inside." You already know that people generally keep valuable things in safes, so your aunt has your complete attention. And since you know generally how combination safes are opened, you know what aspects of her behavior to attend to. Your aunt proceeds to open the safe. She turns the dial clockwise to 20, counterclockwise to 40, clockwise to 20. She pulls down the handle and swings open the door, then immediately closes it.

Now, as you watched your aunt work, you could not make the same responses she made. You could, however, imagine your hand turning the dial to the designated numbers. You could also code this behavior symbolically by picturing a little pot-bellied Santa Claus whose measurements were 20-40-20. More likely, however, you would represent the behavior verbally and rehearse it by repeatedly saying to yourself (or perhaps aloud), "Right 20; left 40; right 20." The point is that you would not merely observe your aunt's behavior; you would be busy behaving (albeit covertly) while you watched her.

Bandura's theory includes other factors that affect the performance of modeled behavior, but it is the attentional and retentional processes that, according to Bandura, account for vicarious instrumental learning. In fact, Bandura insists that vicarious learning cannot be explained without describing the covert behavior involved. His critics might well ask whether it is realistic to assume that bats, pigeons, and other lower animals that learn vicariously do so through symbolic coding and covert rehearsal. Bandura has restricted himself to human vicarious learning, but he might well reply that the fact that lower species learn slowly or not at all through observation supports his belief that attentional and retentional processes are important. One way the role of retentional processes might be resolved would be to test the vicarious learning of chimpanzees before and after they had learned American Sign Language (Gardner & Gardner, 1969). If their vicarious learning improved, this would suggest that retentional processes are useful (though not necessarily essential) to vicarious learning. The fact that such an experiment has not yet been done is indicative of how far we have to go in the study of vicarious learning.

SUMMARY

Vicarious learning has received less attention over the years than Pavlovian and instrumental procedures, partly because of the failures of Thorndike and Watson. Even Warden's successes in the 1930s did not entirely overcome the doubts spawned by the earlier studies, and it was another 30 years before vicarious learning would receive serious attention from a number of researchers. The most important of these researchers was Albert Bandura, who did yeoman's service in documenting the importance of vicarious learning in children. Interest in vicarious learning continues, though it still receives less attention than classical and instrumental procedures.

In vicarious procedures, an observer looks on as a model undergoes direct conditioning. There are, therefore, two kinds of vicarious procedures: vicarious classical conditioning and vicarious instrumental conditioning.

The role of vicarious learning in adaptation can be seen in studies of fear, foraging, and aggression. Vicarious Pavlovian conditioning appears to be important in the development of fears, at least among humans. Vicarious instrumental conditioning is important in foraging and in the development of aggressive behavior.

As with direct conditioning, the effectiveness of vicarious procedures depends upon many variables. Those variables that have received the greatest attention involve characteristics of the model and observer. Observers learn more from models who are competent, attractive, likeable, and prestigious than from models who lack these features. Although vicarious learning has been observed in species as low as the bat, it proceeds much more slowly than in higher species. The age of the observer is another important characteristic, as are the individual's emotional state and previous learning experiences.

There are two prominent theories of vicarious instrumental learning. The Miller-Dollard theory assumes that vicarious conditioning is really a form of direct conditioning, so that learning depends upon reinforcement of the observer's imitative behavior. Bandura's theory argues that learning occurs before imitation, so that what the observer does (in the way of attentional and retentional processes) while observing a model becomes very important.

Many animals get along quite well without vicarious learning. The story is quite different when it comes to people. It is impossible to say what proportion of human learning is due to direct experience and what proportion is due to observation. It is clear, however, that if people suddenly lost their ability to learn vicariously, the effect would be noticeable immediately. Imagine, for example, the difficulties one would encounter in teaching preschoolers to tie their shoes, first-graders to write, or employees to operate machines. Not only would shaping such behavior through reinforcement be much slower, but in many cases, reliance on instrumental conditioning would be dangerous. As Bandura (1971a) has pointed out, it would be extremely unwise to rely solely on direct conditioning in teaching children to swim, adolescents to drive automobiles, or medical students to perform surgical procedures.

This is not to say that classical and instrumental conditioning are unimportant in the lives of human beings. Both procedures have a good deal to do with our daily activities. But compared to the other creatures that inhabit this planet, we humans rely heavily upon vicarious learning in our efforts to cope with the changing world around us.

REVIEW QUESTIONS

1. Define the following terms in your own words:

    vicarious conditioning   attentional process
    covert rehearsal   symbolic coding

2. Distinguish between the procedures of vicarious classical and vicarious instrumental conditioning.

3. Why has vicarious conditioning received less attention than direct conditioning?

4. Design an experiment to determine whether vicarious Pavlovian salivary conditioning is possible.

5. Explain how fear of heights might be acquired through vicarious conditioning.

6. If vicarious learning can lead to the widespread use of some practice, how can one determine whether such behavior is innate or learned?

7. Given what you know about vicarious learning, what advice would you give a friend whose children watch 5 to 6 hours of television daily?

8. How could you use vicarious procedures to create a fad on a college campus?

9. Distinguish between vicarious learning and imitation. Is it possible to have imitation without vicarious learning? Is it possible to have vicarious learning without imitation? Explain your answers.

10. If you wanted to ensure that an observer would learn from a model, what sort of model would you choose?

11. After Marilyn Monroe died, apparently by suicide, many other people took their own lives. Explain these copycat suicides.

12. What is the chief difference between the Miller-Dollard theory and Bandura's theory of vicarious learning?

13. Why does the role of thinking become an issue in vicarious learning?

14. Design an experiment to determine the role of delayed reinforcement of a model's behavior in vicarious learning.

15. According to the Miller-Dollard theory, vicarious conditioning is merely a form of direct conditioning. Explain how this could be the case.

16. Which animals do you think would benefit more from vicarious learning, predators or their prey? Why?

17. What is meant by symbolic coding? How might language aid vicarious instrumental learning?

18. Suppose you proved that vicarious learning ability improves markedly as children develop speech. How would this finding relate to the theories of vicarious learning?

19. How might our view of human nature differ if psychologists had never succeeded in demonstrating vicarious learning in animals?

20. How might superstitious behavior be acquired through vicarious experiences?

SUGGESTED READINGS

Thorndike's experiments on vicarious learning are reported in *Animal Intelligence* (1911) and in a monograph entitled "The Mental Life of the Monkeys," published in 1901. Watson's work appears in "Imitation in Monkeys," an article published in 1908. Their age notwithstanding, all three are readily available in many university libraries and make easy and fascinating reading, despite the fact that the studies are "failures."

Social Learning and Personality Development (1963), by Albert Bandura and Richard Walters, is a fascinating study of how children are influenced by adult models. Neal Miller and John Dollard's *Social Learning and Imitation* (1941) and Bandura's *Social Learning Theory* (1977) offer very different theories of vicarious learning.

SIX

■

Generalization and Discrimination

Learning involves the appearance of behavior in a given situation, that is, in the presence of certain stimuli. Once a new behavior or a new rate of responding is established in one situation, this alters the organism's behavior in other situations. In short, the animal or person behaves in new situations much as it has learned to behave in the conditioning situation. This tendency for learned behavior to "spread" to situations not involved in training is called *generalization;* its opposite, the tendency to behave differently in one situation than in another, is called *discrimination.* In this chapter, we will examine these phenomena and their determinants. Although the patterns of generalization and discrimination that follow vicarious conditioning resemble the patterns that follow direct conditioning, the former has been little studied, so we will restrict ourselves to studies involving Pavlovian and instrumental conditioning.

GENERALIZATION

Generalization involves the tendency for learned behavior to occur in the presence of stimuli that were *not* present during training. For instance, in Pavlovian conditioning, a dog may learn to salivate to the sound of a tuning fork vibrating at 1,000 cycles per second (cps). After this training, the dog may then be found to salivate to the sound of a tuning fork vibrating at, say, 950 cps to 1,100 cps, even though it was never exposed to these stimuli. The conditional response spreads, or generalizes, to stimuli somewhat different from the CS.

The famous Watson and Rayner study (see Chapter 3) provides another example of the generalization of a conditional response. You will recall that Little Albert learned to fear a white rat; that is, a conditioned emotional response could be elicited by presenting Albert with a white rat. After establishing this behavior, Watson and Rayner then tested to see whether other, previously neutral stimuli would also elicit the fear reaction. They presented Albert with a rabbit, cotton wool, and a Santa Claus mask. None of these stimuli had been present when the rat was paired with the loud noise, yet Albert was afraid of them. Albert's fear had generalized from the white rat to other white, furry objects.

Perhaps the first report of generalization following instrumental learning was made by Thorndike (1898) when he observed that "a cat that has learned to escape from [box] A by clawing has, when put into C or G, a greater tendency to claw at things than it instinctively had at the start" (p. 14). In other words, clawing generalized from box A to boxes C and G.

Today, generalization of instrumentally learned behavior is more often studied by training a pigeon to peck a disk of a particular color and then noticing the bird's tendency to peck a different-colored disk. A classic study by Norman Guttman and Harry Kalish (1956) is illustrative. In this study, there were four groups of pigeons, each of which was trained to peck a disk of a particular color. After this training, the birds were exposed to disks of various colors, including the color used during training, for 30 seconds each. Pigeons pecked the disk most frequently when it was the color used during training, but they also pecked the disk when it was a different color. What they had learned in one situation generalized to other situations.

Generalization Gradients

The fact that behavior generalizes to stimuli not present during training does not mean that all new stimuli are equally effective in evoking the response. Nor is generalization an arbitrary and unpredictable phenomenon that occurs in some situations and not others. Indeed, generalization is a reliable and orderly phenomenon that has "a pattern and sense" (Guttman, 1963, p. 144). When stimuli can be arranged in an orderly way along some dimension (such as pitch or hue), from most like the training stimulus to least like it, a clear association between stimulus similarity and generalization can be seen. This can be demonstrated by training an animal to respond in the presence of a stimulus in a particular way and then presenting the animal with several new stimuli of varying degrees of similarity to the training stimulus. The typical finding is that the more similar a novel stimulus is to the training stimulus, the more likely the organism is to respond to it as though it were the training stimulus. When these results are plotted on a curve, they yield a figure called the **generalization gradient**. The slope of the line indicates the amount of generalization: the flatter the line, the more generalization; the steeper the line, the less generalization.

Carl Hovland (1937a) produced a generalization gradient following Pavlovian conditioning. He began by training college students to respond to a particular tone. The US was a mild electric shock and the UR was the galvanic skin response, or GSR (a measure of emotional arousal). The CS was a tone of a particular pitch. After 16 pairings of the CS and US, Hovland then presented four different tones, including the CS. Each tone was presented twice, and the CRs to each were averaged. The results, which showed that the CR diminished as the stimuli grew more unlike the CS, were plotted to produce the generalization gradient shown in Figure 6-1.

A more common way of depicting the generalization gradient is illustrated in Figure 6-2. This gradient, the product of the Guttman and Kalish study of generalization described previously, shows that the greater the difference between a novel stimulus and the stimulus used in training, the less likely a pigeon is to respond to it.

The generalization gradients depicted here are typical of those found in learning texts, but it would be a mistake to assume that all generalization gradients are pretty much alike. The form of the gradient depends upon many variables, including the amount of training, the method of testing for generalization, and the kind of stimuli involved (Honig & Urcuioli, 1981). Nevertheless, there is generally a systematic relationship between an organism's response to a stimulus and the similarity of that stimulus to the stimuli present during training. That systematic relationship is not a mere laboratory curiosity, as studies of semantic generalization make clear.

Semantic Generalization

Most studies of generalization, like those just described, are based on the physical properties of the stimuli involved—color, size, shape, pitch, loudness, and so on. But responses sometimes generalize on

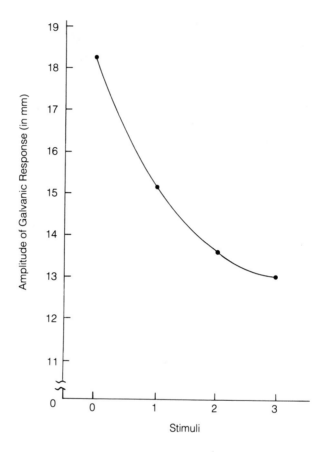

Figure 6-1   Generalization gradient. Average strength of conditional response (GSR) to the CS (0), and to other tones of increasing dissimilarity to the CS (1, 2, 3). (From Carl Hovland, "The Generalization of Conditioned Responses: I. The Sensory Generalization of Conditioned Responses with Varying Frequencies of Tone," *Journal of General Psychology,* 1937, *17,* p. 136, figure 2. Copyright 1937 by the Journal Press. Reprinted by permission of the Helen Dwight Reid Educational Foundation. Published by Heldref Publications.)

the basis of the meaning of the stimulus. This phenomenon is known as **semantic generalization.**

Apparently, the first study of semantic generalization was conducted by Gregory Razran (1939). Razran had 3 adults chew gum, lick lollipops, or eat sandwiches to make them salivate. As they ate, they watched the words *style, urn, freeze,* and *surf* flash on a screen. Then the words were shown alone and saliva was collected in cotton balls that rested under each individual's tongue. Razran weighed the cot-

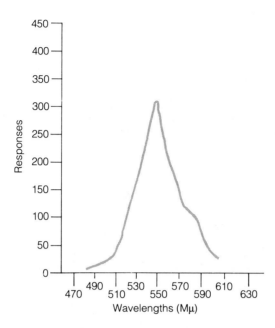

Figure 6-2   Generalization gradient. When pecking a disk of a particular color (in this case, 550 Mμ) had been reinforced, pigeons were likely to peck that disk at a high rate. However, they would also peck disks that were similar to the original disk. (After Guttman & Kalish, 1956.)

ton after each testing period to determine the effectiveness of the procedure. After the people had learned to salivate at the sight of the words, Razran showed them words that were either synonyms (*fashion, vase, chill, wave*) or homophones (*stile, earn, frieze, serf*) of the words used in training in order to determine whether the CR would generalize more to words that had similar sounds or to words that had similar meanings. The average response to the homophones was 37 percent of the average CR. That is, the students salivated about one-third as much to the homophones as they had to the conditional stimuli. However, the average response elicited by the synonyms was 59 percent of the CR. Thus, while there was some generalization based on physical characteristics (the sounds of the words), there was even more generalization based on word meanings.

Semantic generalization has been demonstrated in a number of other studies. John Lacey and his colleagues (1955) paired farm words such as *corn* with electric shocks, so that the word *corn* became a CS that would elicit an increase in heart rate. When the researchers pre-

GENERALIZED THERAPY

The patient was a 37-year-old woman who stood 5 feet 4 inches and weighed 47 pounds. She had a mysterious aversion to eating called anorexia. Arthur Bachrach and his colleagues (1965) used shaping and reinforcement principles to get her to eat more in the hospital. In fact, she gained enough weight to be released. But what would happen when she left the hospital? Would the effects of the therapy carry over? Would the new behavior generalize?

The problem of generalization is a serious one for therapists. One way to attack it is to try to alter the natural environment so that appropriate behavior continues to be reinforced at a high rate. Bachrach and his co-workers used this approach. They asked the patient's family to cooperate in various ways. Among other things, they asked the family to avoid reinforcing invalidism, to reinforce maintenance of weight by, for example, complimenting the patient's appearance, and to encourage her to eat with other people under pleasant circumstances.

With reinforcement of appropriate behavior in the home, the behavior might generalize to other settings. The reinforcement that naturally occurs in these settings would, it was hoped, maintain the desired behavior. The hope seems to have been fulfilled. For instance, the patient attended a social function at which refreshments were served. It had always been the woman's custom to refuse food, but she surprised everyone by asking for a doughnut. All eyes were on her as she devoured the snack, and she later admitted that she got considerable pleasure from all the attention.

Generalization is not always established this easily (Holland, 1978). The juvenile delinquent who acquires cooperative social skills in a special rehabilitation center and then returns to a home and community where aggressive, antisocial acts are reinforced and cooperative behavior is punished is apt to revert to old habits. The chain smoker who quits while on a vacation with nonsmokers must return to a world of smoke-filled rooms. The rehabilitated and repentant child abuser returns to his family. The problem of getting therapeutic gains to generalize to the natural environment is one of the most difficult the therapist faces, but understanding the principles of learning and behavior helps.

sented words that were semantically related (other farm words such as *cow, plow, tractor*), they found that these words also elicited the CR.

These studies demonstrate that, at least among humans, stimulus generalization can be based on abstract concepts as well as physical properties. It is easy to see how this phenomenon may be an important influence on human behavior. There is not much doubt, for example, that during World War II, the word *Japanese* was often paired with unpleasant words such as *dirty, sneaky, cruel,* and *enemy.* As we saw in Chapter 3, such pairing is likely to result in the word *Japanese* eliciting negative emotional reactions. The work on semantic generalization suggests that such emotional responses probably generalize to other words, such as *Oriental, Asian,* and *Chinese,* with similar meanings. Thus, generalization plays an important role in prejudice and other kinds of emotional behavior. It is also of considerable importance in therapy (see Generalized Therapy box).

DISCRIMINATION

Discrimination is the tendency for learned behavior to occur in the presence of certain stimuli, but not in the presence of other stimuli. The organism differentiates, or discriminates, among the stimuli. Discrimination and generalization are inversely related: The more an organism discriminates, the less it generalizes. The procedure for establishing a discrimination (often called **discrimination training**) varies depending upon whether Pavlovian or instrumental learning is involved.

In Pavlovian discrimination training, one stimulus (designated **CS+**) indicates that a US is forthcoming, while another stimulus (designated **CS−**) indicates that the US is not coming. For example, we might put food into a dog's mouth each time a buzzer sounds and give the dog nothing when a bell rings. The result will be that the dog will salivate at the sound of the buzzer (the CS+) but *not* at the sound of the bell (the CS−).

Pavlov (1927) conducted many experiments on discrimination. In one, a dog saw a rotating object. Whenever the object rotated in a clockwise direction, the dog received food; whenever the object rotated in the opposite direction, the dog did not get food. The dog soon learned to salivate to the CS+ (clockwise rotation) and not to the CS− (counterclockwise rotation).

Other experiments yielded similar results. Pavlov's dogs learned to discriminate between different volumes of a particular sound, different pitches of a tone, different temperatures, and so on. Sometimes the level of discrimination was remarkable. One dog learned to salivate when a metronome ticked at the rate of 100 beats a minute, but not when it ticked at a rate of 96 times a minute.

Instrumental discrimination training is somewhat different from the Pavlovian procedure just discussed. In Pavlovian discrimination

WHEN AN S^D IS AN S^Δ

Sometimes what is an S^Δ for one person is an S^D for another. Lately, for instance, there has been a movement to change the traditional skull and crossbones label that graces many poison containers, because it has led to accidental poisonings. The label is supposed to be a warning—an S^Δ—but for children, the skull and crossbones is the mark of pirates and treasures and exciting backyard adventures. For them, a skull and crossbones is an S^D that invites them to gobble the "pirate food" inside (see Figure 6-3). Another label, proposed by the National Poison Center Network, might work better (see Figure 6-4).

Figure 6-3

Figure 6-4

training, a stimulus (CS+ or CS−) indicates whether the US is or is not coming. In instrumental discrimination training, a **discriminative stimulus** indicates whether a particular response, if made, will be reinforced. An **S^D** (pronounced ess-dee) indicates that responding will be reinforced, while an **S^Δ** (pronounced ess-delta) indicates that responding will either not be reinforced or will be punished.

In one kind of instrumental discrimination procedure, a pigeon may receive food after pecking a red disk, but not after pecking a green one. Under such conditions, the bird soon learns to ignore the green disk and pecks steadily at the red one. In another kind of discrimination procedure, Karl Lashley (1930) required rats to jump from a stand to a platform on which they would find food. To reach the platform, they had to jump through a doorway. One door had vertical lines, the other had horizontal lines. If the animal jumped toward the correct door, the door opened, allowing the rat to pass through to the food; if the rat chose the wrong door, it fell to a net below. In this procedure, responding is either reinforced or punished, depending upon the stimulus to which the rat responds. Of course, what happens is that the rat soon learns to jump toward the proper door.

Errorless Discrimination Training

In the procedures just described, the organism undergoing training inevitably makes a number of mistakes. At first, the subject responds at about the same rate to both S^D and S^Δ, but since responses in the presence of S^Δ are not reinforced (and in some instances are punished), they tend to die out. However, in **errorless discrimination training,** it is possible to achieve the same result with almost no errors. Terrace (1964, 1972) presented the S^D in the usual manner, reinforcing appropriate responses. But instead of alternating the S^D (e.g., a blue disk) with the S^Δ (e.g., a yellow disk) he introduced the S^Δ in a form so weak that the birds did not respond to it. Gradually, Terrace increased the strength of the S^Δ until finally it could be presented in full strength yet be ignored by the birds.

Peak Shift

Clearly, discrimination and generalization are integrally related. Discrimination training alters the shape of the generalization gradient so that the slope becomes steeper, but the peak of responding remains at the S^D. When S^D and S^Δ differ in kind, this is the case. For example, if the S^D is a tone and the S^Δ is a light, the animal will soon respond frequently to the tone but rarely to the light. If we then test for generalization by presenting the S^D and other tones, the result is a steep curve with the peak of responding at S^D. However, a peculiar thing happens when the two stimuli differ only in degree, as is the case if an S^D is a tone of 1,000 cps and the S^Δ is a tone of 900 cps. During the test for generalization, the organism may actually show a greater tendency to respond to a novel stimulus than to the S^D. This was first demonstrated in a study by H. M. Hanson (1959).

The stimuli in Hanson's study were disks of different colors. In one condition, pigeons learned to peck a yellowish-green disk (550 nm, or nanometers) and not to peck a slightly different-colored disk (560 nm). A control group did not undergo discrimination training

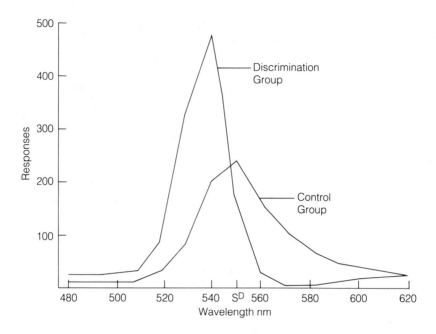

Figure 6-5   Peak shift. Pigeons trained to discriminate between an S^D (550 nm) and an S^Δ (560 nm) responded more often to a 540 nm stimulus than to the S^D. Birds that had been trained only on the S^D (control group) did not show this peak shift. (After Hanson, 1959.)

but did receive food for pecking the yellowish-green disk. After training, the birds were tested by being presented with disks of various colors. The control group showed the expected generalization gradient, with the highest rate of responding in the presence of the yellowish-green disk. But the discrimination training produced a surprising effect: Although trained to peck the yellowish-green (560 nm) disk, these animals were *more* likely to peck a slightly darker green disk (about 540 nm), a color they had not seen during training (see Figure 6-5). As a result of discrimination training, the peak of responding shifted away from the S^D, so this phenomenon is called the **peak shift.**

Peak shift is of interest because it represents a situation in which learning to make one response in one situation (discrimination training) actually leads the organism to make a slightly different response in another situation (during generalization testing). And it suggests that learning to discriminate is more complicated than it appears.

Transposition

There are other indications of the complexity of discrimination training. When an animal learns to respond to an S^D, but not to an S^Δ, is it learning to respond differentially to two independent stimuli, or is it learning something about the relationship between the two stimuli? Some studies indicate that when the stimuli differ only on one dimension (such as color or shape), the latter may be the case.

The classic study of this problem was conducted by the German psychologist Wolfgang Köhler (1939), who trained chickens and chimpanzees to select the lighter of two gray squares. After training, he tested them with the light gray S^D and with a still lighter gray square. Which would the animals select, the stimulus they had previously been reinforced for choosing, or the lighter of the two stimuli? In fact, the animals chose the new, lighter square, though responding to this color had never been reinforced. Köhler called the phenomenon **transposition,** since it seemed analogous to musical transposition, in which a composition is played in a key different from the original. He concluded that what is important in discrimination training is not the individual stimuli involved, but the *relationship* between those stimuli.

If transposition involves relational learning, then how will that learning affect performance in a situation involving a choice between two stimuli, both of which are new to the subject? Apparently anticipating this question, Kenneth Spence (1937) trained chimpanzees to find food under one of two white, metal covers that differed only in size. One chimp got a choice between covers that were 160 and 100 square centimeters. Whenever it chose the larger cover, it found food; whenever it chose the smaller cover, it found nothing. After the chimp had learned to choose the larger cover reliably, Spence presented it with new covers, identical to the first set except that the choice was now between covers that were 320 and 200 centimeters. The chimp chose the larger of the two covers. As in the Köhler study, the animal seemed to have learned something about the relationship between the stimuli, and this learning generalized to a new situation.

Transposition has been demonstrated in humans as well as animals. Elizabeth Alberts and David Ehrenfreund (1951) trained children, age 3 to 5, to find a gumdrop by opening the correct door on a box. The children were trained on one pair of doors, which differed only in size. The smaller door was always the reinforced choice. After the children reached a criterion of 9 out of 10 correct responses, they were tested on a number of new boxes with different size doors. Overall, the results showed that the children continued to choose the smaller doors.

Discrimination Training and Secondary Reinforcement

In instrumental discrimination training, an S^D signals that a response will be reinforced, so it reliably precedes the reinforcer. This pairing of S^D and a reinforcer results in the S^D acquiring reinforcing properties. In other words, one result of instrumental discrimination training is that the S^D becomes a secondary reinforcer (see Chapter 4).

Kent Burgess's (1968) efforts to train Shamu, a killer whale, will serve to illustrate this process. Burgess faced an important problem: How could he reinforce the behavior of a whale effectively with food? He could throw the animal a fish, but it might be some time before the whale found it. This delay of reinforcement would surely slow learning. Not only that, but when the whale found the food, it might be doing something other than performing the response Burgess wanted to reinforce (see Chapter 4 for a discussion of reinforcement delay). Hence, all sorts of extraneous and superstitious behavior might be accidentally shaped up, and this would interfere with training. To avoid these problems, Burgess blew a whistle and then provided food when the animal approached. Thus, the whistle became an S^D for approaching the trainer. When Burgess blew the whistle, the whale swam to him. After this, Burgess could reinforce selected responses by blowing the whistle when the animal made the desired response. If, for example, the whale spouted water, Burgess would blow the whistle; the animal would immediately swim to the trainer and receive a bit of food:

$$R \longrightarrow S^D \longrightarrow R \longrightarrow S^R$$

spout water   whistle sounds   approach trainer   receive food

As this study illustrates, an S^D can also be an effective reinforcer. Other studies show that stimuli that indicate punishment is forthcoming become effective punishers. By saying "No!" when a child begins to toy with some costly china and then punishing when the child does not desist, we establish the word *no* as an S^Δ, a signal to the child to stop whatever he or she is doing. At the same time, the word becomes a powerful secondary punisher, so that we are able to suppress many kinds of behavior simply by saying "No!" (see Dorsey et al., 1978).

Although laboratory studies of discrimination often seem far removed from ordinary experience, research into discrimination has improved our understanding of many important phenomena. Here we will consider two: concept learning and experimental neurosis.

Concept Learning

Transposition appears to involve learning simple concepts (darker than, larger than, etc.) and raises the possibility that many concepts are learned through discrimination training. The word **concept** usually refers to any class or group whose members share one or more defining features. For example, spiders have 8 legs; this distinguishes them from insects, which have less than or more than 8 legs. All ice creams have in common that they are sweet, cold, and soft, and it is these features that allow us to distinguish ice cream from, say, popsicles, which are sweet and cold but hard. Understanding a concept means responding appropriately to any stimulus, not merely the training stimuli, that is a member of the concept class. A child understands the concept "bigger than" when she is able to select the larger of any two objects when asked to; she understands the concept of size seriation when she is able to arrange any series of objects in order according to their sizes.

There is considerable evidence that many concepts are acquired through discrimination training. A study of discrimination training in pigeons (Malott & Malott, 1970) provides an example. In this study, two halves of a key were illuminated independently and could therefore have different colors. When both halves were the same color (either all red or all violet), pecking the key was reinforced; when the two halves were different colors (one half red, the other violet), pecking was not reinforced. After this discrimination was learned, the birds were tested on four new patterns: blue-blue, yellow-yellow, blue-yellow, and yellow-blue. Three out of the 4 pigeons pecked more often when the key halves were the same color than when they were mixed. The concepts the birds learned might be called "sameness" and "difference."

K. Fujita has used a similar procedure to study the acquisition of the sameness concept in monkeys. In one experiment (Fujita, 1983, reported in Pisacreta et al., 1984), monkeys learned to press a lever when two disks were the same color (either red or purple), and not to press the lever when the disks did not match (red and purple). When this discrimination was mastered, Fujita found that the response generalized to novel stimuli. When presented with two yellow or two

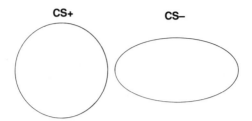

Figure 6-6

green disks, for example, the monkeys pressed the lever; when presented with one yellow and one green disk, they did not press the lever.

Sometimes, very subtle concepts can be learned, even by animals. In one study (Herrnstein et al., 1976), pigeons were exposed to color slides, some of which contained images of people. Pecking was reinforced only when it occurred in the presence of slides containing people. The birds were then tested on new slides to measure the extent to which they had learned the concept of "human being." This was no easy task: Sometimes the people depicted appeared alone, sometimes in groups; they were of different sizes, shapes, ages, and sexes; they wore different kinds of clothing, and even no clothes; they were sometimes in full view, other times partially hidden by objects. Nevertheless, the pigeons demonstrated that they had learned to recognize human beings, despite the fact that the experimenters themselves were unable to pinpoint any single defining feature upon which the birds might have discriminated. The same sort of discrimination training has, of course, produced complex concept learning in humans (see, for example, Bruner et al., 1956).

Experimental Neurosis

N. R. Shenger-Krestovnikova (in Pavlov, 1927), working in Pavlov's laboratory, performed an interesting experiment. Shenger-Krestovnikova trained a dog to salivate at the sight of a circle flashed upon a screen, but not to salivate at the sight of an oval (see Figure 6-6). Next, the researcher modified the oval so that it more closely resembled the circle, and then resumed training (see Figure 6-7). When the animal discriminated between the two figures, Shenger-Krestovnikova modified the oval again, making it still more like the circle, and resumed training. This procedure was repeated again and again. Finally, when the two forms were nearly identical, progress stopped. Not only did the animal fail to discriminate between the two forms, but, as Pavlov (1927) wrote:

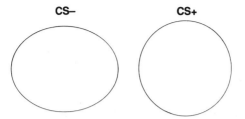

Figure 6-7

The whole behavior of the animal underwent an abrupt change. The hitherto quiet dog began to squeal in its stand, kept wriggling about, tore off with its teeth the apparatus for mechanical stimulation of the skin, and bit through the tubes connecting the animal's room with the observer, a behavior which never happened before. (p. 291)

Pavlov called the dog's bizarre behavior an **experimental neurosis** since it seemed to him that the behavior resembled that sometimes seen in people who had had "nervous breakdowns." Analogous findings had been obtained during instrumental discrimination training (Brown, 1942).

It seems clear that people can find themselves in situations that require extremely subtle discriminations. Teenagers, for example, sometimes are praised by their parents for "accepting responsibility," but on other occasions they are criticized for not "knowing their place." The discriminations the adults require of their children are often nearly as subtle as those Shenger-Krestovnikova required of his dog. And often the results are similar. Whether the "nervous breakdowns" that sometimes result in hospitalization are ever the result of this sort of "discrimination training" is uncertain, but the possibility cannot be ignored.

THEORIES OF GENERALIZATION AND DISCRIMINATION

Pavlov's Theory

Pavlov theorized that conditioning establishes areas of cortical excitation to CS+ and areas of inhibition to CS−. Stimuli that resemble these stimuli excite neighboring areas of the cortex. Thus, stimuli that resemble the CS+ excite areas near the CS+ area of the cortex. This excitation irradiates (spreads) to nearby areas, exciting them. If the

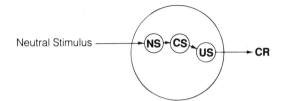

Neutral Stimulus

Figure 6-8

novel stimulus is similar to the CS+, it will excite an area of the cortex near the CS+ area of the brain. The excitation of this area will irradiate to the CS+ area and elicit the CR (see Figure 6-8; a similar explanation can be applied to generalization of instrumental behavior).

According the Pavlov, presenting a CS alone (i.e., without a US) causes cortical inhibition and results in a *decreased* tendency to respond in the presence of the CS. This inhibition, like excitation, irradiates to nearby areas, so that novel stimuli that resemble a CS− inhibit responding.

After pairing a tone with mild shock, Hovland (1937a; see discussion of generalization gradient earlier in the chapter) found a second tone would elicit the CR. Hovland then presented the second stimulus repeatedly in the absence of the US and tested the subjects on the original training stimulus. He found that the subjects were now less likely to respond to this stimulus than they had been following the initial training. That is, the decreased tendency to respond to the second tone generalized to the first. The same phenomenon has been observed in instrumental conditioning (Hearst, 1968; Terrace, 1966).

Pavlov's theory accounts not only for the generalization of excitation and inhibition but also for the steepening of the generalization gradient through discrimination training. One problem with irradiation theory is that the physiological events are merely inferred from observed behavior. Cortical irradiation is presumed to occur only because generalization occurs, but there is no independent validation of its occurrence. The theory therefore suffers from a kind of circularity and is now out of favor with psychologists. Pavlov's ideas have been extended by other theorists, however, most notably Kenneth Spence.

Spence's Theory

Pavlov's theory deals with hypothetical physiological events. What he actually observed, however, was not what went on in the brain, but how an animal responded to different stimuli. Kenneth Spence

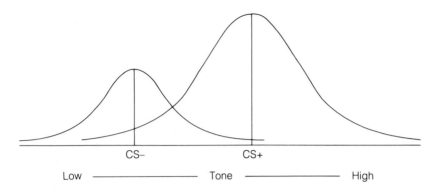

Figure 6-9   Spence's theory of generalization and discrimination. CS+ training produces a gradient of excitation; CS− training produces a gradient of inhibition. The tendency to respond to a stimulus near the CS+ is reduced to the extent that it resembles the CS−. The tendency *not* to respond to a stimulus near the CS− is reduced to the extent that it resembles the CS+.

(1936, 1937, 1960) put Pavlov's physiology aside but accepted the notion that discrimination training does produce generalization to CS− as well as CS+. Pairing a CS+ with a US results in an increased tendency to respond to the CS+ and to stimuli resembling the CS+; the more nearly a stimulus resembles the CS+, the stronger the tendency to respond as if the CS+ were present. The generalization gradient that results is often called an **excitatory gradient.** Presenting a CS− without the US results in a *decreased* tendency to respond to the CS− and a decreased tendency to respond to stimuli resembling the CS−; the more nearly a stimulus resembles the CS−, the stronger the tendency to respond as if the CS− were present. The generalization that results is often called an **inhibitory gradient.**

Spence proposed that the tendency to respond to any given stimulus was the result of the interaction of the increased and decreased tendencies to respond, as reflected in gradients of excitation and inhibition. Consider a dog that is trained to salivate to the sound of a high-pitched tone, and another that is trained *not* to salivate to the sound of a low-pitched tone. The first dog will show generalization of excitation around CS+; the second will show generalization of inhibition around CS−. We can plot the excitatory and inhibitory gradients that result and place them next to one another, as depicted in Figure 6-9.

Notice that the two curves overlap. Discrimination training produces much the same effect within a given organism. That is, the increased tendency to respond to stimuli resembling CS+ overlaps with the decreased tendency to respond to stimuli resembling CS−. What Spence proposed was that the tendency to respond to a given stimulus following discrimination training would be equal to the net difference between the excitatory and inhibitory tendencies. In other words, where the two gradients overlap, the tendency to respond to a particular stimulus will be reduced by the tendency *not* to respond to that stimulus.

Spence's theory accounts remarkably well for various phenomena. It correctly predicts the peak shift phenomenon described earlier, the tendency for the strongest response to shift away from the CS+. And it accounts for the fact that there is no peak shift when CS+ and CS− are widely divergent stimuli (e.g., a very low-pitched tone and a very high-pitched one) or when there are different kinds of stimuli (e.g., a tone and a colored disk), since the generalization gradients of such stimuli will not overlap. Although Spence was concerned primarily with Pavlovian conditioning, his theory can be applied to instrumental conditioning as well. The theory has a good deal to recommend it, but then, so does the Lashley-Wade theory.

The Lashley-Wade Theory

Karl Lashley and M. Wade (1946) proposed an explanation of generalization and discrimination that differs sharply from those of Pavlov and Spence. These researchers argued that generalization gradients depend upon prior experience with stimuli similar to that used in testing. Discrimination training increases the steepness of the generalization gradient because it teaches the animal to tell the difference between the S^D and other stimuli. But the generalization gradient is not usually flat even in the absence of training. Why is this so if the gradient depends on training? The answer Lashley and Wade give is that the animal has, in fact, undergone a kind of discrimination training in the course of its everyday life. A pigeon, for example, learns to discriminate colors long before the psychologist trains it to peck colored disks. The more experience a pigeon has had with colors, especially those resembling the S^D, the steeper its generalization gradient will be; the less experience the bird has had, the flatter the gradient will be.

The theory implies that if an animal is prevented from having any experience with a certain kind of stimulus, such as color, its behavior following conditioning will be affected. If such a color-naive animal is trained to respond in the presence of a red disk, for example, it will later respond just as frequently to a green disk as to a red one. In other words, its gradient of generalization will be flat.

Several researchers have attempted to test this hypothesis. In the typical experiment, animals are reared from birth in the dark in order to deprive them of experiences with color. Then they are trained to respond to a stimulus such as a green disk. After this, the animals are tested for generalization by presenting them with disks of other colors and noting the extent to which they discriminate. The results can be compared to those obtained from animals that had been reared normally. If the gradients of the color-deprived animals are flatter, the Lashley-Wade theory is supported; if rearing in the dark makes no difference in the shape of the gradient, the theory is unsupported.

Unfortunately, the results of such experiments have been ambiguous, with one study tending to support the theory and another study tending to undermine it. Moreover, interpretation of the results is subject to argument. When there is no difference in the gradients of deprived and normally reared animals, proponents of the Lashley-Wade theory argue that the rearing procedure does not entirely preclude experience with the relevant stimuli; when deprivation produces a flat gradient, opponents of the theory argue that the deprivation procedure has damaged the eyes of the animals so that their physical capacity for discriminating colors has been limited. A stronger test of the Lashley-Wade theory is needed than deprivation studies can provide.

If the theory is valid, it can be argued that it should not be necessary to deprive an animal of all experience with a stimulus, but merely to restrict its experience with the stimulus during training. Herbert Jenkins and Robert Harrison (1960) trained pigeons to peck a disk. For some pigeons, a tone could be heard periodically; pecking was reinforced in the presence of the tone, but not during periods of quiet. Other pigeons heard the same tone without interruption. In both cases, then, disk pecking was reinforced in the presence of a tone, but in one case, there were periods of silence during which pecking was not reinforced. The experimenters then tested all the pigeons for generalization to other tones and to periods of silence. Those pigeons that had been exposed to periodic tone had learned to discriminate between periods of silence and tone. As a result, they were much less likely to peck the disk during periods of silence than when the tone sounded. The other pigeons, however, pecked the disk just as much when the tone was on as when it was off. This much is to be expected, since it is analogous to the original training. But what would happen when the pigeons were exposed to different tones, sounds that neither group had heard before? The pigeons that had learned to discriminate between periods of tone and periods of silence also discriminated between the original tone (which, for them, had been an S^D) and other tones. As the Lashley-Wade theory predicts, pigeons that had been reinforced during constant sound pecked as much during one tone as another; in other words, they did not discriminate.

Not all tests of the Lashley-Wade theory have yielded positive results, but it is now generally acknowledged that the steepness of a generalization gradient depends to some extent upon the experience the subject has had with the stimuli under study.

GENERALIZATION, DISCRIMINATION, AND ADAPTATION

We have seen that generalization is the tendency to respond to novel stimuli in much the same way as the organism responds to stimuli used in training. And we have seen that discrimination is the tendency to differentiate between stimuli. Let us now consider the adaptive value of these phenomena.

The tendency to generalize is a blessing bestowed upon us by evolution because it has survival value. Consider the difficulties life would present if what you learned did not generalize. You could, for example, learn how to cross a specific street safely; you could learn how to cross a dozen, or even a hundred, streets. But you would not then know how to cross a street you had never encountered. Generalization can thus be viewed as a kind of bonus from learning: You learn how to perform a particular act in one situation, and *presto!*, you can perform that act in hundreds of other situations.

Generalization is not merely a convenience, it is essential for survival. Conditioned taste aversion offers a powerful illustration of this fact. Animals and people made sick by a particular kind of food refuse to eat not only that food but any item that resembles it. When a blue jay eats a Monarch butterfly and gets sick because of the toxin the butterfly has consumed, it not only refuses to eat any more of that butterfly, it thereafter eschews any Monarch butterfly. In primitive societies, young boys practice the skills of the hunt. The survival of the group depends not only upon the mastery of these skills in the training situation but upon their application to the real world. The skills acquired in shooting an arrow at a tree or at a leaf wafting through the air *must* apply when it comes time to shoot a deer or a bird. The fact that they do is an example of generalization.

As with generalization, discrimination plays an important role in survival. The boy who learns to hunt must learn *not* to shoot animals that his arrows cannot bring down. The girl who learns to gather plants must learn *not* to pick plants that are poisonous or of no nutritional value.

The struggle between predator and prey has a great deal to do with generalization and discrimination. The Viceroy butterfly avoids being devoured because it resembles the Monarch; that is, it survives because the blue jay's behavior toward the Monarch butterfly generalizes to the Viceroy. Similarly, many nonpoisonous snakes resemble poisonous ones and are therefore unmolested by potential enemies. This technique works because potential predators are unable to discriminate between the safe and the dangerous. Predators, too, make use of the tendency to generalize. The angler fish waves a fleshy protuberance about in its gaping mouth, and its victims swim after what looks like a tasty morsel. The angler fish survives partly because its prey cannot distinguish between its lure and the real thing. Some biologists theorize that the rattlesnake's rattle may also provide a kind of lure (Schuett et al., 1984), citing as evidence the fact that frogs fail to discriminate between the insects that are their natural prey and the snake's tail. As the frog lunges for what it takes to be a meal, it instead falls victim to the reptile.

Camouflage may also be viewed as a defense mechanism based upon the principle of generalization. The chameleon escapes its enemies by changing its color to resemble that of its background. The walking stick, a kind of insect, goes unnoticed because it looks like a twig on a tree branch. These disguises are effective survival mechanisms to the extent that the animal's natural predators fail to discriminate between the animal and its surroundings.

We see, then, that learning is not enough for adaptation in a complex world. For both humans and animals, generalization and discrimination are fundamental.

SUMMARY

We saw in previous chapters that learning is an adaptive mechanism that plays an essential role in survival. This chapter has shown that learning would be of limited value were it not for the phenomena of generalization and discrimination.

Generalization is the tendency to respond in situations that are somewhat different from the situation in which the behavior was learned. Without generalization, all learning would be specific to a particular situation. Generalization is tested for by presenting the subject with stimuli not present during training. When the response frequencies are plotted on a graph, the result is a generalization gradient, which shows the frequency of a response in the presence of various stimuli, one of which was present during training. The typical result is a sloping line around the training stimulus; the flatter the line, the more generalization.

Most studies of discrimination involve the physical properties of stimuli—sound, color, shape, and so on. But responses sometimes generalize on the basis of the meaning of a stimulus, a phenomenon called semantic generalization.

Discrimination is also important for adaptation. Behavior that is appropriate in one situation may be highly inappropriate in another. When an organism responds in the presence of a particular stimulus, but not in the absence of that stimulus, we say the organism discriminates. The procedure for establishing a discrimination is called discrimination training. When a discrimination is established, the generalization gradient shows a much steeper slope; that is, there is less generalization. One by-product of instrumental discrimination training is that the S^D and S^Δ become more than signals: An S^D becomes a secondary reinforcer and an S^Δ can become a secondary punisher.

The study of generalization and discrimination has led to an improved understanding of other phenomena. An example is the learning of concepts. Research has also shown that discrimination procedures can produce experimental neuroses, which may provide a model for some naturally occurring human neuroses.

A good deal of research on generalization and discrimination has been aimed at theoretical analysis of these phenomena. Pavlov explained generalization and discrimination in terms of the irradiation of excitation. When generalization occurs, for instance, it is because a stimulus has excited an area of the brain near the part of the brain affected by the CS+. Spence believed that the net difference between gradients of excitation and inhibition predicts the response to novel stimuli. The Lashley-Wade theory maintains that generalization occurs because the organism has had too little experience with the stimuli involved to be able to discriminate among them.

Generalization and discrimination are vital to adaptation. Behavior that does not generalize where appropriate is of limited value, and behavior that generalizes to situations in which it is not appropriate can be dangerous. The use of lures to capture prey and of camouflage to avoid detection are examples of adaptive behavior that depend upon the principles of generalization and discrimination. Predators put evolutionary pressure upon their prey to develop more sophisticated defensive techniques. By developing those techniques, prey animals put evolutionary pressure upon predators to develop more sophisticated predatory techniques. In this way, predator and prey each contribute to the other's evolution.

REVIEW QUESTIONS

1. Define the following terms:

   generalization S^D
   discrimination   discrimination training
   peak shift   transposition

2. Describe the relationship between generalization and discrimination.

3. How is semantic generalization different from other examples of generalization?

4. A student learns to draw human figures. How could you determine if this learning had improved the student's ability to draw animal figures? What phenomenon would you be studying?

5. There is a saying that goes, "He who has been bitten by a snake fears a rope." What phenomenon does this proverb implicitly recognize?

6. Mark Twain once said that a cat that gets burned on a hot stove thereafter avoids hot stoves, but also avoids cold stoves. How could you change the behavior of a cat that fits this description?

7. B. F. Skinner (1951) once taught pigeons to "read." That is, he taught them to peck a disk when a sign said "Peck," and to not peck when a sign said "Don't peck." Describe how Skinner might have accomplished this.

8. Thorndike (1911) wrote that "by taking a certain well-defined position in front of [a monkey's] cage and feeding him whenever he did scratch himself I got him to always scratch himself within a few seconds after I took that position" (p. 236). Explain what sort of training is going on here. Be sure to identify the S^D, the S^Δ, the response being learned, and the reinforcer.

9. Diane says that in the experiment described in question 8, it is not the monkey that is undergoing discrimination training, but Thorndike. Why might she say this? (Hint: The question is, Who is training whom?)

10. Why is generalization important to the clinical psychologist? Why is it important to the teacher?

11. Pavlov trained a dog to salivate at the sight of a circle and then showed that neurotic behavior may be induced by requiring the dog to make finer and finer discriminations between a circle and an oval. How could you cure Pavlov's dog of its neurosis?

12. Most studies of discrimination training use very simple stimuli, such as lights and tones, and very simple responses, such as pecking a disk. How could you use discrimination training to make someone capable of recognizing, from facial features and other "body language," when people were lying?

13. What might be the role of discrimination training in racial prejudice?

14. Explain why it makes sense for feminists to object to the practice of using the pronoun *he* to refer to doctors, lawyers, accountants, and scientists while chambermaids, homemakers, prostitutes, and baby-sitters are referred to as *she*.

15. How does Spence's theory account for the phenomenon of peak shift?

16. Explain the importance of the phenomenon of transposition.

17. What is a concept? How could you teach a child the concept *automobile?*

18. What implications does research on errorless discrimination training have for the construction of educational software?

19. Explain why a stimulus that becomes an S^D also becomes a secondary reinforcer.

20. Explain why a person who is red-green color blind (that is, red and green objects look gray) is at a disadvantage compared to his or her peers.

SUGGESTED READINGS

Most of the important works on generalization and discrimination are technical papers published in professional journals. They are difficult reading and tend to focus on narrow aspects of these phenomena. However, there are some publications that the interested student will find both readable and intriguing.

Two are books already recommended: Pavlov's *Conditioned Reflexes* (1927) and Thorndike's *Animal Intelligence* (1911). Both books treat generalization and discrimination, though the authors may not always discuss the phenomena as they have been described here. (Remember that generalization and discrimination were newly discovered phenomena when these books were written.)

Another person who has written lucidly about topics covered in this chapter is B. F. Skinner. His article, "How to Teach Animals," published in *Scientific American* in 1951, shows how discrimination training can be used to teach all sorts of behavior. It also demonstrates the value of secondary reinforcers in teaching. The principles Skinner describes are not limited to animals.

One of Skinner's most important books, *Science and Human Behavior* (1953) deals in part with topics covered here. See especially Chapters 7, "Operant Discrimination," and Chapter 8, "The Controlling Environment."

■

SEVEN

Schedules of Reinforcement

In everyday parlance, we use the term *learning* to refer to the acquisition of new behavior. A pigeon that rarely or never turned in counterclockwise circles when a light was turned on now does so reliably and efficiently. A child who could not ride a bicycle at all now rides with skill and confidence. A college student for whom the equation F = ma previously meant nothing now can use the formula to solve physics problems.

In addition to referring to the appearance of new behavior, we have seen that learning also refers to changes in the rate at which existing behavior is performed. A pigeon that has learned to turn in counterclockwise circles in the presence of a red light may make the turns at the rate of 3 or 4 a minute. If we can train the bird to make 9 or 10 circles a minute, this change in behavior is a form of learning. No new behavior occurs, but the bird has learned to make the response more often in a given period.

Learning sometimes means reducing the rate at which a response occurs. Small children often go through a phase in which they repeatedly ask the question "Why?":

"Daddy, why are you hanging up the clothes?"

"So they'll get dry."

"Why?"

"So we'll be able to wear them."

"Why?"

"Because . . ."

Whether (as most parents think) the reinforcer that maintains this behavior is the knowledge that is provided or whether the reinforcer is adult attention (both are known to be reinforcers for most children) is not clear. What is clear is that the incessant repetition of "Why?" soon begins to make most parents a little crazy. Eventually, they stop answering the questions. Sooner or later, the child learns that questioning adults pays off *only if it is done at a relatively low rate.* Learning is this case means a reduction in the rate of responding.

Learning can mean a change in the pattern of responses as well as the rate. If a pan of cookies must bake for 10 minutes, it is pointless to check the cookies during the first 5 minutes or so, but it is essential to check on them after an interval of about 8 or 9 minutes. Thus, learning in this situation means changing not only the rate at which the response occurs but also the temporal pattern of responding.

We can see the same phenomenon in the workplace. Consider two factory workers, one paid an hourly wage for spray-painting lawn chairs and the other paid piece work (so much per chair) for the same work. Both employees are allowed to take a 15-minute coffee break every 2 hours. Very likely there will be a difference in the response rates of the two employees: The one on piece work will turn out more lawn chairs each day, since that worker's pay varies according to the number of chairs painted. But it is also likely that there will be a difference in the response patterns of the two workers. The one on an hourly wage will stop every 2 hours for the 15-minute break that is allowed and may even stretch the break into 20 minutes if the supervisor isn't around. By contrast, the employee on piece work is likely to take shorter breaks and may even work right through the breaks without a pause. There is, then, a difference not only in the response rates of the two workers but in the pattern of their responses.

As the previous examples indicate, the pattern and rate of a response vary with the response consequences in force. Thus, the hourly wage earner takes the breaks allowed because that worker is paid the same amount whether he or she rests for those 15 minutes or works. The worker on piece work, however, works faster and takes fewer breaks because his or her paycheck depends upon the number of appropriate responses emitted (e.g., chairs painted) during the workday. Such workers sometimes cut short a break with the comment, "Back to work for me; I can't make any money here."

The pattern of response consequences is called a **schedule of reinforcement.** A particular kind of reinforcement schedule tends to produce a particular pattern and rate of responding, and these effects are incredibly reliable. When a given schedule is in force for some time, the organism responds in a very stereotypic way as long as that schedule is in force. If the organism is removed from the training environment for a prolonged period and then returned to it, it often resumes the previous pattern of responding almost as if it had never left. Moreover, if different schedules are in force for different kinds of behavior, the organism will display different rates of responding appropriate to the different schedules. In this chapter, we will consider some of the more basic kinds of schedules and their effects, beginning with simple schedules.

SIMPLE SCHEDULES

Continuous Reinforcement

The simplest of simple schedules is called **continuous reinforcement, or CRF.** In continuous reinforcement, each response of a designated nature is reinforced. If, for example, a rat receives food each time it presses a lever, lever pressing is on a continuous reinforcement schedule, as is the disk pecking of a pigeon if it receives a bit of grain each time it pecks a disk. Likewise, a child's behavior is on CRF if she is praised every time she hangs up her coat without being reminded to do so, and your behavior is on CRF when you operate a vending machine if, each time you insert the requisite amount of money, you receive the item selected.

Because a response is strengthened (i.e., made more likely to occur) each time it is reinforced, continuous reinforcement leads to very rapid increases in response rates. It is especially useful, then, when the task is to shape up some new behavior or chain of responses. You can see that it would be much easier to teach a pigeon to make counterclockwise turns by reinforcing each successive approximation of the response than it would be if one were to reinforce successive approximations only occasionally.

Although continuous reinforcement typically leads to the most rapid changes in behavior, it is not the most common schedule in the natural environment. Most behavior is reinforced on some occasions, but not on others. A teacher is not able to praise a child each time she hangs up her coat, and vending machines sometimes take our money and give us nothing in return. When reinforcement occurs intermittently, the behavior is said to be on an **intermittent schedule.** There are many kinds of intermittent schedules (see Ferster & Skinner, 1957), but the most important fall into four groups.

Fixed Ratio Schedules

In ratio schedules, reinforcement is delivered when a response has occurred a certain number of times. In a **fixed ratio,** or **FR, schedule,** reinforcement occurs after a fixed number of responses. In the laboratory, a rat may be trained through CRF to press a lever for food. After the response is established, the experimenter may switch to a schedule in which every 3rd lever press is reinforced. In other words, the rat must press the lever 3 times before it receives a bit of food. The schedule is usually indicated by the letters *FR* (for fixed ratio), followed by the number of responses required for reinforcement. The lever pressing of our hypothetical rat, for example, is on an FR 3 schedule. Continuous reinforcement is actually a kind of fixed ratio schedule, then, and may be designated FR 1.

Animals on fixed ratio schedules respond at a high rate, punctuated by pauses after each reinforcement. A rat that lever presses on an FR 5 schedule will press the lever quickly 5 times, eat the food that appears in the food tray, pause for a moment, and then return to work at the lever. A rat on an FR 50 schedule will show much the same pattern, except that the **postreinforcement pauses** (as they are called) will be longer. The greater the number of responses required for reinforcement, the longer the postreinforcement pause. Thus, reducing the ratio of responses to reinforcers from, say, 50:1 to 10:1 (i.e., from FR 50 to FR 10) does not substantially increase the rate at which the animal responds *once it has set to work;* what it does do is shorten the "breaks" it takes after each reinforcer (see Figure 7-1a).

The reason for postreinforcement pauses in FR schedules is not clear. It is tempting to assume that they are due to fatigue. The animal makes a number of responses and then pauses as if to "catch its breath" before starting the next long run. But animals on other types of schedules often work even harder without pauses. Surely if fatigue were a factor, animals on these schedules would have to stop periodically.

Fixed ratio schedules are common outside the laboratory. Many games make use of fixed ratio schedules; in board games, players often get one point for each correct answer. Perhaps the best examples of FR schedules involve work. As noted, many employees work on some sort of fixed ratio schedule, though it is usually called piece work. Often, they are paid a certain amount for each piece they produce, as in the case of the garment worker who is paid so much for each shirt sewn. Sometimes, payment is based indirectly on the number of items produced, as in the case of the farm worker who is paid so much per pound of fruit or vegetables picked. Actually, in

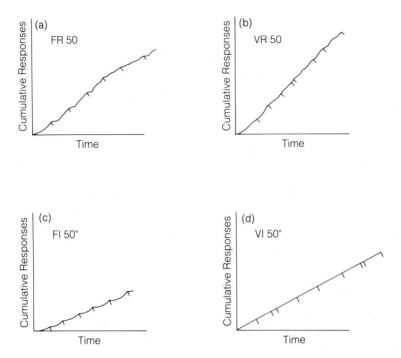

Figure 7-1   Intermittent schedules of reinforcement. In an FR 50 schedule (a), every 50th response is reinforced; in a VR 50 schedule (b), an average of 50 responses is required for each reinforcement; in an FI 50″ schedule (c), a response is reinforced when it occurs after a 50-second interval; in a VI 50″ schedule (d), a response is reinforced after an average interval of 50 seconds. Short, diagonal lines indicate delivery of a reinforcer. (Hypothetical data.)

these two examples, payment is not usually made upon completion of a set number of responses, but rather at the end of some period, such as the workweek (in the case of the garment worker) or the workday (in the case of the farm worker). Nevertheless, it is fair to call these FR schedules, because some record is kept of the number of responses and this record serves as a secondary reinforcer. The farm worker may, for example, receive a token for each pound of berries picked. This token is a secondary reinforcer since it can be exchanged for payment at the end of the day.

Variable Ratio Schedules

Instead of reinforcing after a fixed number of responses, it is possible to vary the number of responses required around some average. For example, instead of reinforcing every 5th lever press, we might reinforce after the 2nd response, then after the 8th response, then the 6th, the 4th, and so on. On such **variable ratio schedules,** usually abbreviated **VR,** the number of responses required for reinforcement varies around some average. In a VR 5 schedule, an average of 5 responses is required for each reinforcement.

Variable ratio schedules produce higher response rates than fixed ratio schedules. Thus, an animal on a VR 50 schedule will produce more responses in an hour than an animal on an FR 50 schedule. The difference is partly due to the pauses in the FR schedule, since such pauses are not a regular feature of VR schedules. But even if these pauses are ignored, we see that the animal on variable ratio reinforcement works harder (see Figure 7-1b). This is so even though the actual payoff is the same for both animals. That is, the animal on FR 50 earns as much food for its 50 responses as the animal on VR 50 does (on average) for its 50 responses.

Variable ratio schedules are quite common in natural environments. As fast as the cheetah is, it does not bring down a victim every time it gives chase, nor can it depend on being successful on the second, third, or fourth try. There is no predicting which particular effort will be successful. All that can be said is that, on average, one in every so many attempts will be rewarded. All predatory behavior is reinforced on VR schedules, though the exact schedule varies depending upon many factors. For instance, if the elk in a particular area are heavily infested by parasites, they will be easier for wolves to take down. However, if the elk are parasitic, then their predators will be too, and the weakened wolves may be less efficient hunters. At first, then, attacks on elk by wolves will be on a low ratio schedule, but as the wolves themselves become infested, the ratio may rise.

Variable ratio schedules are important in human society as well. A teacher may praise a student for good attendance, but not ordinarily after every 50 days of uninterrupted attendance; the teacher may praise the student after 30 days, then after 60 days, then after 40. (This is not to say that the teacher works out this schedule in advance. Nevertheless, a schedule of reinforcement is in force.) College students find themselves on a VR schedule when their instructor bases their grades on unannounced quizzes given once or twice a week. Since the opportunities for reinforcement (and the avoidance of punishment) are unpredictable, students on such schedules who find good grades desirable (reinforcing) tend to study frequently during the week.

Gambling provides a particularly interesting example of VR schedules in human life, since gambling is a serious problem for many people. Gambling casinos have made profitable use of the distinctive features of VR schedules. Slot machines, for example, pay off on a high VR schedule that necessarily results in the player losing in the long run. Nevertheless, the unpredictability of reinforcement ("This next quarter could be the one, Maybel!") makes it very difficult for some people to let go of the "one-armed bandits." Other games of chance, such as roulette and craps, operate on the same sort of VR schedule. The casino's only real problem is to get their patrons to persist at gambling long enough to establish a steady response rate. One way that they do this is to provide free chips, so that the novice is not initially gambling his or her own money. By the time the chips run out, the patron is likely to be "hooked."

Fixed Interval Schedules

Reinforcement need not be based solely on the number of responses. In interval schedules, reinforcement is dispensed following a response, but only when the response occurs after a given period of time. In **fixed interval, or FI, schedules,** the response under study is reinforced the first time it occurs after a specified interval. Note that the reinforcer is not delivered merely because a given period of time has elapsed; a response is still required. For example, a pigeon that has learned to peck a disk may be put on an FI 5" (read FI 5 second) reinforcement schedule. The first time the bird pecks the disk, food is delivered into its food tray, but for the next 5 seconds, disk pecking produces no reinforcement. Then, at the end of the 5-second interval, the very next disk peck is reinforced.

Like fixed ratio schedules, fixed interval schedules produce post-reinforcement pauses. Typically, the animal on an FI schedule makes few or no responses for some time after reinforcement, but gradually increases the rate of response so that by the time the interval has elapsed, the response rate is quite high. Thus, animals on FI schedules typically produce a scalloped-shaped response curve (see Figure 7-1c).

Why should FI schedules produce a scalloped-shaped curve while animals on FR schedules respond at a steady rate between pauses? Apparently, the animal on FR is reinforced for responding steadily, while the animal on FI is not. Consider first the case of a rat pressing a lever on an FR 50 schedule. The animal has a lot of work to do before it receives its next reinforcer, and any pause delays its arrival. Now consider the rat on an FI 50" schedule. No responses will be reinforced until 50 seconds have passed, so responding during this period brings the animal no closer to reinforcement. The animal therefore waits until just before the time has elapsed and then begins responding. The rat could, of course, wait until *after* the interval had elapsed before beginning to respond rapidly. This would reduce the number of responses per reinforcer, but it would necessarily increase the interval between reinforcers. The most efficient policy, then, is to begin responding shortly before the interval has ended and continue responding rapidly until the reinforcer is delivered. This is precisely what the animal on an FI schedule does.

Good examples of FI schedules in the animal world are hard to come by. Many female animals become sexually receptive at fairly regular intervals, and attempts by males to mate with them at other times are seldom reinforced. This therefore looks like an FI schedule. But estrus (sexual receptivity) is indicated by specific odors, and male sexual behavior is more likely to be under the control of such stimuli than the passage of time.

Examples of fixed interval schedules in humans are easier to come by, perhaps because we more often "live by the clock." Your behavior is on an FI schedule when you bake bread in an oven since checking the bread will be reinforced only when it occurs after a specified period. The first time you bake bread, you may open the oven door repeatedly "to see how it's doing." But you soon learn to wait until the required baking time has nearly elapsed before peeking inside the oven. We are also on FI schedules when we meet people at specific times. You may meet a fellow student for lunch each weekday at noon. If you show up an hour earlier or an hour later, you are not likely to be reinforced by your friend's company, so you will usually arrive at the meeting place a little before or just after noon. Similarly, college students are on FI schedules when their grades depend solely upon their performance on midterm and final exams. Typically, student responding follows the scalloped curve. That is, they do little studying for the midterm until a week or two before the test, when their efforts intensify. After the midterm, they usually leave off studying for awhile (this is the postreinforcement pause). Then, as the end of the semester approaches, they begin to hit the books again in preparation for the final exam. If the instructor determines grades on the basis of quizzes given each Friday, the same sort of scalloped curve will appear on a weekly basis. Student procrastination, it would seem, is partly the result of FI schedules.

Variable Interval Schedules

Instead of reinforcing a response after a fixed interval, it is possible to vary the interval during which responses are not reinforced around some average. For example, instead of reinforcing disk pecking after a fixed interval of 5 seconds, we might reinforce a response after 2 seconds, then after 8 seconds, 6 seconds, 4 seconds, and so forth. On such **variable interval,** or **VI, schedules,** the average length of the interval during which responses are not reinforced varies around some average. In a VI 5″ schedule, the interval between reinforced responses averages 5 seconds.

Variable interval schedules produce higher response rates than FI schedules, though not so high as FR and VR schedules. As with VR schedules, variable interval schedules are free of postreinforcement pauses. The animal responds at a steady rate, pausing only long enough to consume the reinforcers delivered to it (see Figure 7-1d).

We can find VI schedules in natural environments as well as in the lab. Leopards often lie in wait for their prey rather than stalking it. Sometimes the wait may be short, sometimes long, but remaining alert and waiting quietly are eventually reinforced by the appearance of prey. The same sort of thing may be seen in many other species, including spiders and snakes. Similarly, the naturalist or nature photographer is often on a VI schedule since he or she must wait varying lengths of time before having the opportunity to get a good shot. The air traffic controller who watches a radar screen and the submariner who watches a sonar screen are also on VI schedules, since the signal for which they watch occurs at irregular intervals. We also find ourselves on VI schedules when we must wait in line at the bank or the theater.

Stretching the Ratio

Once an animal has learned to perform a particular response, it can be required to respond for very few reinforcers. Rats will press levers and pigeons will peck disks thousands of times for a single reinforcer, even if that reinforcer is a small amount of food. It should be noted, however, that the experimenter does not merely train a rat to press a lever and then put the animal on, say, an FR 1,000 schedule. The experimenter must begin with a relatively low ratio, such as FR 1. Then, when the animal is responding at a steady rate on that schedule, the experimenter may increase the ratio to FR 3; when this schedule has been in force a while, the experimenter may go to FR 7, then FR 15, and so on. This procedure is known as **stretching the ratio** (Skinner, 1968), but the concept applies to interval as well as to ratio schedules. Stretching the ratio (or interval, as the case may be) must be done with some care because, if the experimenter stretches too rapidly, responding will be disrupted, a phenomenon called **ratio**

strain. If ratio strain is severe, the animal may stop responding entirely.

It may have occurred to you that stretching the ratio is similar to a procedure discussed in Chapter 4—shaping. The procedures are indeed very much alike. The difference is that shaping produces new responses, while stretching the ratio affects the rate of old responses and the ratio of responses to reinforcers. By stretching the ratio, animals and people can be induced to make thousands of responses for very little "pay."

COMPLEX SCHEDULES

The simple reinforcement schedules just reviewed can be combined to create various kinds of complex schedules. In a **multiple schedule,** for example, a response is under the control of two or more schedules, each associated with a particular stimulus. A pigeon that has learned to peck a disk for grain may be put on a multiple schedule in which pecking is reinforced on an FI 10″ schedule when a red light is on, but on a VR 10 schedule when a yellow light is on; the two reinforcement schedules alternate, with the changes indicated by changes in the light. The experimenter refers to this as a multiple FI 10″ VR 10 schedule. The bird's responses show the familiar scalloped curve of FI schedules when the red light is on, followed by the rapid, uninterrupted pecking associated with VR schedules when the yellow light is on (see Figure 7-2).

Multiple schedules produce the same sort of behavioral shifts in human beings. For instance, a seventh-grader named Billy is a hellion in Mr. Smith's history class, but an angel in Ms. Jones's English class. Very likely the reason for the difference in behavior has to do with different reinforcement schedules. Mr. Smith may inadvertently reinforce disruptive behavior by attending to Billy when he misbehaves, perhaps on the misguided theory that his misconduct means that he "needs attention." Ms. Jones, on the other hand, ignores Billy when he misbehaves, but reinforces desirable behavior. Billy responds "appropriately" to the two different schedules: His rate of disruptive behavior is high in the presence of Mr. Smith, but low in the presence of Ms. Jones.

A **chain schedule** is similar to a multiple schedule except that reinforcement is delivered only upon completion of the last in a series of schedules. Suppose that a pigeon pecks a red disk on an FI 10″ schedule. At the end of 10 seconds, the next disk peck does *not*

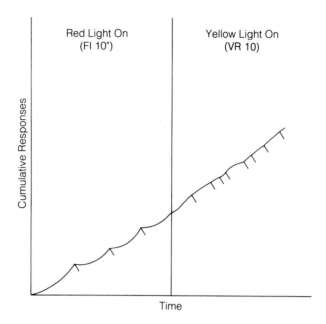

Figure 7-2   Multiple schedule. A pigeon's rate and pattern of responding changes when a stimulus indicates a change in the reinforcement schedule in force. (Hypothetical data.)

produce reinforcement, but the light changes from red to yellow. Responses on the yellow disk are reinforced with food on an FR 50 schedule. After 50 responses, the bird receives food, the disk changes back to red, and the FI 10″ schedule is once again in effect. A chain schedule thus differs from a multiple schedule in that reinforcement is delivered only upon completion of the last schedule of reinforcement.

The question arises as to why an animal responds in the presence of a stimulus when these responses are not reinforced, as is the case in a chain schedule. The most likely explanation is that the change in stimulus, which indicates not only that a new schedule is in force but that the organism is one step closer to reinforcement, is a secondary reinforcer (see Chapter 4).

In multiple and chain schedules, only one schedule is available at any given moment. In **concurrent schedules,** two or more schedules are available at once. A pigeon may have the option of pecking a red disk, in which case responses are reinforced on a VR 50 schedule, or pecking a yellow disk on a VR 20 schedule. In other words, the concurrent schedule involves a choice. In the case of a concurrent VR

SCHEDULED NEUROSIS

There are many ways to become neurotic. We saw in Chapter 6 that an animal will behave bizarrely if required to make increasingly subtle discriminations for reinforcement. Other research shows that animals behave peculiarly under certain reinforcement schedules. Schedules that include both reinforcement and punishment are especially likely to produce neurotic symptoms.

For instance, Jules Masserman (1943) taught a cat to lift a cover to find food. When this response was well established, Masserman changed the consequences: Now when the cat lifted a cover, it would find food, but sometimes it would receive a blast of air or a brief electric shock as well. The result was that the cat quickly learned not to make the response, but in addition, it displayed rather unusual behavior. "For instance," writes Masserman, "Cat 53 was a moderately quiet animal in which two air-blasts abolished further feeding responses but produced a fidgety, incessant pacing and shifting from side to side" (p. 67) among other symptoms. Other cats became extremely passive. One animal would lay so still "he appeared to be asleep; moreover, he could be placed in various cataleptic postures for periods of from ten to twenty minutes" (p. 67).

All of us have had experiences similar to those of Masserman's cats, though usually the consequences involved are secondary reinforcers and punishers. The woman who feels she is due for a raise may become irritable and fidgety before she knocks at the boss's door if, in the past, her requests have been acceded to only after an unpleasant scene. The man who has trouble getting dates may go out with a woman who treats him with contempt, but he probably will struggle with his mixed feelings before dating her again.

It is not certain whether such mixed consequences play an important role in human neurosis, but it does seem certain that they complicate our lives. If only the environment would answer us in a clear and consistent manner—a simple "Hell, Yes!" or a simple "Hell, No!" Life might not be perfect, but it would be a lot less complicated.

50 VR 20 schedule, the animal would soon choose the yellow disk and the VR 20 schedule.

Since much of human behavior can be thought of as involving choices, studies of concurrent schedules have received considerable attention in recent years. One particularly interesting finding from this research concerns the matching law.

CHOICE AND THE MATCHING LAW*

As noted, a concurrent schedule represents a kind of choice. The pigeon on such a schedule may make one response (peck the red disk) or another (peck the yellow disk). It cannot do both simultaneously, so a choice exists. In recent years, psychologists have become increasingly interested in the study of behavior in such choice situations.

Making a choice may involve a great deal of thought. Human beings faced with a choice often verbalize silently, and sometimes aloud, about the relative merits of the various response alternatives. It is possible that animals engage in analogous behavior when faced with a choice. However, our interest in choice is not in these cogitations, but in the effect that the reinforcement schedules have upon the choices made. The task is to be able to predict, from the reinforcement schedules in force, how the person or animal will respond in a choice situation.

In certain situations, this is easily done. Imagine a rat in a T-maze arranged so that if the rat enters the arm on the right, it will receive food, but if it enters the arm on the left, it will receive a shock. We have no difficulty in predicting that after a few trials, the rat will regularly choose to turn right rather than left. A choice situation in which response A is always reinforced and response B is always punished quickly results in the reliable performance of response A. Given a choice between sleeping in either of two beds, one smooth and firm, the other soft and lumpy, you will almost always select the former. We can also predict with confidence the outcome of a choice between a response that is always reinforced and one that is neither reinforced nor punished.

Prediction becomes more difficult, however, when both alternatives offer rewards and the only difference is in their relative frequency. But animals have an uncanny knack for selecting the "better-paying" work. Consider the case of a pigeon given a choice between pecking either of two disks, where pecking the red disk is reinforced on an FR 50 schedule and pecking the yellow disk is reinforced on an FR 75 schedule. What will the pigeon do? Perhaps it will go back and forth repeatedly between the two disks. Or perhaps it will work steadily at one disk, but the disk will be selected at random, so that one pigeon will peck at yellow, another at red. In fact, what happens is that the pigeon initially spends some time at each disk, moving

---

* I am grateful to Howard Rachlin for helpful comments on an earlier version of this section.

back and forth between them, but it eventually settles on one disk, and that disk is nearly always the one associated with the higher reinforcement rate. Humans display the same ability to discriminate between reinforcement schedules (Pierce & Epling, 1983).

The tendency to choose the better of two reinforcement schedules can be expressed by the formula

$$\frac{R_1}{R_2} = \frac{r_1}{r_2}$$

What this formula means is that, given two responses, R_1 and R_2, each on its own reinforcement schedule, r_1 and r_2, respectively, the relative frequency of each response equals the relative frequency of reinforcement available. This statement is called the **matching law** since the response frequency *matches* the reinforcement frequency (Herrnstein, 1961, 1970).

You can see that a choice situation involving different schedules of reinforcement can be viewed as a kind of discrimination task (see Chapter 6). In the case of two ratio schedules, such as FR 30 and FR 40, the subject samples each and then settles on the more desirable schedule. In concurrent ratio schedules, it makes sense to identify the higher-paying schedule as quickly as possible and remain loyal to it. Switching back and forth between two ratio schedules, one of which "pays better" than the other, is pointless. In the same way, if you can pick beans for Farmer Able or Farmer Baker, and Able is paying $5 a bushel compared to Baker's $4, it makes little sense to switch back and forth. Rather, your behavior will follow the matching law—you will pick for Farmer Able.

Switching makes more sense when concurrent *interval* schedules are involved. Consider the case of an animal on a concurrent FI 10″ FI 30″ schedule. Clearly, the payoff is better on the FI 10″ schedule, so it makes sense for the animal to spend most of its time working on that schedule. But even on that schedule, there are periods during which responding is useless. Some of this time could be spent responding on the FI 30″ schedule. And the longer the animal works on the FI 10″ schedule, the more likely it is that a response on the FI 30″ schedule will be reinforced. It therefore makes sense for the animal to devote most of its effort to the FI 10″ schedule, but occasionally make a few responses on the FI 30″ schedule. In fact, this is exactly what happens.

What about concurrent VI schedules? Suppose a rat has a choice between VI 10″ and VI 30″ schedules. Once again it makes sense for the rat to devote most of its time to the VI 10″ schedule, but the longer it does not respond on the VI 30″ schedule, the more likely such responding is to be reinforced. This is so even though delivery of reinforcement is variable and therefore unpredictable. And once again, animals behave in the most sensible manner: They focus their attention on the VI 10″ schedule, but periodically abandon this schedule to respond to the VI 30″ schedule. In this way, they receive the maximum amount of reinforcement possible. Even when the differences in schedules are fairly subtle, animals usually respond in a manner that is in their best interests.

We have seen that, given a choice between two interval schedules, an animal will alternate between them. Is it possible to predict, on the basis of the schedules in force, how often an animal will respond on each schedule? Richard Herrnstein (1961, 1970) has found that it is indeed possible. He reports that in a two-choice situation, response choice may be predicted according to the mathematical expression

$$\frac{R_A}{R_A + R_B} = \frac{r_A}{r_A + r_B}$$

where R_A and R_B represent two responses, A and B, and r_A and r_B represent the reinforcement rates for responses A and B, respectively.

This equation is merely a reformulation of the matching law and states that the proportion of responses matches the proportion of reinforcement available. Take the case of a rat trained to press a lever for food. Presses on lever A are reinforced on a VI 10″ schedule; presses on lever B are reinforced on a VI 30″ schedule. If the rat were to respond solely on the VI 10″ schedule, it would receive a maximum of 6 reinforcers per minute. If it occasionally responded to the VI 30″ schedule, it could obtain a maximum of 2 more reinforcers. Thus, of the total reinforcers obtainable, 75 percent (6 out of 8) are available on the VI 10″ schedule and 25 percent are available on the VI 30″ schedule. The value of r_A is therefore about .75; that of r_B is about .25. Inserting these numbers into the previous equation, we obtain

$$\frac{R_A}{R_A + R_B} = \frac{r_A}{r_A + r_B} = \frac{.75}{.75 + .25} = \frac{.75}{1.00} = .75$$

The formula predicts that the rat will devote approximately three fourths of its responses (.75 = 75 percent) to schedule A (the VI 10″ schedule) and one fourth of its responses to schedule B (VI 30″).

Herrnstein has extended the matching law beyond the two-choice situation, claiming that every kind of behavior represents a choice. Consider the pigeon that receives food when it pecks a disk. There are many responses the pigeon may make besides pecking the disk. Some of these responses are innate, while others are apparently under the control of natural reinforcers. The bird may, for instance, groom itself, wander around the cage, peck at objects on the floor or on the walls, or sleep. In pecking the disk, it is therefore making a choice between that response and various alternative responses. Indeed, even when the pigeon pecks the disk at a high rate, it continues to engage in other kinds of behavior, such as head bobbing, turning its head left and right, and so forth. Theoretically, it is possible to identify all of these responses and the reinforcers that maintain them and to predict the relative frequency of any one of them. This idea can be expressed by the formula

$$\frac{R_A}{R_A + R_O} = \frac{r_A}{r_A + r_O}$$

where R_A represents the particular response we are studying, R_O represents all *other* responses, r_A represents the reinforcers available for R_A, and r_O represents all reinforcers available for all other responses (Herrnstein, 1970). This formula has less predictive value than the formula for the two-choice situation, since it is not generally possible to specify all the responses that may occur, nor all the reinforcers those responses may produce. (Some responses may, for example, be reinforced by physiological events not readily subject to observation, as in the case of the reinforcer a rat receives when it scratches an itch.)

Although it is not clear how animals and people are able to discriminate between subtle differences in reinforcement schedules, it is clear that the ability to do so is highly adaptive. The value of matching response choice to reinforcement schedules is easily seen in foraging for food. If food is more plentiful in one area than another, the animal that responds by choosing to forage where food is more abundant has a better chance of surviving. Similarly, predators often have a choice of prey animals. The lion may take a very young wildebeest with little difficulty, but since other lions will claim a share, the hunter may receive too little food to justify the effort. On the other hand, if it pursues a large healthy adult, the chase is apt to be fruitless and can result in injury to the predator. The lion works on the best schedule when it pursues animals that are old, sick, or injured, and this is what it generally does. It fares even better if it chooses to take a prize away from a weaker predator, such as the cheetah, and it will do this when the opportunity arises.

Humans likewise benefit from the ability to match responses to reinforcement. No doubt for most of human existence, people have made good use of the ability to apportion responses appropriately among the hunting and foraging areas available. Today, a farmer does this by devoting most available farmland to a crop that produces a nice profit under typical weather conditions, and planting a smaller area in a less lucrative crop that does well under adverse weather conditions. The rest of us do the same thing when we spend more time at a high-paying job than at a low-paying one. College students obey the matching law when they devote more time to a five-credit course than to a one-credit course, since a high grade in the former pays better (contributes more to grade point average) than a high grade in the latter. We all follows the same principle when we spend more time with someone whose company we enjoy than with someone we find tiresome.

The matching law has been found to be a robust phenomenon, but it has its limits. For instance, studies of choice involve the tendency to choose one response over another over a period of time, but many life choices essentially represent one-shot situations. Upon graduating from college, you may have your choice of two different jobs. If you could switch back and forth between the two, your behavior would probably conform to the matching law. But as a practical matter, you will have to choose one job and turn down the other.

Nevertheless, the matching law holds for a wide variety of species, including humans, and for a wide variety of responses, reinforcers, and reinforcement schedules (see deVilliers, 1977, for a review). It holds, for example, whether we are considering different rates of reinforcement (Herrnstein, 1970), different amounts of reinforcement (Todorov et al., 1984), or different reinforcement delays (Catania, 1966). And it holds for punishment schedules as well as reinforcement schedules (Baum, 1975). Because of its robustness, the study of choice and the matching law have helped to provide a foundation for a new field, experimental economics (see Experimental Economics box).

In light of the apparent relevance of reinforcement schedules to everyday human behavior, there would seem to be no doubt about the value of research in this area. However, the importance of reinforcement schedules is under debate.

EXPERIMENTAL ECONOMICS

Some psychologists and economists have drawn a parallel between research on reinforcement schedules and economics and have founded a new field called **behavioral,** or **experimental, economics.** They note, for instance, that pressing a lever or pecking a disk for food is analogous to working for pay. One naturally seeks out the highest-paying job available, and this is what studies of choice and the matching law are about.

Other economic principles have been found to hold in animal experiments. For instance, economists know that when the price of a luxury item rises, the consumption of that item declines. But when the item is an essential, such as food, large increases in price produce only small decreases in consumption. The same phenomenon has been demonstrated in rats. Rats will work for psychoactive drugs (a luxury), but increases in the price of the drugs (an increase in the number of lever presses required for a given amount of drug) usually result in decreased consumption; yet large increases in the price of food (an essential) do not lower consumption substantially (Hursh, 1980, 1984). It is possible, then, to study economic principles experimentally with animals.

It is also possible to study such principles in human groups. In one study, Ray Battalio and John Kagel (reported in Alexander, 1980) studied the effects of a token economy on the behavior of female patients in the psychiatric ward of a state hospital. Tokens could be earned for performing various tasks, such as making one's bed or working in the laundry, and exchanged for cigarettes, candy, and other items. This can be construed as a choice between various activities for which tokens are available and other activities (watching television, sleeping) for which, presumably, other reinforcers are available. The situation resembles the society outside the hospital, where people generally have a choice between working for pay or participating in various leisure activities. One thing the researchers were interested in was how the reinforcers would be distributed among the patients. That is, would each person earn about the same number of tokens or would some people earn far more than others, as is the case for the United States population as a whole? The results revealed that the distribution of wealth in the psychiatric ward closely paralleled that of the general population. For example, those in the top 20 percent of token earners owned a total of 41.2 percent of all tokens earned, while the bottom 20 percent earned only 7.4 percent. The top 20 percent of the U.S. population as a whole earns 41.5 percent of all income, while the bottom 20 percent earns 5.2 percent. Thus, the figures for patients earning tokens is virtually identical to the figures for money earned in the larger society.

THE IMPORTANCE OF
REINFORCEMENT SCHEDULES

A great deal of research has been done on schedules of reinforcement and their differential effects. But some psychologists have raised doubts about the significance of this research (see, for example, Schwartz et al., 1978). Some argue that the schedules of reinforcement studied in the laboratory are artificial constructions not found in the real world. Others complain that research on schedule effects has generated reams of data on hundreds of schedules, but that these data contribute little of real importance to an understanding of behavior.

It is true that schedules found outside the laboratory are seldom as simple as those created by an experimenter. But this is true of all laboratory science; researchers take a problem into the lab precisely because the lab allows them to simplify it. Thus, a psychologist studies a rat's behavior on a concurrent VR 10 VR 15 schedule not because this schedule is particularly representative of the rat's natural environment, but because it is a convenient way of determining the animal's ability to discriminate between similar schedules. The goal is to discover rules that describe the way the environment affects behavior. Such rules cannot easily be discovered unless the experimenter simplifies the environment.

The second charge is that studies of schedules generally produce trivial findings. But it is not trivial to note that personality (which is to say the characteristic behavior of a given individual) is a function of the individual's history of reinforcement. Traditional explanations attribute personality differences to qualities of mind: John is said to be overweight because he "lacks will power"; Mary is a compulsive gambler because of "masochistic urges"; Bill is persistent in his efforts to break the school track record because he "has stick-to-itiveness"; Phyllis comes up with novel ideas because she "has a lot of imagination." The trouble with all such "explanations" is that they merely name the thing to be explained. John's tendency to overeat is called a lack of willpower; Phyllis's ideas are called imaginative. The study of reinforcement schedules gives us a more scientific way of accounting for such behavior, an intermittent schedule of reinforcement will result in the behavior occurring at a high rate. This means that Phyllis's creativity is very likely a function of the schedule of reinforcement this behavior has been under (see Pryor et al., 1969). If Bill is persistent, the chances are that his history of reinforcement has shaped up this behavior.

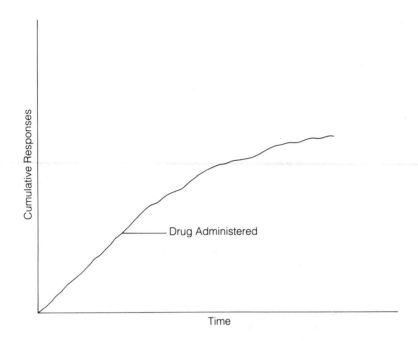

Figure 7-3   Use of schedules in pharmaceutical research. Behavioral effects of a drug may be studied by administering it to an animal responding steadily on a given schedule. (Hypothetical data.)

Research on schedules has proved valuable for another reason. Because intermittent schedules produce extremely steady rates and patterns of responding, they have improved our ability to study the effects of *other* variables on behavior. For instance, one may study the effects of a new drug by giving it to an animal that is responding steadily on a VR 5 schedule. If the rate of response increases or decreases, or if the pattern of responding changes, we may attribute these changes to the drug (see Figure 7-3). In this way, we have a clear indication of the effect the drug has on behavior. Similar approaches can be used to study the effects of food deprivation, brain stimulation, the relative power of different reinforcers, and so on. Whether reinforcement schedules deserve to be called the "sleeping giant" of behavioral research (Zeiler, 1984) remains in doubt, but the importance of research in this area to an understanding of behavior seems clear.

SUMMARY

Learning is a change in behavior, and that includes changes in the rate and pattern of a response over time. Response rates and patterns are functions of the schedule of reinforcement in effect.

There are several kinds of reinforcement schedules, each of which has distinctive effects on behavior. In continuous reinforcement, or CRF, each time an organism makes the response under study, it receives food or another reinforcer. Continuous reinforcement results in rapid increases in the rate of response and is therefore very effective in shaping new behavior. Continuous reinforcement differs from intermittent schedules in that, in the latter, responses are not always reinforced.

One kind of intermittent schedule is the fixed ratio, or FR, schedule. In this kind of schedule, every nth response is reinforced. Thus, a lever-pressing response on an FR 10 schedule is reinforced after a lever is pressed 10 times. FR schedules produce bursts of rapid and continuous responding punctuated by pauses after each reinforcement. The length of these postreinforcement pauses varies with the schedule: the higher the ratio of responses to reinforcers, the longer the pauses. Piece work, in which an employee is paid so much for each item of work completed, is a common example of a fixed ratio schedule.

In variable ratio, or VR, schedules, the number of responses required for reinforcement varies around an average. An animal on a VR 50 schedule makes an average of 50 responses for each reinforcer. Like fixed ratio schedules, variable ratio schedules produce high rates of responding. However, VR schedules do not produce postreinforcement pauses; instead, the organism responds at a steady, uninterrupted pace. A good example of variable ratio schedules in human society is gambling.

Ratio schedules are based on the number of responses made. Interval schedules reinforce a response only when it occurs after a specified interval. In fixed interval, or FI, schedules, a response is reinforced the first time it occurs after a given interval. An animal on an FI 50" schedule receives food or another reinforcer when it performs a specified response after an interval of 50". Once a response is reinforced, responding has no effect until the 50 seconds have elapsed. The result is that animals on FI schedules make few responses during the early part of the interval, but respond more frequently as the end of period approaches. College students often find themselves studying very little during the early part of the semester and then burning the midnight oil near midsemester when reinforcers for studying become available.

In variable interval, or VI, schedules, a response is reinforced only after a period of time, but the interval varies around some average. An animal on a VI 50" schedule receives reinforcement for responding after intervals of varying lengths that average 50". Variable interval schedules produce higher response rates than fixed interval schedules, but not as high as ratio schedules. Like VR schedules, VI schedules produce steady response rates without postreinforcement pauses. Predatory animals lying in wait for prey and air traffic controllers watching a radar screen provide examples of VI schedules.

Animals and humans have been known to perform hundreds of responses for a single reinforcer, but it is necessary to begin with a relatively rich schedule and gradually stretch the ratio. That is, the number of responses required for reinforcement is gradually increased. An analogous procedure is applied to interval schedules.

Two or more simple schedules can be combined to form various kinds of complex schedules. When the schedules alternate and each is identified by a particular stimulus, a multiple schedule is said to be in force. A chain schedule resembles a multiple schedule except that reinforcers are delivered only during the last schedule in the chain. In concurrent schedules, two or more schedules are available simultaneously, so that the organism must choose between them.

Humans and animals have a remarkable ability to obtain the maximum amount of reinforcement available under concurrent schedules. The tendency to apportion responses in proportion to the reinforcement available is so reliable it is called the matching law. In the case of a choice among ratio schedules, the matching law correctly predicts responding on the schedule with the highest reinforcement frequency. In the case of a choice among interval schedules, the matching law predicts responding to each schedule in proportion to the amount of reinforcers available on each.

The significance of research on schedules has been challenged in recent years. Some argue that laboratory studies of schedules are artificial because the schedules studied are seldom, if ever, found in nature. But the artificiality of laboratory studies allows the researcher to arrive at reliable generalizations which, when tested in natural environments, often hold true. The analysis of reinforcement schedules has provided new insights into behavior previously attributed to "character" and other vague constructs. Finally, the study of schedule effects has led to the development of new methodologies for studying behavior.

REVIEW QUESTIONS

1. Define the following terms:

   CRF   stretching the ratio
   intermittent schedules   matching law
   FR 20   postreinforcement pause
   VR 20   complex schedule

2. Give an example (not provided by the text) of a decrease in responding that indicates learning has occurred.

3. John wants to teach Cindy, age 5, the alphabet. He plans to reinforce correct responses with praise and small pieces of candy. What sort of schedule should he use?

4. Mary complains that her dog jumps up on her when she gets home from school. You explain that she reinforces this behavior by petting and talking to the dog when it jumps up, but Mary replies that you must be wrong, since she "hardly ever" does this. How would you respond to Mary's comment?

5. Five-year-old David gives up easily in the face of frustration. How could you develop his persistence?

6. Joyce is annoyed because some of her employees fail to take the periodic rests breaks required by the union and the state's safety regulations. Why do you suppose this happens, and what can Joyce do to correct the problem?

7. Every Saturday at noon, the local fire department tests the fire signal. Is this a reinforcement schedule and, if so, what sort of schedule is it?

8. Many people regularly check the coin return after using a telephone even though their call went through. Explain this behavior.

9. Mr. Smith and Ms. Jones both give their students new spelling words on Friday. Mr. Smith always tests his students on the following Friday. Ms. Jones also tests her students once a week, but the day varies, and she does not announce the test day in advance. Whose students are more likely to study on Tuesday nights?

10. How might casino operators increase their income by "stretching the ratio?"

11. Concurrent schedules are said to represent a choice situation. Why is a multiple schedule not said to represent a choice?

12. Describe the similarities and differences between multiple and chain schedules.

13. Explain the expression

$$\frac{R_A}{R_A + R_B} = \frac{r_A}{r_A + r_B}$$

14. Rat X's lever pressing is put on a concurrent FR 10 FR 20 schedule. Rat Y's behavior is put on a concurrent VR 10 VR 20 schedule. Which rat is likely to select the more reinforcing schedule first?

15. How might you use what you know about reinforcement schedules to study the effects of the presence of observers on human performance?

16. Someone says to you, "George is a nasty fellow. It's just his nature." How could you account for George's personality in a more scientific way?

17. A student tells you that studying reinforcement schedules is a waste of time. Give arguments for the opposing view.

18. How can an experimenter avoid developing ratio strain in his or her subjects?

19. This chapter describes schedules of reinforcement. How would schedules of punishment work? Use, as an example, a VR 10 punishment schedule.

20. Pretend you are a behavioral economist who wishes to know the effect of inflation on purchasing. Describe an experiment that will shed light on the problem.

SUGGESTED READINGS

The classic work on schedules is *Schedules of Reinforcement* by C. B. Ferster and B. F. Skinner (1957). It describes the basic kinds of reinforcement schedules and provides many charts illustrating the response rates and patterns associated with each.

The matching law was formulated in an article by Richard Herrn-stein entitled "The Law of Effect" (1970). Howard Rachlin's learning text *Behavior and Learning* (1976) deals with this subject in more detail than the present chapter.

A nontechnical survey of research on the application of reinforce-ment schedules to problems in economics is provided by Tom Alex-ander (1980) in a *Fortune* magazine article called, "Economics Accord-ing to the Rat." A sample of more technical treatments in this area can be found in Hursh (1984).

For a discussion of the relevance of reinforcement schedules to the analysis of human behavior and to concepts such as personality, see Skinner's *Behaviorism at Fifty* (1963) and *Science and Human Behavior* (1953).

EIGHT

■

Extinction and Forgetting

We saw in the last chapter that once a response has been learned, the schedule of reinforcement in force has a profound effect upon the rate at which that response occurs. Even a complex response that took a long time to learn may be maintained at a steady rate with surprisingly little reinforcement. What happens, though, if the reinforcement is terminated? For example, what if we trained a rat to press a lever and then stopped reinforcing this behavior? Or what would happen if we removed the rat from the training cage, so that it had no opportunity to press the lever at all, and then returned it to the cage? It is these two topics, extinction and forgetting, that will concern us in this chapter.

EXTINCTION

Extinction involves dissolving the contingency that maintains behavior. In terms of classical conditioning, extinguishing a conditional response means presenting the CS alone, that is, without the US. When this is done repeatedly, the CR becomes weaker and appears more slowly and less reliably. Eventually, the CR ceases to occur, or occurs only about as often as it did before conditioning, at which point it is said to have been extinguished.

Pavlov (1927) was probably the first person to study extinction in

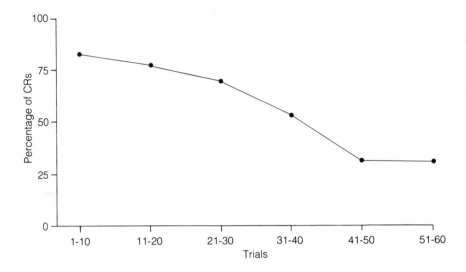

Figure 8-1   Extinction. Average percentage of CRs declines with repeated presentation of the CS alone. (After Hilgard & Marquis, 1935.)

the laboratory. After training a dog to salivate at the sound of a metronome, Pavlov repeatedly presented the sound without pairing it with food. The number of drops of saliva in response to each appearance of the CS steadily declined. A similar pattern emerged when response speed was used as a measure of the CR. Repeated exposure to the CS, without pairing with the US, resulted in the CR latency getting progressively longer.

A study of eyelid conditioning by E. R. Hilgard and D. G. Marquis (1935) provides another example of Pavlovian extinction. In that study, dogs learned to blink in response to a light. By the fifth day, 3 of the 4 dogs gave conditional responses to the CS over 90 percent of the time; the 4th dog responded 76 percent of the time. When the experimenters put the dogs on extinction, the CR declined steadily, and after 50 extinction trials, the response rate had declined to about 25 percent for each dog (see Figure 8-1).

An instrumentally conditioned response is extinguished by withholding reinforcement following the response. Skinner (1938) trained rats to press a lever and then, after about a hundred responses had been reinforced, he disconnected the feeding magazine. Everything was as it had been during training, except that now the response no longer produced food. The result was a gradual decline in the rate of lever pressing (see Figure 8-2).

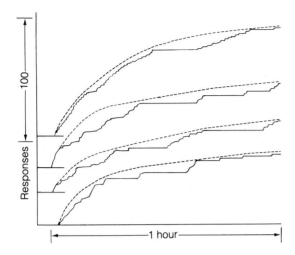

Figure 8-2 Extinction curves. Lever pressing was reinforced on a CRF schedule, then put on extinction. The curves show typical decreases in response rate in four rats. (From B. F. Skinner, *The Behavior of Organisms: An Experimental Analysis,* © 1938, Renewed 1966, p. 75. Reprinted by permission of B. F. Skinner.)

A well-known example of the application of extinction is a study by Carl Williams (1959). A 21-month-old boy who had been seriously ill for much of his young life insisted that someone stay with him when he was put to bed for an afternoon nap. If the adult left the room before the child was asleep, the boy would go into a rage and cry until the adult returned. Of course, when the adult returned, this reinforced crying. What were the parents to do? Williams advised them to put the tantrums on extinction: The child was to be put to bed and left alone. No matter how loudly the child protested, the parents were not to return to the room until the child's nap time was over. As you can see from Figure 8-3, the result was a steady decline in the time spent throwing tantrums.

The facts concerning extinction are pretty much the same whether the response being extinguished is respondent or operant behavior. We will therefore focus here on the extinction of operant responses.

Extinction Effects

The principle effect of extinction is a decline in the rate of the previously reinforced response. The frequency of the response drops grad-

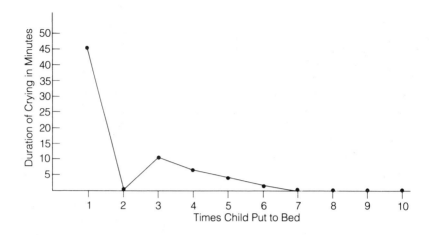

Figure 8-3   Extinction of crying. (After Williams, 1959.)

ually until it approaches its baseline level—the level maintained before the response was reinforced. At this point, the response is said to
have been extinguished. However, the extinction procedure may not
entirely undo the effects of conditioning. Even after many hours of
extinction and hundreds of nonreinforced responses, the behavior
may occur with a frequency that exceeds its baseline level. There is
considerable doubt, in fact, as to whether a well-established response
can ever be truly extinguished, that is, returned to baseline level (see,
for example, Razran, 1956). What's done, to paraphrase Shakespeare,
can n'er be undone.

A second effect of extinction is an increase in the variability of
behavior. A rat that has learned to press a lever for food may, when
put on extinction, press the lever harder, or use its nose instead of its
forepaw, or use two forepaws instead of one. Other behavior, not
previously much in evidence, may become more common. The rat
may sniff about the lever, move about the cage, look into the empty
food tray, and stand on its hind legs. We see the same phenomena in
people. A person who puts a coin into a vending machine only to
have the coins fall into the coin return tray is apt to insert the coins in
a slightly different way, perhaps altering the order of coins, shoving
them into the slot more forcefully or more gently, and so on. If these
efforts are not reinforced, other behavior will appear: The customer is
apt to look around, press the coin return several times, reach into the
tray the food normally falls into, and so forth.

A related effect of extinction is the appearance of emotional behavior. Rats that have received food for pressing a lever have been known to bite the lever when that response is no longer reinforced. When another animal is present in the Skinner box, animals undergoing an extinction procedure sometimes attack them, as if *they* were responsible for the failure of the reinforcer to arrive (Azrin et al., 1966; Rilling & Caplan, 1973). Skinner (1953) writes:

> A pigeon which has failed to receive reinforcement [for pecking a disk] turns away from the [disk], cooing, flapping its wings, and engaging in other emotional behavior. The human organism shows a similar . . . effect. The child whose tricycle no longer responds to pedaling not only stops pedaling but engages in a possibly violent emotional display. The adult who finds a desk drawer stuck may soon stop pulling, but he may also pound the desk, exclaim "Damn it!," or exhibit other signs of rage. (pp. 69–70)

We have all seen people strike vending machines that failed to reinforce previously reinforced behavior. Telephones, typewriters, and automobiles also suffer abuse under these circumstances.

Spontaneous Recovery

One extinction session is often not enough to thoroughly extinguish a response. This is so even though the extinction session may last for several hours and involve hundreds or even thousands of nonreinforced responses. What often happens is this: The response rate declines and finally stabilizes at some very low level. Extinction appears to be complete, and the animal is returned to its home cage. If, however, the animal is later put back into the training situation, it will once again respond as it had during training. This reappearance of a previously extinguished response is called **spontaneous recovery.** The longer the interval between the two sessions, the more nearly the response rate recovers.

In the absence of reinforcement, the animal does not continue to respond for very long, so that what we see is a second extinction curve. This second extinction occurs much more rapidly than the first. We may witness the same phenomenon in human beings. In the Williams experiment described previously, crying recovered spontaneously and was inadvertently reinforced. The response thus had to be extinguished all over again. Similarly, a person who has made a number of unsuccessful attempts to get food from a defective vending machine may give up only to try once again when passing by the machine later in the day. Likewise, for the employee who finds that there is no connection between hard work and success (e.g., workers receive promotions, raises, and bonuses strictly on the basis of seniority), hard work is on extinction. The employee is likely to put less and less effort into the job until the minimum effort required to hold the job is exerted. The employee will continue to work, but working *hard* will have been extinguished. However, if the employee takes a leave of absence for, say, additional training, he or she may once again make a strong effort after returning to the job. The previously extinguished behavior will reappear, but this time, if efforts continue to go unrewarded, the employee will quickly give up the attempt.

Resurgence

Let us now consider a phenomenon closely related to spontaneous recovery. Suppose a pigeon is trained to peck a disk on a VI schedule, and then this response is extinguished. Now suppose some new response, such as flapping its wings, is reinforced. Finally, all reinforcement is withheld. During this extinction period, the frequency of wing flapping declines as expected, but something unexpected also occurs: The bird begins to peck the disk it had been reinforced for pecking in the past. As the rate of wing flapping declines, the rate of disk pecking increases (see Figure 8-4). This phenomenon is known as **resurgence,** since the earlier behavior resurges (Epstein, 1983).

Resurgence has only recently been submitted to experimental analysis (Epstein, 1983, 1985a), but it has been observed by many researchers over the past 50 years. Epstein (1985a) notes that Clark Hull (1934), among others, described the phenomenon, and Wolfgang Köhler (1927/1973) alluded to it in his famous studies of insightful problem solving in chimpanzees (see Chapter 9). In one experiment, Köhler gave a chimpanzee named Sultan two bamboo sticks with which to retrieve some fruit that lay outside of its cage. The animal had had experience retrieving fruit with sticks, but in this instance, the sticks were too short to reach the fruit; the solution required that Sultan insert one stick into the hollow end of the other, thus making one long stick. After some futile attempts to reach the prize, first with one stick and the the other, Sultan committed what Köhler called "a great stupidity" (p. 126). The chimp laid aside the bamboo sticks, walked to a large box in the back of the cage, and moved the box toward the bars. This was, of course, of no help whatever. However, Köhler (and no doubt thousands of his readers)

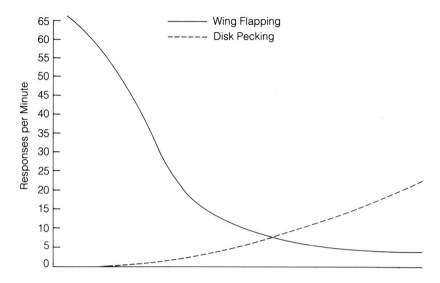

Figure 8-4   Resurgence. When a response (wing flapping) is put on extinction, a previously reinforced response (disk pecking) reappears. (Hypothetical data.)

failed to appreciate that this "great stupidity" was not a random event. The chimp dragged the box as near the goal as it could, an act that had been reinforced in situations requiring the retrieval of fruit. As the use of sticks to retrieve the fruit was extinguished, previously effective behavior reappeared, or "resurged."

Sigmund Freud offered another example of resurgence. Freud described a phenomenon he called **regression,** the tendency to return to more primitive, infantile modes of behavior. The man who is unable to get his wife to behave as he would like by asking her nicely may resort to having a tantrum, a form of behavior that got good results with his mother when he was a boy. Epstein (1983, 1985a) points out that this regression is an example of resurgence. The behavior "asking nicely" is on extinction, and the man reverts to a form of behavior that had been reinforced in similar situations in the past. However, Epstein notes that there is no need to assume, as Freud did, that the response that resurges will be more primitive than the behavior it replaces. It need only be a response that had earlier been effective (i.e., reinforced); it may be more primitive than the behavior now on extinction, but it need not be.

Generalization of Extinction

We saw in Chapter 6 that when an organism learns to respond in the presence of a stimulus in a given way, it also tends to respond in much the same way in the presence of other, similar stimuli. This is generalization. An analogous phenomenon occurs in extinction, as Skinner (1938) demonstrated. He put rats into an experimental chamber with a light in it and trained the rats to press a lever with the light on. The next day he extinguished lever pressing with the light *off*. Notice that the response was extinguished in a slightly different situation (light off) than the learning situation (light on). The response declined in the predictable fashion. Then, after 55 minutes, Skinner turned on the light. The idea was to see whether the results of extinction in the dark would generalize or whether the response would have to be extinguished all over again. The results showed that turning on the light had the effect of increasing the response rate, but only for a moment. The second extinction proceeded much more rapidly than the first, and the response rate was soon very low again. Extinction in the first situation (light off) had generalized to the second situation (light on).

Generalization of extinction also occurs in humans. If a child's tantrums at home are no longer reinforced, the behavior will disappear. The child may still throw a tantrum in other settings, such as the grocery store or a restaurant, but if these tantrums are not reinforced, the behavior will extinguish relatively rapidly. In other words, the effects of the extinction procedure carried out in the home will spread, or generalize, to other settings.

Of course, extinction will not generalize from one situation to another unless the consequences are the same in both situations. If parents cease reinforcing their child's tantrums, but a babysitter continues to reinforce them, the child will soon discriminate: The child will not have tantrums when the parents are present, but will scream like a siren when alone with the babysitter.

Variables Affecting Rate of Extinction

The phrase "resistance to extinction" refers to the endurance of a response placed on extinction. A response on extinction occurs less and less frequently, usually leveling off, near the level that existed before conditioning. But how long does it take to reach this point? And how many responses will the organism make before reaching it? The longer it takes and the more responses made, the greater the resistance to extinction. There is tremendous variability in resistance to extinction. Sometimes a response extinguishes in a few minutes, after only a few nonreinforced responses; on other occasions, it takes many hours and thousands of nonreinforced responses before the behavior finally reaches an extinction level. This variability in resistance to extinction is due to a number of factors, some of which we will now consider.

Number of Reinforced Responses   It stands to reason that the more times a response has been reinforced, the more responses it will make during extinction. This was demonstrated experimentally by Stanley Williams (1938). First, Williams trained rats to press a lever. Each rat received a food pellet for each lever press, but some rats were allowed only 5 reinforced lever presses, while others were allowed 10, 30, or 90. The next day, Williams put lever pressing on extinction. The results clearly showed that the more training a rat had (the more reinforced trials), the more slowly extinction proceeded (see Figure 8-5).

Reinforcement Schedule   Probably the most important variable affecting resistance to extinction is the schedule of reinforcement prior to extinction. Continuous reinforcement produces the most rapid learning, but it also leads to the most rapid extinction. Intermittent reinforcement during instrumental conditioning results in far greater resistance to extinction, a phenomenon known as the **partial reinforcement effect**. The effect is not limited to animals. Harlan Lane and Paul Shinkman (1963) put a college student on extinction after reinforcing responses on a VI 100″ schedule. The student then made over *8,000 unreinforced responses* during extinction!

Effort Required in Responding   Another variable that affects extinction is the amount of effort a response requires. Jack Capehart and his co-workers (1958) trained rats to press a lever. Sometimes a lever press required a force of only 5 grams, other times it required 40 grams, and sometimes it took 70 grams. All rats learned to press the lever at the three different weights. Then the experimenters put lever pressing on extinction, but varied the amount of effort required to depress the lever. For some rats, depressing the lever required only 5 grams of pressure, for others 40 grams, and for others 70 grams. The question was, Would the amount of effort required during extinction influence the total number of responses? The results showed that the more effort required to make a response, the fewer responses were

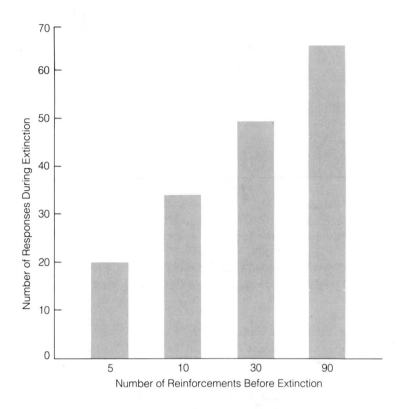

Figure 8-5   Extinction as a function of reinforcement. The average number of responses made during extinction increased with the number of reinforced responses prior to extinction. (After Williams, 1938.)

likely to be made in extinction (see Figure 8-6). It is likely, then, that a child whose tantrums threaten to break the eardrums of those nearby will give up such rages more rapidly than a child who whimpers and whines in a barely audible fashion.

Nature of the Learned Response   The kind of response involved may affect the rate of extinction. An animal may be particularly disposed, as a result of genetic evolution, to respond in certain ways but not in others. Raccoons have a tendency to manipulate objects in their forepaws, but not to stand on their forepaws. As we shall see in Chapter 10, these innate predispositions make it easy for animals to learn certain responses, but difficult to learn others. It seems likely that behavior that an animal is slow to learn because of genetic predis-

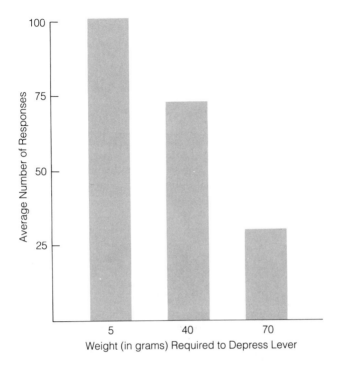

Figure 8-6 Effort and extinction. The more force required to depress a lever, the fewer responses made during extinction. (Compiled from data in Capehart et al., 1958.)

positions will be quick to extinguish, while behavior that is readily learned will extinguish slowly.

The predispositions referred to are specific to a given species. But even across species, certain kinds of responses extinguish more readily than others. The most striking example of this is the avoidance response. We saw in Chapter 4 that an animal will learn to make a response if that response results in avoiding an aversive stimulus. A dog will, for example, learn to jump a hurdle when a light comes on if, by doing so, it avoids an electric shock. Each time the dog jumps the hurdle, jumping is reinforced by not receiving a shock. Even if we break the electrical circuit, so that the animal no longer needs to jump the hurdle to avoid the shock, when we turn on the light, the dog will persist in jumping the hurdle, thereby "avoiding" the shock.

We can see the same thing in human beings. Certain forms of superstitious behavior are said to ward off danger (see the discussion of superstition in Chapter 4). In Europe during the Middle Ages, many people wore some sort of amulet to prevent evil spirits from causing illness. Every day spent without disease could be attributed to the amulet, so wearing the amulet was reinforced by the avoidance of illness. If a person did succumb to an illness, one might argue that the amulet had "lost its power" and replace it with a new one. We are not so far removed from this sort of superstitious behavior as we like to think. Many of us still wear amulets "for luck" and feel strangely vulnerable without them.

Avoidance responses are so resistant to extinction that once such a response has been well established through negative reinforcement, it is extremely difficult to extinguish it. One technique that is effective is to prevent the avoidance response from occurring. When no aversive stimulation is forthcoming, the response begins to weaken. The dog that learned to avoid a shock by jumping a hurdle may be prevented from jumping the hurdle. If this is done repeatedly without the dog receiving a shock, the dog will no longer jump the hurdle when given the opportunity to do so. The same technique works with people. If, for example, you can persuade a superstitious friend to go out several times without a favorite good luck charm, he or she may give up using it. But this is true only if no aversive event occurs in its absence. If your friend has an accident while not carrying the amulet, he or she will be all the more convinced that it works.

Punishment in Combination with Extinction   Another factor in the rate of extinction should be mentioned. If punishment is combined with extinction, the response disappears faster than if it is merely placed on extinction. Punishment and extinction are quite different procedures, but when used in combination, they quickly reduce the rate of a previously reinforced response.

There are, of course, other variables that affect the rate at which extinction occurs, but those described here are among the most important. Let us now turn to efforts to explain extinction effects.

Theories of Extinction

Amsel's Frustration Hypothesis   A. Amsel (1958, 1962) proposes what he calls the **frustration hypothesis:** Nonreinforcement of previously reinforced behavior is frustrating. Frustration is an aversive emotional state, so anything that reduces frustration will be reinforcing. In continuous reinforcement, there is no frustration because there is no nonreinforcement. But when the response is placed on extinction, there is plenty of frustration. With each nonreinforced response, frustration builds: Each nonreinforced response elicits a more aversive state. (Anyone who has repeatedly lost coins in a pay phone or a vending machine is familiar with the aversive state created by nonreinforcement of a response that is normally reinforced.) Any behavior that avoids or reduces an aversive state is reinforced, so during extinction, the rat increasingly avoids pressing the lever. (In the same way, you will quickly abandon a pay phone that cheats you, thereby reducing your annoyance.) Two responses then compete with one another during extinction: the lever-pressing response (previously reinforced by food) and the lever-avoidance response (currently reinforced by the reduction of frustration).

But when behavior is reinforced intermittently, there are periods of nonreinforcement—and frustration. The organism continues to respond during these periods of frustration and eventually receives reinforcement. Thus, responding *while frustrated* is reinforced; that is, the intermittent schedule teaches the organism to respond when frustrated. Put another way, the emotional state called frustration becomes an S^D (see Chapter 6) for responding. Now when the response is placed on extinction, the organism becomes frustrated, but the frustration is an S^D for responding. Responding is not reinforced, which elicits frustration, which is an S^D for responding, which elicits frustration, and so on.

The thinner the reinforcement schedule (the more responses required for each reinforcer) during training, the higher the level of frustration when the rat finally receives food. For the rat on a thin schedule, then, high-level frustration becomes a cue for lever pressing. With continued responding during extinction, the organism becomes increasingly frustrated. But since high-level frustration is an S^D for responding (the more frustrated the rat gets, the closer it gets to food), extinction proceeds slowly.

Capaldi's Sequential Theory   E. J. Capaldi's (1967, 1971) **sequential theory** proposes to explain extinction without recourse to the concept of frustration, yet Capaldi does focus on the cues present during training. Capaldi notes that during training, each lever press is followed by one of two events: reinforcement or nonreinforcement. In continuous reinforcement, all lever presses are reinforced, which means that reinforcement is an S^D for lever pressing. During extinction, no responses are reinforced, so an important cue for responding (the presence of reinforcement) is absent. Extinction proceeds rapidly after continuous reinforcement, then, because an important cue for responding is not present.

During intermittent reinforcement, some responses are followed by reinforcement, some by nonreinforcement. The sequence of reinforcement and nonreinforcement becomes important in that it provides a signal for responding. A rat on an FR 10 schedule, for example, must respond 9 times without reinforcement before it responds the 10th time and receives reinforcement. The nonreinforced lever presses are a kind of S^D for lever pressing. The thinner the reinforcement schedule, the more resistant the rat will be to extinction, since a long stretch of nonreinforced responses has become the cue for continued responding. In other words, the rat responds in the absence of reinforcement because, in the past, long strings of nonreinforced responses have reliably preceded reinforcement.

These two theories of extinction have much in common. Both assume that extinction is an active learning process, and both assume that it is, in some sense, a kind of discrimination training procedure. Both Amsel and Capaldi assume that stimuli present during training become S^Ds for responding. The chief difference seems to be that Amsel finds the S^D inside the organism (the physiological reaction called frustration) and Capaldi finds the S^D in the organism's external environment (the sequence of reinforcement and nonreinforcement).

Extinction is a complex and important phenomenon. Through it, behavior that is no longer functional dies out, the way a species that is no longer adapted to its environment becomes extinct. There is, however, another way that behavior may die out: forgetting.

FORGETTING

Forgetting refers to a change in a learned response following a lack of opportunity to make the response. In forgetting, there need be no change in the contingencies in force, as is the case with extinction; all that is required is that the organism be deprived of the opportunity to make the response.

Consider the case of a pigeon that has learned to peck a disk for food. After training, the bird is removed from the experimental chamber and returned to its home cage. Note that it has not been punished for pecking the disk, nor has it been allowed to peck the disk without being reinforced. It is simply deprived of the opportunity to practice what it has learned. A month passes, during which time the bird has no opportunity to obtain food by pecking on a disk. If, when given the opportunity to peck the disk for food, the pigeon fails to do so, then we may say that the response has been forgotten.

This example implies that forgetting means a decline in the probability of some behavior, but this is not always the case. Forgetting involves a change in behavior, but the change is not necessarily a decline in response probability. In one study, Henry Gleitman and J. W. Bernheim (1963) trained rats to press a lever on an FI schedule and then removed the animals from the training cage for either 24 hours or 24 days. The cumulative records showed that there was less of the scalloping associated with FI schedules after the longer interval. After a period of 24 hours, rats were likely to pause following reinforcement; after a period of 24 days, they were likely to continue responding. In other words, after a long interval the animals forgot to pause immediately after reinforcement. In this case, then, forgetting was indicated by an *increase* in responding. The same measure of forgetting applies in other situations. For example, a rat that has learned to press a lever for food may, as a result of discrimination training, learn *not* to press the lever when a red light is on. After a long interval without practice, the rat may forget what it has learned and press the lever whether the light is on or not.

Of course, forgetting is often incomplete. An organism may fail to respond in exactly the same way it did at the conclusion of training, yet some evidence of the effects of training may linger. There are several ways that the degree of forgetting can be measured.

Measuring Forgetting

One way we can measure forgetting is by reinstating the training procedure. This **relearning method** allows us to see how long it takes to reach the performance level in effect at the end of the training period. The longer the recovery takes, the more forgetting has occurred. Hermann Ebbinghaus, the German psychologist who conducted the first experiments on forgetting (Ebbinghaus, 1885/1913), used the relearning method. Ebbinghaus memorized lists of nonsense syllables, such as ZAK, KYL, and BOF. When he was able to recall every item on a list, he would put the list aside for a time before relearning it. The number of times he had to go through a list in order to attain a perfect performance indicated the amount of forgetting.

Another way of measuring forgetting is the **extinction method.** A rat might be trained to press a lever, be removed from the training cage for a time, and then be put back into the training cage. We can compare this rat's performance with that of a rat that has undergone extinction immediately after training. If the delay between training and extinction results in fewer responses during extinction, forgetting has occurred.

In the **free recall method,** the subject is asked to produce responses learned earlier. For example, a person might memorize a list of words or a string of digits and then, after a specified period without practice, be asked to reproduce it. The less accurate the reproduction, the greater the amount of forgetting.

A variation of this technique is known as **prompted recall,** where stimuli associated with the learned response are presented. These hints, or **prompts,** increase the likelihood that a response will be remembered. A student who is unable to recall a list of foreign terms when asked to do so may nevertheless be able to recall some of them if given the first letter of each term. Those words still not recalled may be remembered if their first and second letters are presented. The stronger the hint, or prompt, required to elicit the response, the more forgetting has occurred.

Another measure of forgetting is called **delayed matching to sample,** or DMS (Blough, 1959). In a typical DMS study, a pigeon is presented with a row of three disks. The middle disk is illuminated for a brief period by either a yellow or a blue light. After this, the two disks on either side are illuminated, one with a yellow light, the other with a blue one. If the bird pecks the disk that matches the sample, it receives food. Once the bird has learned to "match the sample," the experimenter introduces a delay between the offset of the sample disk and the illumination of the two alternative disks. Failure to match the sample indicates forgetting.

Although we all complain about forgetting, the fact is that retention of learning is really quite remarkable, even among animals. Thorndike (1911) reported retention of learning in monkeys after an interval of 8 months. Skinner (1950) trained pigeons to peck a target for food and then retested them after an interval of 4 years. When returned to the training chamber, the birds immediately began pecking the target and made hundreds of responses during extinction. Nevertheless, forgetting does occur and so is an important behavioral phenomenon; the rapidity with which forgetting occurs depends upon a number of variables.

Variables Affecting Rate of Forgetting

We saw earlier that the speed with which a response extinguishes is referred to as its resistance to extinction. You are not likely to see the phrase "resistance to forgetting" in any psychology text, but it is clear that one learned response may be forgotten more readily than another. Resistance to forgetting, like resistance to extinction, depends upon a number of variables.

Retention Interval   The most obvious variable in forgetting is the length of the **retention interval,** the time between training and testing: the longer the interval, the greater the degree of forgetting. In one study, R. M. Gagne (1941) trained rats to run down an alley to find food. When the training was completed, the rats were tested after intervals of from 3 to 28 days. The results showed clearly that the longer the interval between training and testing, the greater the deterioration in performance (see Figure 8-7).

Degree of Original Learning   One variable that affects the rate of forgetting is how well the behavior is learned in the first place. Ebbinghaus learned each list of syllables to a criterion of one errorless performance. That is, when he could go through a list one time without a mistake, he counted the list learned and put it aside. Many other early studies of forgetting used the same criterion. But Ebbinghaus also demonstrated that going beyond this minimal criterion—a practice called **overlearning**—greatly increases resistance to forgetting.

Overlearning is certainly important in areas other than nonsense syllables. Harry Bahrick (1984) found that the degree of original learning affects how well people recall Spanish learned in high school. People who studied Spanish for only a year and earned a grade of C remembered little of what they had learned when tested years later. But those who studied Spanish for 3 years and earned As did very well when tested, even 50 years later. The difference was not attributable to differences in the opportunity to practice the language, but to how well the language was learned originally. Findings of this sort have obvious implications for students who want to retain what they learn in their courses beyond the end of the semester.

It should be noted that differences in original learning are responsible for what appears to be a distinct factor in forgetting, the meaningfulness of what was learned. Various studies have shown that

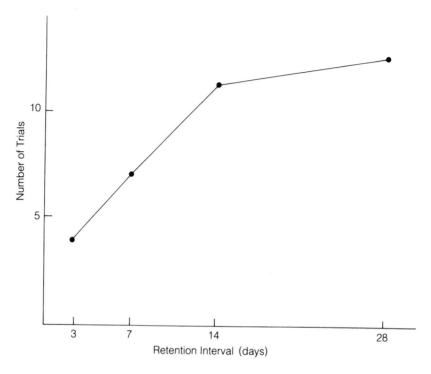

Figure 8-7   Retention interval and forgetting. Average number of trials required to relearn a response increased with the length of the retention interval. (After Gagne, 1941.)

meaningful material, such as words and phrases, is better recalled than meaningless material, such as nonsense syllables. But Benton Underwood (1966) showed that this finding is due to the failure to control for differences in original learning. Meaningful material is almost by definition material with which one has had some previous experience; that is, it is material about which one has learned something. Underwood demonstrated that when both meaningful and meaningless materials are learned to the same degree, differences in the rate of forgetting disappear.

Intertrial Interval   When training takes the form of discrete trials, the interval between trials (intertrial interval, or ITI) affects the rate of forgetting (see, for example, Gleitman et al., 1963). In general, the longer the ITI, the better retention is. It may occur to you that an ITI is similar to a retention interval, only shorter. The ITI is usually a matter of seconds or minutes, while the retention interval is usually a matter of hours or days. What if we were to begin a training program with a short ITI and gradually increase the ITI as training proceeded? Suppose, for example, that we train a rat to run a maze by giving it 10 trials a day, with each trial separated by 30 seconds, and that the time it takes the animal to run the maze decreases steadily for 5 days and then levels off. Now suppose that we begin increasing the ITI each day. After several days of training, we might work up to a 1-hour ITI; after several weeks, we might reach an ITI of 24 hours. It is clear that if we now test for forgetting after an interval of 12 hours, a period shorter than the ITI, we should see no signs of forgetting whatsoever. And it seems likely that even if we increase the retention interval to 48 hours, there will be less forgetting than would be the case for a rat that had undergone the same number of trials with a stable ITI of 30 seconds. So far as I know, no experiment of the sort just described has been done, but it is interesting to speculate about the possibility of shaping resistance to forgetting by gradually increasing the ITI.

Nature of Learned Response Some responses—emotional responses, for one—seem much more resistant to forgetting than others. Gleitman and P. Holmes (1967) established a conditioned emotional response in pigeons and then tested them after intervals of 1 or 90 days. They found no evidence of forgetting, even after 3 months. An earlier study found no evidence of forgetting a conditioned emotional response even after 2-1/2 *years* (Hoffman et al., 1963).

Various studies have demonstrated that taste aversions are also remarkably persistent. You may recall the study of taste aversion in cancer patients described in Chapter 3. In this study, patients ate a distinctively flavored (maple-walnut) ice cream before receiving chemotherapy. Nausea is a common side effect of chemotherapy, and the pairing of the ice cream and nausea produced a taste aversion. An average of 4-1/2 months after conditioning, which involved only one trial, the patients were asked to choose between two ice creams, after first tasting each. Only 3 out of 12 patients who had undergone conditioning chose the maple-walnut ice cream, while 8 out of 14 control subjects chose that flavor. In other words, though the taste aversion was acquired in only one trial, it was not forgotten. Other research suggests that everyday taste aversions may last a lifetime even though people assiduously avoid the foods involved, thereby providing ample opportunity for forgetting to occur (Garb & Stunkard, 1974; Logue, 1979).

Most of these studies indicate that forgetting is a slow process, far slower, at least, than learning. But forgetting does occur; let us now turn our attention to the question of why.

Theories of Forgetting

Disuse Theory   Many people assume that the explanation for why forgetting occurs is very simple: It is caused by the passage of time. Ask a random passerby if he or she knows how to determine the area of a cone, and that person very likely will not know, adding by way of explanation, "It's been 20 years since I studied that!" In other words, the 20 years have caused the forgetting. Sometimes people offer a slightly different excuse for the failure to remember something: "If you don't use what you've learned, you forget it." This sounds different from saying forgetting is caused by time, but it's really just another way of saying the same thing. The implication is that the time since the last use causes forgetting. Like the image of a photographic print exposed to the sun, the memory of an experience is assumed to fade with time. This theory is often referred to as the **theory of disuse.**

One reason that this theory is intuitively attractive is that it is consistent with everyday observations. Chief among these is that there is a very strong relationship between forgetting and the time that has elapsed since training. Most people learn to ride a bicycle in their early years and may continue doing so even in college. But somewhere along the line, the bicycle is replaced by speedier and less enervating means of transportation. One day we wake up and find that it has been 10 or 15 years since we last rode a bike, and we wonder whether we can do it at all. We get on a bike and discover that, although we can still get around on two wheels, the years without practice have taken their toll. It is safe to say that most 12-year-olds can ride circles around their parents if those parents have not continued to cycle.

This subjective observation is supported by data on the role of retention interval length in forgetting. Such studies leave no doubt that forgetting is a function of the passage of time. The question is whether the passage of time *explains* the forgetting that occurs. The answer, as John McGeoch (1932) showed, is that it does not. Time does not explain forgetting because time itself is *not* an event. Time is not something that occurs but rather an invention for talking about the occurrence of events. An hour, for example, is approximately 1/24 of the time it takes for the earth to rotate on its axis; a week is seven complete rotations of the earth; a year is one complete revolution of the earth around the sun, and so on. Time itself is not an event and can therefore not be said to cause other events. The image on a film fades with time, but it is the action of sunlight, not time, that causes the fading. Similarly, forgetting occurs *in* time, just as people grow sick in time; but it is not time that causes forgetting any more than it is time that causes illness. "Time, in and of itself," wrote McGeoch (1932), "does nothing" (p. 359). To explain forgetting, one must identify the events that account for its occurrence. One attempt to do just that is called interference theory.

Interference Theory   Early evidence that events rather than the passage of time are responsible for forgetting came from a classic study by John Jenkins and Karl Dallenbach (1924). Two college students learned lists of 10 nonsense syllables in the morning and before retiring in the evening. They were retested after 1, 2, 4, or 8 hours. The results showed significantly less forgetting after a period of sleep than after a similar interval of activity. Indeed, after 2 hours of sleep, additional time had no effect on the recall of sleepers (see Figure 8-8). Other studies corroborated the finding that periods of inactivity produce less forgetting than comparable periods of activity. In one, for example, human subjects forgot less after a period of sensory deprivation than people in a more ordinary environment (Grissom et al., 1962), while in another study, immobilized roaches forgot less than those allowed to run around (Minami & Dallenbach, 1946).

Clearly, events that occur as an organism interacts with its environment contribute to forgetting. But what events? What is it that happens during the retention interval that causes the deterioration of performance? McGeoch (1932) hypothesized that the solution to the problem of forgetting was learning, and he proposed an **interference theory** of forgetting. Forgetting is not due to the passage of time, he argued, but rather to the learning that occurs during the passage of time. It is, he suggested, "a result of an active interference from interpolated events" (p. 364). Or, as another psychologist phrases it, "We forget because we keep on learning" (Gleitman, 1971).

Two kinds of interference have been proposed. In **retroactive interference,** new learning reaches into the past, as it were, to interfere with earlier learning. Retroactive interference is often studied in humans by means of **paired associate learning.** Typically, the object is to learn a list of word pairs, such as cow-table, so that when given the first word (cow), the subject names the second (table). Usually, the list is taught by repeatedly presenting the subject with the first

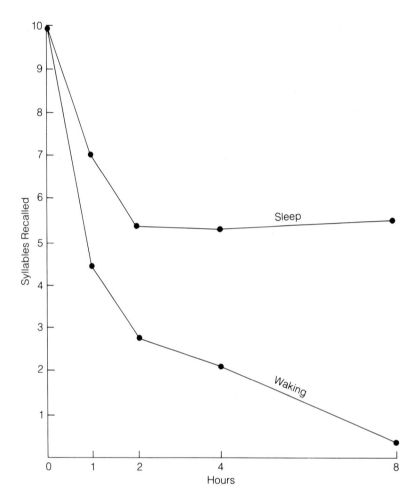

Figure 8-8   Forgetting and sleep. Average number of syllables recalled by one subject after intervals of sleep and waking. (After Jenkins & Dallenbach, 1924.)

word in each pair, asking for the word that goes with it, and then presenting the correct answer. (This is, of course, an instrumental learning procedure.) To study retroactive interference, two or more lists of paired associates are used. In one experiment, Leland Thune and Benton Underwood (1943) had college students learn lists of 10 paired associates made up of adjectives. Each subject learned an A-B list (e.g., hungry-beautiful), then an A-C list (hungry-powerful), and then relearned the A-B list. The results showed that learning the A-C list interfered with recall of the A-B list. Moreover, the better the A-C list had been learned, the more it interfered with recall of the A-B list.

We have seen that the passage of time does not explain the fact that forgetting increases as the retention interval increases. However, retroactive interference predicts this phenomenon, since the longer the retention interval is, the greater the opportunity for learning something that will interfere with past learning. You experience this in your everyday life when, for example, you find that after learning your new license plate number, you have difficulty recalling the old one. The passage of time is not the culprit, since you were previously able to recite the number despite periods of several weeks or months without practice. Similarly, if you learn Italian in college, you may find that it interferes somewhat with your ability to recall the Spanish you learned in high school. In other words, new learning interferes with old learning, and the more new learning, the more forgetting.

In **proactive interference,** past learning reaches into the future, so to speak, to interfere with new learning. What you learned earlier interferes with your ability to recall what you have learned recently. Proactive interference has been demonstrated in dozens of experiments, often involving pairs of words. Typically, in these studies, all subjects learn an A-C list, but some subjects first learn an A-B list. Differences between the two groups in learning the A-C list reveal the degree of interference from the A-B list. Such studies reliably show that learning the first list interferes with recall of items on the second list.

Once again, you can see the same phenomenon in your everyday life. If someone is introduced to you as John and you later learn that his name is Bill, you may have trouble recalling his name correctly. Similarly, if you study Italian in college, your attempts to recall the Italian word for a common object may be thwarted by your having learned the Spanish word for that object in high school. In other words, old learning interferes with new learning.

Proactive interference, like retroactive interference, increases with the interval between learning and testing. In retroactive interference, this makes sense because the longer the interval, the more we learn that can interfere with past learning. But why should the length of the retention interval affect proactive interference? Underwood (1948, 1957) studied this problem using paired associate learning. He theorized that when a subject is learning words on the second list, the first list is, in essence, on extinction. But we know from other studies that responses placed on extinction are apt to recover spontaneously. It follows, reasoned Underwood, that list A-B responses will show

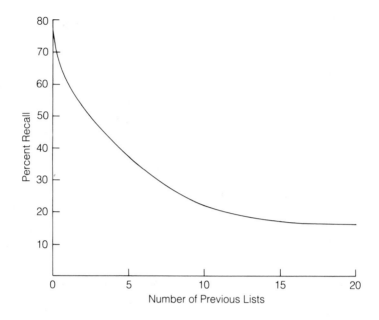

Figure 8-9   Interference and forgetting. Underwood plotted data from a number of studies and found that forgetting increased with the number of previously learned lists. (After Underwood, 1957.)

spontaneous recovery during testing on list A-C. The longer the retention interval, the more likely spontaneous recovery becomes and the more likely proactive interference is to occur. Consistent with this argument, Underwood found that after a delay of 5 hours, retroactive interference was greater than proactive interference, but after a 2-*day* interval, there was almost no difference between them.

Underwood (1957) demonstrated that interference theory could account for another puzzling phenomenon. Ebbinghaus found tremendous amounts of forgetting after short retention periods. Underwood showed that Ebbinghaus's poor recall was at least partly due to interference from other lists he had learned. In a replication of Ebbinghaus's work, Underwood discovered that experienced list learners forgot more than inexperienced ones. The more lists subjects had learned previously, the less well they recalled the new list (see Figure 8-9). This fits perfectly with interference theory, since the more learning that has occurred in the past, the greater the opportunity for proactive interference.

Interference theory accounts for several forgetting findings in a parsimonious and elegant manner and is, for that reason, very popular among psychologists today. Consider, for example, the findings of a study of forgetting of meaningful verbal material (Coleman, 1962). In this study, the experimenter gave a person a 24-word passage with the words arranged in random order. The task was to study the list and then reproduce it in its scrambled order. The result was given to another subject, who attempted to memorize the reproduced version; this person's effort was turned over to a third subject, and so on. The result was that the arrangement of words became less and less random and more and more meaningful. The finding may be interpreted in terms of proactive interference. In learning a language, we learn a great deal about the way words are related to one another. Prepositions ordinarily appear before articles, articles before nouns, nouns before verbs, and so on. Interference theory predicts that such prior learning will intrude upon the learning of a disorderly arrangement of words. Thus, interference theory offers a simple explanation of these results.

Interference does not, however, account for all phenomena associated with forgetting; some of these phenomena can be explained by context theory.

Context (Stimulus Change) Theory Although McGeoch (1932) himself believed that interference was important in forgetting, he did not believe that it was sufficient to account for all forgetting. He proposed what is now known as **context, or stimulus change, theory,** which states that forgetting is a function of the difference between the situation in which a response is learned and the situation in which the test for forgetting takes place. The idea is that when learning occurs, it occurs within a particular context, that is, in the presence of a set of stimuli. These stimuli act as cues that serve to elicit the response. If, later on, these cues are absent, performance suffers.

This idea is easily illustrated from everyday experience. For instance, you may know the name of the person who sits next to you in history class, but if you see him or her while off campus, you may find that the name escapes you. Most of us have also had the experience of learning a speech to perfection, only to stumble over it when in front of an audience. We usually attribute the poor performance to "nervousness," but evidence indicates that the difference between the practice setting (e.g., an empty classroom) and the crowded lecture hall is at least partly responsible.

It follows that the more the context changes, the greater the degree of forgetting will be. Suppose that a boy spends the first 5 years of his life in France and then emigrates to America. Once in America,

---

THE STATE OF LEARNING

So far, we have discussed the ways in which changes in the external environment affect forgetting. But there is an environment inside the skin as well as outside of it. Do changes in this internal environment affect recall? D. Overton (1964) conducted experiments to answer this question (see also Girden & Culler, 1937).

Overton gave rats a tranquilizing drug and then taught them to run a simple T-maze. Later, when the effects of the drug had worn off, Overton tested the rats and found that they appeared to have forgotten their earlier learning. There is nothing very startling about this; we might easily believe that the drug interfered in some way with the brain's functioning. But Overton took one more step. He tranquilized the rats again and put them back into the maze. This time they performed well! The earlier forgetting was due to a change in the animal's internal state. Thus, behavior that is learned during a particular physiological state is lost when that state passes, a phenomenon now called **state-dependent learning** (see Ho et al., 1978, for a review).

There is some evidence that changes in emotional state may also produce state-dependent learning. Gordon Bower and his colleagues (1978) used hypnosis to induce people to feel happy while learning one list of words and sad while learning another list. When the subjects were tested, their recall varied sharply with their mood. If their mood during testing matched their mood during training, their recall was very good; if not, their performance was poor.

---

the child begins to learn English, and if his parents avoid speaking French, there will be little opportunity for the child to practice his native language. Gradually, the child will lose the ability to speak French. At middle age, he may insist that he has forgotten virtually everything he once knew about his original language. Now suppose that the man returns to France to visit the place where he was born. When he gets on the plane in New York, he is unable to speak French or to understand more than a few words of the announcements made in French during the flight. But a curious thing happens when he reaches the airport in France. He begins to understand a few more words, and perhaps some short phrases. He finds that when the taxi driver speaks to him, or when he overhears people talking in a restaurant, though he does not understand every word, he gets the gist of what is being said. The French that he was sure he had forgotten quickly returns, and in a few weeks, he is speaking the language as well as he did when he left those many years ago. But why should a person who is unable to remember something in one country be able to recall it in another? The answer seems to be because of the different cues in the two countries. When forgetting is due to a difference in the stimuli present during learning and recall, it is said to be **cue-dependent forgetting** (Tulving, 1974).

Context theory implies that forgetting is a kind of discrimination learning. A response is reinforced in the presence of certain stimuli, so it is likely to be elicited by those stimuli. These stimuli may include not only those the experimenter identifies as S^Ds but also background stimuli—the context in which training occurs. Changes in the environment (the context) can play an important role in forgetting.

EXTINCTION AND FORGETTING COMPARED

Both extinction and forgetting normally refer to a steady decline in learned behavior and are therefore easily confused. Perhaps a few words should be said to make the distinction between them clear.

First, let us consider procedural differences. In extinction, a stimulus (a US or an S^R) that had regularly appeared in association with a stimulus or a response no longer does so. Extinction is actually a form of training in which the organism learns *not to respond* in a particular way. The dog that had learned to salivate at the sound of a bell learns through extinction *not* to salivate when the bell rings. A rat that had learned to press a lever for food learns *not* to press the lever. In forgetting, there is no change in the training procedure whatsoever; training is merely discontinued.

Second, let us consider the effects of extinction and forgetting. As a result of an extinction procedure, a response that had occurred at a high rate comes to occur at a low rate. This is not to say, however, that the response is lost, that the organism is incapable of making it. Children who have learned to "get their way" by throwing tantrums will show a sharp decline in this behavior if those around them cease reinforcing it. But this does not mean that the children no longer know how to throw tantrums; they simply do not do so. Indeed, the response is likely to continue to occur, though at a very low frequency. And if the reinforcement contingency is reinstated, the old behavior will quickly reemerge as if it had never been extinguished. The forgetting "procedure" also normally results in a decline in the frequency of a response, but forgetting implies the inability of the organism to make the response when the situation calls for it. Thus,

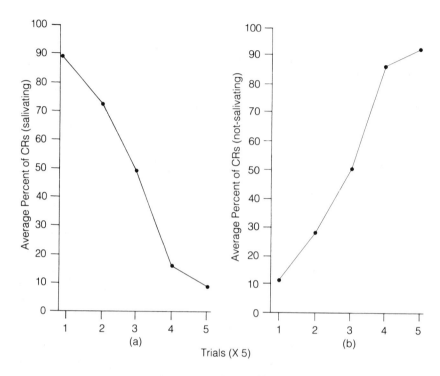

Figure 8-10   Extinction as learning. The extinction of the salivary response may be plotted as the decrease in the salivary response (a) or as the increase in the "not-salivating response" (b). (Hypothetical data.)

the student may feel inclined to recall the name of the inventor of the steam engine, but be unable to do so. Often, the response appears to have been lost and cannot be elicited even with prompting. Extinction implies a reluctance to perform a response; forgetting implies an inability to do so.

Far from being a form of forgetting, then, extinction is probably best viewed as a kind of learning (Estes, 1959; Guthrie, 1960). The rat that had learned to press a lever for food learns from the extinction procedure not to press the lever; the dog that had learned to salivate at the sound of a buzzer learns not to salivate on hearing the buzzer. At the same time that a response is being lost, a new response is being acquired. Thus, instead of plotting the disappearance of, say, the salivating response as an extinction curve, we might just as logically plot the appearance of the not-salivating response as a learning curve (see Figure 8-10).

So far in this chapter, we have said nothing about the adaptive value of extinction and forgetting. Both are often viewed as weaknesses, or limitations to the ability to adapt. But if we take the view that extinction is merely learning, we can see that it has considerable survival value. It is important to learn, for example, that food may be found in a particular place; but it is equally important to learn not to waste one's time exploring an area when the food supply has run out. Remember that the environment is constantly changing, and it is necessary to modify one's behavior in accordance with these changes. Extinction is part of that adaptive process.

What about forgetting? Everyone considers forgetting a nuisance, but can it, like extinction, be said to have benefits? At first glance, it would seem not. After all, it is generally true that the more one learns, the better off one is, and to forget is to lose what one has learned, which certainly seems to be a step backward. Indeed, there is no denying that forgetting can be very costly, even life-threatening. But remember once again that no organism lives in a stable environment. The constant changes to which we must adapt mean that what was important to remember several weeks ago is no longer important today and, in fact, may be detrimental.

It is also interesting to consider what life would be like if we never forgot anything. Actually, there have been a few people who seemed almost to have achieved this state: Once they learned something, they never seemed to forget it. But at least one such person complained that the inability to forget proved a serious handicap (see Luria, 1968). This person was constantly being bombarded by memories brought to mind by events in his daily life. He might see a license plate number on a passing car, and that might trigger a series of associations. This sort of unwanted recall constantly interrupted his thoughts and made it difficult for him to pursue a line of thought or even to engage in a conversation. Forgetting may be a nuisance, but it would seem to be preferable to never forgetting.

One final word needs to be said about extinction and forgetting: Neither procedure entirely eradicates the effects of earlier training. A long period of extinction may seem to have returned an organism to its original response tendencies, while another organism may seem to have completely forgotten a response learned earlier. But in both cases, appearances are misleading. This can be demonstrated by retraining the response that has been extinguished or forgotten. Inevitably, the response is relearned faster than it was learned originally. This means that in some way, we are permanently changed by learning experiences. Sometimes this is to the good. The student who seems to have forgotten all of the algebra he or she once knew will find relearning it much easier than learning it the first time was. But sometimes the lingering effects of learning are less desirable. The person who grows up in an environment filled with racial hatred may appear to cast aside those prejudices, but the evidence suggests that the hatred is still there, lying in a shallow grave, as it were, sleeping but not dead.

SUMMARY

Both extinction and forgetting involve a decline in the probability of a learned response and both are, in some sense, adaptive.

Extinction is a procedure in which the contingency that had established a response is changed. In extinction following Pavlovian conditioning, this means presenting the CS alone; in extinction following instrumental conditioning, it means withholding stimuli that previously reinforced a response. Vicarious extinction procedures involve applying the procedures just mentioned to a model as an observer looks on.

The principal effect of extinction procedures is a steady decline in the probability of the response on extinction. When the response reaches a steady rate, it is said to have been extinguished. An extinguished response may continue to occur at a rate higher than the original (preconditioning) baseline.

When a response is placed on extinction, there is typically an increase in the variability of behavior. The form of the response being extinguished may change, and other responses may increase in frequency. Negative emotional behavior, such as aggression, is likely to occur.

A response that has been extinguished may reappear following an interval, a phenomenon known as spontaneous recovery. If the extinction procedure remains in force, the response will once again extinguish, this time more rapidly than the first time. A related phenomenon is called resurgence: When a response is placed on extinction, other previously effective responses will begin to appear.

The effects of extinction tend to generalize. A response that has been extinguished in one situation will tend to occur at a similar low rate in similar situations.

The number of times a response is performed during an extinction procedure varies. Resistance to extinction is a function of the number of times the response had been reinforced prior to extinction, the effort required in responding, the kind of response involved, and whether extinction is combined with punishment. Probably the most important determinant of resistance to extinction is the schedule of reinforcement in effect prior to extinction. Intermittent reinforcement produces much greater resistance than continuous reinforcement, a phenomenon known as the partial reinforcement effect.

Efforts to explain extinction effects include Amsel's frustration hypothesis and Capaldi's sequential theory. Both assume that stimuli present during training become cues for responding during extinction.

Forgetting is a deterioration of learned behavior associated with the passage of time. In forgetting, the organism is denied the opportunity to make the learned response. Forgetting usually means a decrease in the probability of a response, but under certain circumstances, it can mean an increase in response probability.

Forgetting may be measured in various ways, including relearning, extinction, free recall, prompted recall, and delayed matching to sample.

Variables affecting the rate of forgetting include the retention interval, degree of original learning, intertrial interval, and the nature of the learned response.

The disuse theory of forgetting assumes that forgetting is caused by the passage of time. This theory is popular among laypersons, but psychologists argue that time is not an event and therefore cannot provide an explanation of forgetting.

Interference theory proposes that forgetting occurs because of new learning. Learning response A interferes with response B. Interference is retroactive or proactive, depending upon whether learning interferes with past learning or future learning.

Context, or stimulus change, theory maintains that forgetting is due to differences in the stimuli present during training and during testing. When the changes are in the organism's external environment, we refer to cue-dependent forgetting; when they are inside the organism, we refer to state-dependent forgetting.

Extinction and forgetting are similar phenomena, but there are important differences between them. Extinction involves a change in the training contingencies, while forgetting involves an interval of time between training and testing. Responses that have been extinguished are not necessarily lost, whereas forgetting implies at least a momentary inability to make the response. Extinction is clearly useful in adapting to changing conditions, and even forgetting has its uses, up to a point.

REVIEW QUESTIONS

1. Define the following terms:

extinction	forgetting
spontaneous recovery	generalization of extinction
resistance to extinction	paired associate learning
overlearning	state-dependent learning

2. Why do some teachers ask their students to take the same seat at each class meeting?

3. John was determined to do well on the final exam in biology, so he studied from 10:00 P.M. to 2:00 A.M. each night for the 2 weeks before the test. To keep from falling asleep, he took "uppers." The night before the 8:00 A.M. exam, he made sure he got a good night's sleep, but he did not do nearly as well on the test as he thought he should. What explanation can you offer? Describe how you could test the accuracy of your explanation.

4. Mary and Hilda each train a roach to run a maze. Mary uses an intertrial interval of 10 seconds, while Hilda runs one trial every hour. The training continues until both roaches run the maze in the same time, and then training ceases. Then each roach runs the maze again one week after its last training trial. Which would be likely to run the maze in the shortest time?

5. Harvey and Harry each train a rat to press a lever using continuous reinforcement to shape the behavior. When Harvey's rat is pressing the lever at a steady rate, he switches to an FR 50 schedule, while Harry keeps his rat on CRF. After 3 hours of training, both men put lever pressing on extinction. Which animal will make the greater number of responses during extinction?

6. Hilda and Ethel work together to train a rat to press a lever. When they are satisfied that the response has been well learned, Hilda suggests that they remove the lever from the cage for awhile and then reinstall it to see what happens. Ethel proposes that they leave the lever in place but disconnect the feeding mechanism. Then they begin to wonder whether they would be studying different phenomena or the same thing. What do you think?

7. Jerry trains a rat to press a lever, then studies the effects of various reinforcement schedules on the rat's performance. He begins with FR 5, then switches to FI 30", then VR 20, then VI 30". Then Jerry switches to an extinction schedule. He predicts that the

pattern of responses during extinction will reflect the schedules of reinforcement used during training, beginning with VI 30″ and followed in order by VR 20, FI 30″, and FR 5. Explain why Jerry thinks this might happen.

8. A teacher complains that his sixth-graders are always getting out of their seats for one thing or another. You visit the class and find out that the teacher inadvertently reinforces this behavior by attending to the children when they are out of their seats. You advise the teacher to withhold reinforcement for this behavior, to put the response on extinction. He agrees to try it but a few days later says, "It worked beautifully for a while, but then they were back to their old habits." Explain what probably happened.

9. A woman asks you for advice about a child whose nap-time tantrums are so fierce that the neighbors have complained to the police. You advise her to put the response on extinction and explain to the neighbors that things will get worse before they get better. She follows your advice but later complains that the benefits were only temporary: "We went out of town for a couple of days and the tantrums started up all over again." Explain what went wrong and what the parents should do about it.

10. Two pigeons are trained to peck a disk and then each is put on a different reinforcement schedule. Bird 1 is put on a VI 5″ schedule; bird 2 is put on a VR 5 schedule. After 100 reinforced responses, the schedules are reversed. The experimenter notes that in each case, the second schedule takes longer to stabilize than the first. Explain.

11. Design an experiment to determine whether there is such a thing as generalized forgetting. (Hint: See discussion of generalized extinction.)

12. Give an example (not taken from the text) of resurgence.

13. Which of the two theories of extinction do you prefer? Defend your choice.

14. A researcher once trained raccoons to climb a cage for food when a particular stimulus, a card, appeared. If they did not find food on these occasions, they tore up the card. How do you account for this behavior?

15. Some psychologists maintain that spontaneous recovery is a form of forgetting. Explain this. Include an original example of sponta-

neous recovery and identify what has been forgotten when it occurs.

16. The text describes paired associate learning as a form of instrumental conditioning. Explain why this is so. Be sure to identify the response and reinforcer involved.

17. Give an example of both retroactive and proactive interference from your own experience.

18. What is wrong with the idea that forgetting is caused by the passage of time?

19. The text describes the hypothetical case of a person who left France as a boy and returned years later and found that the French he thought he had forgotten came back to him. This actually happened. But people in France laughed at him because he spoke like a 5-year-old. Explain this.

20. Some people say that what happened in Nazi Germany in the 1930s and 1940s could never happen here. What have you learned about extinction and forgetting that would make you doubt the truth of this statement?

SUGGESTED READINGS

Important early work on extinction is described in Pavlov's *Conditioned Reflexes* (1927) and in Skinner's *The Behavior of Organisms* (1938).

The classic work on forgetting is Hermann Ebbinghaus's *Memory*, first published in German in 1885. An English translation is available and is surprisingly readable. For a fascinating look at someone who had difficulty forgetting, see Luria's *Mind of Mnemonist* (1968).

NINE

■

Thinking

DEFINING THINKING

"Cogito ergo sum." Every educated person has heard those words, the words of the 17th-century French philosopher René Descartes. Yet few people realize the significance of Descartes's observation, "I think, therefore I am," which formed the foundation of his philosophy. Descartes found that while he could doubt everything else, he could not doubt the fact that he doubted, that thinking was taking place. And if thinking occurred, then there must be a thinker. If I think, I must exist.

It did not take until 1637, when Descartes wrote his famous *Discourse on Method*, for people to know that they thought or to be certain of their existence. The import of the Cogito, as it is called, is that it made thinking central to philosophy. Thinking became more certain, more real, than the physical environment. For while a person might see a flower where in fact there is none (we have all known our eyes to play tricks on us), the *experience* of seeing a flower is undeniable. This line of reasoning had a profound effect not only upon philosophy but upon psychology. The first fact of psychology, to paraphrase the famous psychologist William James, is that thinking exists.

But what exactly *is* thinking? There are many answers to this question; one that has proved its scientific utility is that **thinking** is behavior.* Much of the behavior we call thinking is not readily observed by others. My pain is a private experience. I may describe my pain, but the verbal description is not the pain. Other people can hear my moans or the verbal report about the pain ("My back aches"), but no one observes the pain itself. Other forms of thinking are likewise private. I see, hear, smell, taste, and feel, but these are private events that no one else shares, even though they may see, hear, smell, taste, and feel much the same thing.

Even though a good deal of thinking is private, the distinction between overt (public) and covert (private) behavior is often arbitrary. Much of our thinking consists of silent speech, but when we "talk to ourselves," we are doing essentially what we do when talking to another person. Indeed, we typically use the same vocabulary, the same grammar, and even the same musculature in private speech as we do in public speech (McGuigan, 1978). The only important difference is that when we talk to ourselves, our speech is usually inaudible to others. Similarly, when we feel emotion, we react to the stimulus concerned not merely by feeling angry but in various physiological ways, such as a change in heart beat or respiration. No one can observe my joy, but with the proper monitoring equipment, anyone can observe the physiological responses that are part of the feeling I call joy.

We have seen in the previous chapters that environmental events change behavior in predictable ways. If thinking is behavior, then it ought to be possible to show that events in the thinker's environment are systematically related to the thinker's thoughts. In other words, we ought to be able to demonstrate that thinking is at least partly under the control of the environment.

The idea that thinking is behavior and that, like any other behavior, it is subject to the vagaries of a changing environment is difficult for many students (and for some psychologists) to accept. Therefore, while much more might be said in a general way about this subject (see, for example, Skinner, 1957), it may be more fruitful (and more convincing to the skeptical reader) to focus on examples of thinking that would seem to be particularly difficult to treat as behavior: self-awareness, seeing, remembering, insightful problem solving, and delusions and hallucinations.

---

* While most psychologists probably agree that much of thinking can be viewed as behavior (especially private behavior), some psychologists take a very different approach to thinking than that presented in this chapter. See, for example, Bransford (1979).

SELF-AWARENESS

Self-awareness seems so basic, so fundamental to experience, that we rarely examine the concept closely. But what is the self of which we are aware, and how do we become aware of it?

Descartes believed that thoughts and feelings were fundamentally different from overt behavior, but we have just seen that the distinction is often arbitrary. Our anger becomes overt when our hands tremble and we make a fist in response to an insulting remark. If the self is our thoughts, then it appears that the self is not entirely housed within our skin, but sometimes spills out into the open. The self is, then, *all* of our behavior, overt as well as covert. We are what we do.

We are concerned here not so much with the self, however, as with self-awareness. What does it mean to be self-aware? Let us consider first what it means to be aware of someone else. Suppose you are sitting at a table in a school cafeteria. A friend sits across from you and engages you in conversation. She has recently taken an important test that you will soon have to take, so you are intensely interested in what she has to report. During the conversation, another student sits next to you and listens silently to the conversation, but you are so absorbed in what your friend is saying that you are later surprised to find someone sitting next to you. We say that we are aware of someone, then, when we observe their behavior.

If the self is our behavior, then we are aware of the self when we observe our own behavior. "I was angry" means that I observed myself behaving in ways commonly identified as anger. A more scrupulous self-observer might say "I noticed that my voice trembled, my face and neck felt warm, I clenched my teeth, made fists with my hands, felt my heart beat fast, and cursed silently."

B. F. Skinner (1953) notes that we often observe subtle forms of behavior in ourselves and make inferences from them about our future behavior. We do this all the time when we speak of future plans. When we say, for example, "I think I'll quit school," we are really saying "I have observed myself behaving in ways that suggest I will quit school." Saying "I think I'll quit school" is not, in any fundamental way, different from saying "I think Joe will quit school." The events that lead to either observation will be nearly identical: negative statements about school, failure to attend classes, poor grades, unsuccessful efforts to make friends or join social clubs or athletic teams, and so on. In other words, we make observations about our own behavior that are essentially the same as the observations we make about others.

To be aware of one's self means, then, to observe one's own behavior, just as we observe the behavior of others. How is it that we come to observe our behavior? Why do we become self-aware?

It is easy to see why we observe the behavior of others: doing so is reinforced. We may notice that Mary is "in a good mood," and our efforts to engage her in conversation are, on such occasions, reinforced. Or we may notice that Mary is "in a foul mood," and this allows us to avoid the aversive consequences that are likely to follow certain kinds of behavior, such as attempting to engage her in conversation. We never actually observe the private events that are Mary's feelings, of course; rather, we observe subtle forms of behavior such as a smile or a frown. Such behavior serves as discriminative stimuli, that is, as signals that certain kinds of behavior will be reinforced and other kinds of behavior will be punished. The signals vary from person to person, which is why it takes a while to learn a person's moods. When we know someone well, however, we say that we "can read her (or him) like a book." And so we do.

We become expert at "reading" a person's behavior because it pays to do so, but why do we observe our own behavior? Again, the answer is that it pays to do so. If we are able to detect from our own behavior that we are in the early stages of flu, we may speed our recovery by getting additional rest before the symptoms hit with full force. Similarly, if we notice that we are "in a bad mood," then we may avoid an unpleasant argument by postponing a meeting to discuss wedding plans with our in-laws. Or consider the case of a man who is not a careful observer of his own behavior. When such a person says at various times during a conversation that he's going to college, that he's going to join the Navy, and that he's going to work in his uncle's garage, we say that he doesn't know what he will do. But there are aversive consequences for being a person who "doesn't know his own mind": People may not take such a person's statements seriously (remember the little boy who cried wolf); a banker may be reluctant to loan money to a person who "changes his mind" so often; and people are apt to deny opportunities to someone who seems "so immature." When we observe our behavior carefully, however, we can better predict what we will do, just as we can predict the behavior of a close friend. This sort of insight, or self-awareness, is reinforced because it allows us to behave more effectively.

It was once thought that such self-knowledge was available only to humans. Two prominent psychologists not so long ago wrote in a popular psychology text that "one of man's unique distinctions, setting him off most sharply from other animals, may be just this extraordinary capacity *to look at himself*" (Krech & Crutchfield, 1961, p. 202). But recent research has shown that other animals appear to be quite capable of at least a primitive form of self-awareness.

Gordon Gallup (1970, 1979) was apparently the first to provide experimental evidence of self-awareness in a subhuman species. In his first study (Gallup, 1970), he exposed chimpanzees to a full-length mirror for several days. Initially, the animals responded to their reflection as if to another animal, but these social responses were gradually replaced by self-directed behavior. Increasingly, the animals used the mirrors to groom parts of their bodies they could not otherwise see, to pick food from between their teeth, to look at themselves as they made faces or blew bubbles, and so on. After this, each animal was anesthetized and dabbed with an odorless red dye on one eyebrow ridge and the upper part of one ear. Upon recovering from anesthesia, the animals were observed for 30 minutes with the mirror removed and then for 30 minutes with the mirror present. The chimps made almost no effort to touch the dyed parts of their bodies when there was no mirror, but made from 4 to 10 responses with the mirror present. Sometimes the animals would look in the mirror, touch the dye with their fingers, and then examine their fingers closely. When chimps that had not had experience with mirrors were anesthetized and dyed, they did not touch the dyed spots and showed no signs of using the mirror to inspect themselves. Gallup concluded that "insofar as self-recognition of one's mirror image implies a concept of self, these data would seem to qualify as the first experimental demonstration of self-concept in a subhuman form" (p. 87).

Gallup repeated his experiment with monkeys but was unsuccessful. He concluded that "the capacity for self-recognition may not extend below man and the great apes" (p. 87). But other research has proved him wrong.

Robert Epstein and others (Epstein et al., 1981) found that even the lowly pigeon is capable of performing in the manner of Gallup's chimps. These researchers first trained pigeons to peck dots on their own bodies, then to peck a wall after seeing a dot flashed there, and then to peck the wall after seeing the flashing dot reflected in a mirror. After this, the researchers put a blue dot on each bird's breast beneath a bib. The bib prevented the bird from seeing the dot directly, but it could see the dot reflected in a mirror. Each bird was

THE SHAPING OF AWARENESS

Even more basic than self-awareness is awareness of the external environment. Ordinarily, we lose this awareness of the outside world only when we sleep, but people who suffer serious brain injuries often lapse into a sleep-like state known as coma.

Most people think of coma as deep sleep, but in long-term cases, patients often engage in behavior that suggests they are about to awaken. They may open their eyes, turn their heads, move a hand. Often, they seem trapped in a fog-like state somewhere between sleep and wakefulness. Recent research suggests that reinforcement may help some coma victims break through the fog.

Mary Boyle (Boyle & Greer, 1983) worked with 3 people who had been comatose for at least 6 months. Each of the patients made some slight spontaneous movements, such as squinting or moving the head from side to side. Boyle tried to increase the frequency of these acts by reinforcing them with music. First, she asked the patient to make some movement that he or she had been seen to make spontaneously. Then she encouraged the desired act by, for example, moving the patient's head from side to side. After this, she repeatedly asked the patient to make that movement. Each time the patient complied within 10 seconds of the request, Boyle played a selection of the patient's favorite music for 15 seconds. Training continued for 2 sessions a day, 7 days a week, for 4 months.

There was nothing new about the idea of playing music for coma victims; what was new was making music contingent on the patient's behavior. This instrumental procedure would, in a healthy, conscious person, result in a rapid increase in response rate. But coma victims are, by definition, not responsive to the environment. Would the procedure modify *their* behavior?

Results varied. One patient's left hand was thought to be paralyzed. Boyle reinforced movement of the left hand as well as the right, and it too began to move. Eventually, the patient came to use his left hand to tug at the gastric tube on his left side, probably because it was a source of irritation; no such behavior had ever been observed in this patient before. The patient who had been in coma for the shortest period of time produced the best results: a clear increase in the likelihood of making a response when asked to do so.

Boyle conducted this study with the hope of demonstrating that reinforcement procedures could be used to assess the severity of a coma patient's condition, the assumption being that those who responded best to reinforcement would have the best chance of recovering. Indeed, her best pupil did eventually come out of coma. But did Boyle do more than assess this patient's condition? Could it be that the reinforcement procedure had something to do with the

> patient's recovery? Boyle is cautious, but she thinks the answer is yes.
>
> Boyle holds out the hope that reinforcement of spontaneous behavior will one day be part of the standard treatment for coma. Perhaps successively more wakeful behavior (e.g., opening the eyes, keeping the eyes open for longer periods, tracking moving objects with the eyes, and so on) could be reinforced. In essence, therapy would consist of reinforcing successive approximations of wakefulness. In other words, awareness would be shaped up.

tested first with the mirror covered; none of the animals tried to peck the blue dot. Next, the birds were tested with the mirror uncovered, and each of them soon began pecking at a spot on the bib corresponding to the dot on its breast.

Whether chimpanzees and pigeons really are self-aware in the same sense as humans is a matter for conjecture. These studies demonstrate that animals can become careful observers of their own bodies, at least the outer surface of their bodies. They do not, of course, demonstrate that animals observe their own moods and thoughts and other private behavior the way humans do. But the experiments do offer support for the notion that self-awareness means observing one's own behavior and that such self-awareness "can be accounted for in terms of an environmental history" (Epstein et al., 1981, p. 696). In other words, self-awareness is learned.

Humans learn to observe themselves—to be self-aware—not so much from mirrors as from other people. "Strangely enough," writes Skinner (1953), "it is the community which teaches the individual to 'know thyself' " (p. 261; see also Cooley, 1902; Mead, 1934). Skinner adds that we teach a child to say "that itches," "that tickles," "that hurts," by suggesting such terms when we observe behavior or events that ordinarily accompany such experiences. For instance, scratching suggests itching, giggling when brushed with a feather suggests tickling, moans and tears suggest pain. By observing and commenting upon behavior that suggests certain experiences, we teach the child to observe those private events.

Skinner also notes that we teach children to make comments upon and predictions from self-observations. We do this, in part, by asking the child questions: What are you doing? What are you going to do? Why are you doing that? How do you feel? Are you in a good mood? Do you want to play? Are you sleepy? These and countless other questions direct the child to observe and comment upon private experiences, that is, thoughts and feelings. When the observations are accurate, they are likely to be reinforced. At noon, we ask a child if she is hungry, and if she says yes, we provide food. If the child has accurately reported her private state (if she is correct in saying she is hungry), food will reinforce her observation. If the child says she is hungry when she is not, the food may not be reinforcing and may even be aversive is she is made to eat it. By means of such experiences, the child learns to observe herself carefully.

SEEING

Seeing is a response to light waves emanating from or reflected by objects in the environment. Seeing is, in some sense, an innate response to light waves, but it is nevertheless a response that is affected by experience. In fact, some aspects of seeing that seem to be innate may be largely learned, an idea nicely illustrated by the phenomenon of **size constancy.** Suppose that you stop along a roadside in the country and see a deer grazing in a distant field. The image that falls upon your retina is much smaller than it would be if the deer were nearby, yet you do not see a miniature deer. In a sense, we make allowances for the distance. This tendency toward size constancy is so common that it seems innate, but there is evidence that learning is involved.

Colin Turnbull (1961) is an anthropologist who studied the BaMbuti pygmies of the Belgian Congo, who live in forests so dense that they rarely have the opportunity to see more than several yards away. Turnbull took a young pygmy man named Kenge on a trip outside the forest. From a hillside overlooking a clearing, they could see distant mountains. Kenge asked Turnbull what they were. Were they hills? Were they clouds? Then, from another high point overlooking a plain, they could see a herd of buffalo grazing in the distance. To Kenge, they appeared small, and he asked what kind of insects they were. When he was told that they were buffalo twice the size of those he had seen in his forest, Kenge laughed and told his guide not to tell such stupid stories. When Turnbull insisted the animals were buffalo, Kenge "talked to himself, for want of more intelligent company, and tried to liken the buffalo to the various beetles and ants with which he was familiar" (p. 305). Turnbull drove down toward the buffalo and noted Kenge's reaction. "He watched them getting larger and larger . . . [and] muttered that it was witchcraft" (p. 305). Even after Kenge realized that the animals really were large buffalo, he remained puzzled about why they had been so

---

LEARNING TO SEE

A normal, healthy, 14-year-old girl choked on some candy, and suddenly she was neither normal nor healthy. Because of the accident, she suffered brain damage that left her unable to walk, interfered with her ability to speak, and slowed her ability to learn. It also left her blind.

Learning principles have proved remarkably useful in the rehabilitation of brain injury victims (Chance, 1986), but could such principles help a person regain her sight? Kay Merrill and Donald Kewman (1986) think so.

Their client was not wholly blind. Her eyes reacted to light, and she should correctly identify the color of notebook-sized objects such as her hospital chart cover. But she was unable to point to the features of a person's face and did not react normally when an object was thrust toward her eyes. Though she had some sight, she was, for all practical purposes, blind.

Merrill and Kewman set about improving the girl's vision. The training procedure was fairly complicated, but basically involved presenting her with objects of various shapes and colors and asking her to identify them. After each response, she was told whether she answered correctly or not. Under these circumstances, positive feedback is a powerful reinforcer. The results showed that her ability to answer correctly improved. As she progressed, she received training in more difficult tasks.

After 2 years of training, which included remediation of intellectual and motor as well as visual deficiencies, she returned to school. Amazingly, she was able to see well enough that she did not require special visual aids. The researchers admit that some recovery would have taken place even if the girl had received no special training. But they also clearly believe that, to some extent at least, the girl actually learned to see again.

---

small. Later on, the two came upon a large lake. Kenge had never seen a body of water larger than a small river, nor a boat larger than a canoe, and he could not believe that a fishing boat 2 miles out contained several people. "But it's just a piece of wood," he said (p. 305).

Size constancy is apparently learned, yet we may assume that Kenge saw the buffalo that Turnbull saw and merely failed to appreciate their true size. Other studies, however, indicate that given different experiences, people actually see different things. In one study (Siipola, 1935), students were asked to report what words they saw flashed on a screen. Interspersed among the words were some non-sense words such as *wharl, pasrot,* and *dack.* Before the test began, half of the students were led to believe they would be seeing words that dealt with animals, while the other half were told they would see words having to do with transportation. The researcher was interested in what the students would see when the nonsense words appeared briefly on the screen. The result was that what they saw depended upon what they had been told they would see. For instance, when the nonsense words *wharl, pasrot,* and *dack* appeared, students in the animal group saw *whale, parrot* and *duck,* while those in the travel group saw *wharf, passport* and *deck.*

Another experiment showed that learning makes us likely to see familiar items when unfamiliar ones are present. Jerome Bruner and Leo Postman (1949) flashed playing cards on a screen for brief periods. Some of the cards were ordinary, but some had colors opposite to their suit, that is, a black five of hearts or a red three of spades. What did people see when the odd cards appeared? They saw normal cards. A black five of hearts, for instance, was seen as either a red five of hearts or a black five of spades. When the experimenters increased the exposure time (the time the cards appeared on the screen), people tended to see a kind of compromise, so that a red three of spades was seen as purple.

It might be said that the students in these experiments saw what they expected to see. But even if this is so, we have to ask the source of their expectation. The answer is to be found in their learning histories, which changed both what the students expected to see *and* what they saw. It is, for example, unlikely that students unfamiliar with playing cards will see red when what is presented is black. These experiments make clear that what one sees is the product of past learning as well as the immediate stimulus.

Imagination

We have been discussing ordinary seeing—visual experiences elicited by the thing seen. But we also sometimes see things that are not present. We may dream of apples, and if we do, the experience of seeing them occurs in the absence of the thing seen. Or we may daydream of apples, again without the presence of apples or apple-like objects. In both cases, we literally see what is not before us. Skinner (1953) suggests that such seeing may be a conditional response. A person may "see X, not only when X is present, but when any stimulus which has frequently accompanied X is present. The dinner bell not only makes our mouth water, it makes us see food" (p. 266). Deprivation increases the likelihood that a conditional response will be elicited by a CS. If someone describes food to us, we often say we can see it, but we see the food especially clearly if we happen to be very hungry at the time.

Some daydream seeing (or imagining) may be a conditional response, but in other instances, it seems to be operant behavior maintained by its consequences. In solving a problem involving spatial relationships, for example, it is often helpful to manipulate objects. If the objects are not present, we may manipulate them "in our head"; that is, we may see them even though they are not present. We do so apparently because such behavior is reinforced. Consider this problem: Martha walks north 1 mile, turns east and walks 3 miles, turns south and walks 1 mile, turns west and walks 3 miles. How far is she from her starting point? To solve a problem of this sort, many people draw a little sketch with pencil and paper to indicate Martha's travels. But if writing materials are not available, we can visualize the course taken without drawing it, and if doing so helps us achieve the correct solution, the behavior—seeing—is reinforced.

REMEMBERING

Forgetting is the inability to make a response that was previously in the organism's repertoire. We discussed forgetting in Chapter 8, so a discussion of remembering here might seem redundant. But remembering means more than the absence of forgetting. When a person is unable to make a previously learned response, that person may do things in an effort to elicit the response. We say that he or she is "trying to remember." It is this meaning of the word *remembering*— the effort to produce a weak response—that we will consider here.

How do we remember? Traditionally, we are said to remember by "calling to mind" (the word *remember* comes from Latin words meaning "mindful again"). Today we dress up this traditional view in computer metaphors: We speak of "searching our memory banks." But people in the act of remembering are not searching memory banks, any more than they are, to use an older metaphor, searching through filing cabinets in their heads. In some sense, past experiences may be recorded in the brain, but if those records are "searched," the term refers to some sort of physiological process that has nothing to do with our behavior when trying to remember.

What *do* people do when remembering? To illustrate, try answering the following question: What were you doing on Monday afternoon in the third week of September 2 years ago? (Though the question may seem impossible to answer, give yourself a least 2 minutes to work on it before reading further. You might think aloud and record your thoughts on tape.) Peter Lindsay and Donald Norman (1972) suggest that a typical answer to this question might go something like this:

> OK, let's see. Two years ago . . . I would be in high school in Pittsburgh . . . That would be my senior year. Third week in September—that's just after summer—that would be in the fall term. . . . Let me see. I think I had chemistry lab on Mondays. I don't know. I was probably in the chemistry lab. . . . Wait a minute—that would be the second week of school. I remember he started off with the atomic table—a big, fancy chart. I thought he was crazy, trying to make us memorize that thing. You know, I think I can remember sitting . . . (p. 379)

If you tried this exercise, you probably behaved in much the same way as this student, that is, you talked to yourself. But why talk to yourself when trying to recall an event? The answer is that in talking to yourself about the event to be recalled, you provide discriminative stimuli (see Chapter 6) that may elicit the desired response. Remembering is largely a matter of using various kinds of discriminative stimuli, or prompts, to elicit weak responses.

Consider the common task of trying to remember someone's name. Suppose you see a familiar face at a party, but can't recall the name that goes with it. What do you do in your effort to remember the name? You might begin by asking yourself what sound the name begins with. If you can't say, you might go through the alphabet. If this is successful ("I think it starts with an 'S' sound"), you might go through a list of common names starting with this sound. ("Was it Smith? Shelly? Snyder?") You may hit upon the right name or upon a name that is so similar that it triggers the correct response. If not, you might think of other things you know about the name. ("Was it one syllable, like Sharp? Two syllables, like Sandburg? Three, like Sambino?") Often we can say a good deal about a person's name even when we can't remember what it is. And sometimes, recalling these related facts helps us recall the name itself.

Another way of prompting a name involves recalling things about the person named. Often we know a great deal about a person even though we cannot say the person's name. You may remember what sort of work he does, who his friends are, what his politics are, how and where you met him, and many other facts. Pondering these facts may prompt the missing name. For instance, in thinking about the circumstances under which you met, you may recall the introduction, including the part that goes "I want you to meet . . ." Sometimes, recalling the introduction will enable you to fill in the name. Or you may recall a feeling about the person or his name, and contemplating this may help. You may find yourself thinking, "There's something about him or his name that's connected with primitive cultures. Maybe he's an archeologist. No, that doesn't sound quite right. But I do think I met him at the college." Eventually, this sort of ruminating can result in your suddenly recalling that the person is Dr. Savage, the history professor.

Notice that the process you go through when trying to recall someone's name is the same process that you might go through trying to help someone *else* recall a name. And such prompting helps as well when trying to recall other kinds of responses. A weak response is elicited by stimuli associated with it. When we produce those stimuli ourselves, we are helping ourselves remember.

Mnemonics

There is a good deal of evidence that recall is affected by the way in which behavior is learned originally. For example, read the following number once, then cover it and try to recall it: 165561. Check your recall. Don't be surprised if you didn't do too well. Now try this set of numbers: 264-462. That series probably was much easier, but look again—both tasks involve the same number of digits. There are other things one can do to make a series of digits easier to recall. For instance, you might group the numbers in pairs, so that it sounds like a person's body measurements; the second series thus becomes 26-44-62. Another memory aid is to imagine something associated with what you have to recall. In the case of the number series, you might imagine a cone-shaped person who has the measurements 26-44-62.

All of these memory tricks come under the heading of **mnemonics,** a word that denotes any technique for improving recall. Mnemonics can be used to improve recall of all sorts of things, not just numbers. One technique for remembering names is to conjure up an image that in some way depicts the name. To recall Dr. Savage, for example, you might picture a witch doctor preparing a batch of missionary stew. It is even possible to devise mnemonic systems for recalling long strings of facts. In one, called the peg word system, you memorize an image for each of the first 20 or more integers. These images can be any word that designates a concrete object, and they can be made easy to recall by making them rhyme with the numbers: One is a bun, two is a shoe, three is a tree, four is a door, five is a hive, and so on. Once you've mastered the peg word list, you "hang" new things on the pegs by picturing them in some way. If you want to remember a store list, you imagine each item connected in some way to a peg word image. To remember lightbulbs, adhesive tape, and index cards, you might picture a lightbulb standing upright in a bun, adhesive tape wound around a shoe, and index cards hanging from the branches of a tree. With a little practice, you can recall long lists of items in this way.

There is no doubt that mnemonics improve recall (Bower, 1970). The question is, Why? In some cases, they help by reducing what is to be learned. If you are asked to remember the number 264462 and happen to notice that 462 is 264 backwards, then you need only remember 264. But in most cases, mnemonics improve our ability to remember by providing us with prompts to use when trying to make the desired response. If, when you meet Dr. Savage, you make a point of imagining a witch doctor preparing missionary stew, you will provide yourself with a prompt to use later when remembering his name. So long as you remember the prompt, your chances of coming up with the name are good. If you forget the prepared prompt, you will have to fall back upon other prompts, such as those described earlier. The peg word system is simply a formal way of providing prepared prompts. When you want to recall your store list, you recall the peg words. In imagining each peg word, you have a prompt for recalling the image of the item attached to it, so that when you picture the bun, you see a lightbulb sticking up in it.

Animals appear to use prompts to elicit responses from themselves in much the same way as humans do. Walter Hunter (1913) performed an experiment of the type that is now called delayed matching to sample (see Chapter 8), in which an animal could enter one of three compartments. A light appeared briefly over the door to the one compartment containing food. Hunter noticed that once an animal had learned to enter the previously illuminated door, it sometimes displayed an "orienting attitude" during the retention interval. That is, it leaned toward the door that had just been illuminated. The animals were evidently using their own body posture as a means of prompting themselves to make the appropriate response—in other words, to remember.

Remembering is often viewed as a mysterious process, sometimes involving dark, unconscious forces. There are many things about remembering that are not well understood, and there is no doubt that it involves unconscious physiological processes. But it seems clear that remembering is, in essence, a matter of doing things to elicit responses that are in the repertoire but not presently available.

INSIGHTFUL PROBLEM SOLVING

Problem solving is another area that is shrouded in mystery. It is often spoken of in conjunction with references to "the mysteries of mind" and is said to be one of those subjects that defy scientific analysis. However, psychologists who have approached problem solving from the standpoint of instrumental conditioning have given the lie to this view.

A problem exists when an organism is in a situation in which reinforcement is available but the response necessary to produce reinforcement is not currently in the organism's repertoire. In everyday parlance, we say that a problem exists when a goal is blocked. Thus, a cold mouse has a problem if the entrance to its warm nest is guarded by a cat; a hungry monkey has a problem if it cannot reach the fruit that hangs from branches too small to support its weight; and you have a problem if you are to attend a party, but cannot find the host's house. If the situation has been faced before and resolved satisfactorily, it is not truly a problem since the organism merely does what it did before. In true problem situations, the necessary response may be in the organism's repertoire, but it is, at the moment, not forthcoming. Thorndike's cats were capable of pulling the cord that would open the cage door, but the probability of this response was initially quite low. Through reinforcement, the response became stronger, until the cat quickly and easily pulled the cord when placed in the box; at this point, the box no longer presented a problem.

Problem solving would seem, then, merely to be instrumental conditioning. But there are instances of problem solving in which the solution does not occur in the slow, piecemeal manner that characterized Thorndike's cats, nor is it gradually shaped up in the way that Skinner's pigeons learned to peck a disk. Sometimes the solution suddenly appears in full form, like Athena springing fully grown from the head of Zeus. The best-known experiments on such insightful problem solving are those described in *The Mentality of Apes* by the German psychologist Wolfgang Köhler.

In a typical experiment, Köhler suspended fruit from the ceiling of a cage in a corner and placed a large box in the center of the cage. The chimpanzees under study attempted to reach the fruit by jumping, but the fruit was too high. One of the chimps, Sultan, "soon relinquished this attempt, paced restlessly up and down, suddenly stood still in front of the box, seized it, tipped it hastily straight towards the objective, but began to climb upon it at a (horizontal) distance of half a metre, and springing upwards with all his force, tore down the banana" (1927/1973, p. 40).

In such instances of problem solving, the solution's abrupt appearance is said to be an inexplicable "act of mind," not to be accounted for in terms of the reinforcement of previous responses. Such insight is different from the gradual selection of correct responses seen, for example, in Thorndike's cats. But is insight really independent of prior reinforcement? Unfortunately, Köhler's records of the experiences of the animals prior to testing are spotty. In the case just cited, it is not clear what sort of experiences Sultan had had with respect to the use of boxes or the retrieval of fruit from high places. However, if the same sort of spontaneous insight could be demonstrated in animals with a particular reinforcement history, this would suggest that the insight was due to that reinforcement history.

In a brilliant experiment, Robert Epstein and his colleagues (1984) taught a pigeon (1) to push a small box toward a target and (2) to climb on a box that was already beneath a toy banana and then peck the banana. Once this was accomplished, the researchers hung the toy banana from the ceiling of one corner and put the box in another corner. Note that this represented a new situation for the bird, a situation quite similar to that confronted by Sultan. The bird's behavior was also remarkably like that of Sultan: "It paced and looked perplexed, stretched toward the banana, glanced back and forth from box to banana and then energetically pushed the box toward it, looking up at it repeatedly as it did so, then stopped just short of it, climbed, and pecked. The solution appeared in about a minute for each of three birds" (Epstein, 1984b, p. 48f.). One could, of course, argue that the birds had solved the problem through some mysterious process (e.g., the workings of the unconscious); but it is more parsimonious to attribute the solution to the animal's reinforcement history.

Numerous other experiments demonstrating insightful problem solving have been reported. But it is likely that these, too, will succumb to an analysis in terms of reinforcement. In one of Köhler's most famous experiments (see Chapter 8), Sultan was given two hollow bamboo rods, one of which was small enough that it could be pushed into the end of the other. Outside the animal's cage lay a bit

NO SMOKING SECTION

The research by Robert Epstein and his colleagues shows how insightful solutions result from previously learned behavior. But new behavior can sometimes be composed of genetically acquired behavior as well.

Paul Silverman, an ethologist, describes an experiment that started out as a study of the effects of smoke inhalation on rodents but turned into a study of insightful problem solving (Silverman, 1978). Each of the rats, hamsters, and mice in this study was placed in a glass cylinder, and cigarette smoke was piped in through a narrow inlet. The animals "plainly disliked even the very diluted smoke, and from the second day onwards they started to do something about it" (p. 367). What they did was to block the inlet pipe with the only materials at hand, their own fecal pellets (see Figure 9-1). "One rat stuffed the inlet pipe only ten seconds after being put in the cylinder for the third day, before the first cigarette had even been lit" (p. 368).

Silverman notes that while the rodents's behavior seemed to appear rather suddenly, it was actually the result of the gradual integration of preexisting behavior. The rodents had, in their smoke-free home cages, engaged in the same sort of behavior (scratching, kicking with the hind legs, carrying fecal pellets or food, etc.) involved in stuffing the inlet. But whereas the research of Epstein and his co-workers shows the role of previously learned behavior in insightful problem solving, the present study shows that innate behavior is often also involved. Once again we see that experience interacts with heredity to produce behavior.

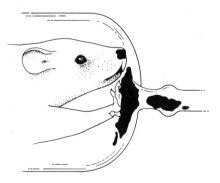

Figure 9-1   Rodents blocked the inlet through which smoke entered their glass cells. Their "insightful" solution consisted of innate responses. (After Silverman, 1978. Used by permission of Universe Books and Chapman & Hall Ltd.)

of fruit, just far enough from the bars that it could not be reached with either stick alone. After an hour of unproductive work, Sultan sat down on a box and examined the sticks. His keeper wrote that "while doing this, it happens that (Sultan) finds himself holding one rod in either hand in such a way that they lie in a straight line; he pushes the thinner one a little way into the opening of the thicker, jumps up and is already on the run towards the railings . . . and begins to draw a banana towards him with the double stick" (p. 127). What the descriptions of this experiment typically neglect to point out is that Sultan had had considerable experience in the use of sticks in the retrieval of fruit before being given this problem.

The influence of previous learning is sometimes seen in the form of problem-solving errors. In the two-stick experiment described above, Sultan at one point committed what Köhler called "a great stupidity" (p. 126). Unable to reach the fruit with either stick, he pulled a box from the back of the room toward the bars. This was, of course, of no help in this situation, but it is understandable given the chimp's history of reinforcement; that is, moving a box toward a goal had, in the past, proved helpful. It is interesting that when Köhler's animals behaved in ways that Köhler recognized as useful in the solution of a problem, he called their behavior insightful; when the behavior appeared to be useless, he called it a great stupidity. Ironically, in both cases, the appearance of the behavior seems to have been determined by the animal's reinforcement history.

Problem solving is obviously of considerable importance to survival for both animals and humans. It now appears that whether the mouse gets by the cat, whether the monkey reaches the fruit in the tree, and whether you find your way to the party depends to a large extent upon the reinforcement history of each with respect to responses that are relevant to the problem. We humans are, of course, far better at solving problems than are lower animals. But this may be largely because we are more adept at learning from the consequences of previous experiences. As Thorndike observed in 1911, "Because he learns fast and learns much, in the animal way, man seems to learn by intuitions of his own (p. 281)." The point of all this is not that insight does not occur, but that insight does not explain problem solving. Rather, insight is what needs to be explained. Efforts to account for insight in terms of instrumental conditioning have not solved all the "mysteries" of problem solving, but they have cleared away some of the clouds in which this subject has for so long been shrouded.

DELUSIONS AND HALLUCINATIONS

Ordinary thoughts and sensory experiences appear to fall within the realm of behavior and to be the products of previous experience, but what about bizarre thoughts and sensory experiences? People in mental hospitals have delusions (false beliefs such as "Everyone is out to get me" or "There are little green men inside my stomach") and hallucinations (such as hearing voices that say "You're no good"). Are not such delusions and hallucinations the products of "disordered minds"?

It should be noted that delusions and hallucinations can have an organic basis. Schizophrenia is probably a disease of the brain, and its symptoms include delusions, hallucinations, and other forms of bizarre behavior. Senile paresis, Alzheimer's disease, brain damage, and some drugs can also induce such behavior. But even when an organic problem exists, bizarre behavior may be largely under the control of reinforcement.

Let us take up an actual case of bizarre thinking in a psychiatric patient. Joe Layng and Paul Andronis (1984) provide an example. The woman, a patient in a mental hospital, began to complain that her head was falling off. She seemed quite frightened, so a member of the staff sat with her to calm her down, but the delusion got worse. She began to hear popping sounds that preceded the feeling that she was losing her head. A discussion with the patient led to the discovery that she found it very difficult to approach the staff members to engage them in conversation. Sometimes when she approached them, they responded with obvious annoyance. Her delusional behavior produced the desirable effect (interaction with the staff) without the risk of hostile reactions. In other words, the delusion was reinforced. Once the woman learned how to approach the staff without incurring hostile reactions, the delusion disappeared, and her head seemed securely attached.

Layng and Andronis (1984) also describe the case of a middle-aged man admitted to a locked hospital ward after he tried to pull a pair of clothesline poles out of the ground in his backyard. He shouted that the poles were blasphemous statues of the cross and that Jesus had told him to tear them down. It turned out the man's efforts to involve his wife in his demanding business problems had been unsuccessful and that she showed concern only when he became morose. In other words, she reinforced disturbed behavior. She inadvertently shaped up increasingly pathological behavior, until he finally behaved in a way that resulted in his hospitalization. When

EXORCISING WITCHES

Schizophrenia is a serious form of psychosis. Its origin is uncertain, but many psychologists believe that it is a brain disease. From the standpoint of behavior, however, a schizophrenic can be thought of as a person who displays a high rate of bizarre behavior. It follows that one goal of treatment is to reduce the rate of such behavior. One way to do this is with antipsychotic drugs; another way is to apply learning principles.

An example of how this may be done is provided by Brad Alford (1986), who worked with a young schizophrenic patient in a psychiatric hospital. The man was greatly helped by medication but continued to experience some symptoms, including the delusion that a "haggly old witch" followed him about. Alford decided to focus on getting rid of the witch. He did this by having the patient keep a record of his feeling that he was being followed. The patient also indicated the strength of his belief, from 0 (certainty that the belief was just his imagination) to 100 (certainty that the belief reflected reality).

Alford used an ABA design. During the treatment (B) phases, he reinforced expressions of doubt about the veridicality of the delusional belief. The result was that the patient's reported confidence in the delusion declined (see Figure 9-2).

It might be argued, however, that the patient believed in the witch as much as ever and merely learned not to admit it. To test this idea, Alford looked at the medication the patient received before and during the study. He found that the man received one kind

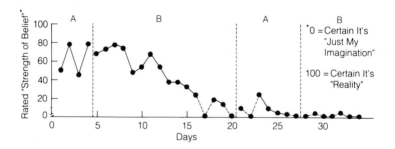

Figure 9-2   Strength of delusional belief. During treatment (B) phases, the patient's confidence in the reality of the "haggly old witch" declined. (After Alford, 1986. Copyright 1986 by the Association for Advancement of Behavior Therapy. Reprinted by permission of the publisher and author.)

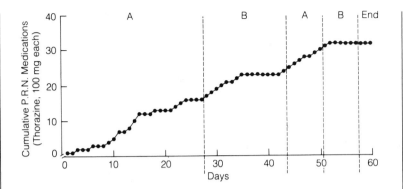

Figure 9-3 Tranquilizer consumption. During treatment (B) phases, the rate at which the patient received tranquilizer pills declined. (After Alford, 1986. Copyright 1986 by the Association for Advancement of Behavior Therapy. Reprinted by permission of the publisher and author.)

of medication routinely, but the nurses gave another drug, a tranquilizer, only when he seemed agitated. If the patient became convinced that the witch wasn't real, then there should have been a decline in the rate at which he received tranquilizers. And indeed there was a decline (see Figure 9-3).

To the extent that schizophrenia means displaying a high rate of bizarre behavior, then, this study demonstrates that schizophrenics can be made less schizophrenic by the application of learning principles.

she learned to show concern for her husband's business problems instead of his bizarre behavior, his symptoms began to subside.

It might be asked whether these cases involve true delusions and hallucinations. The woman might not really have *believed* that her head was coming loose; the man might not really have *heard* voices. But what proof do we have that anyone's report matches his or her experience? How do you know that I see an apple when I say I do? That you see an apple corroborates the presence of the apple, but not my seeing it. A blind person might detect the presence of apples from their fragrance and say that he or she sees them. We have no reason to doubt that people accurately report their private experiences when they tell us about delusions and hallucinations. But whether delusions and hallucinations occur as private events misses the point, as Layng and Andronis point out. Bizarre behavior has consequences, and when the consequences are reinforcing, the bizarre behavior is likely to persist.

Goldiamond's Paradox

One objection to this analysis is that bizarre behavior often occurs even when it is not reinforced. Goldiamond (1975) describes a woman virtually paralyzed by fear of cockroaches. She remained in bed, too afraid to move about. Her husband was sympathetic and gave her the attention she had previously been denied. This attention was apparently the reinforcer that maintained her phobic behavior. But this introduces a dilemma in that the woman's husband was not always at home. Ordinarily, we would expect that discrimination would take place: The woman would become an invalid when reinforcement was available for invalidism (i.e., when the husband was present), but would go about her business when reinforcement was not available (when the husband was absent). But this did not occur: The woman stayed in bed whether her husband was present or not. This is what might be called **Goldiamond's paradox**, which states that in order for bizarre behavior to be reinforced, it must sometimes occur on occasions when it cannot be reinforced (Goldiamond, 1975).

The reason is simple. If a person behaves bizarrely only when reinforcement for bizarre behavior is available, people catch on. The reinforcer controlling the behavior becomes apparent and is soon withheld. Reinforcement for bizarre behavior is therefore often contingent not only upon the occurrence of the behavior but upon the occurrence of the behavior *at times when reinforcement is unavailable.* "In other words," write Layng and Andronis (1984), "the apparent absence of maintaining consequences or the presence of aversive consequences on some occasions, may be requirements that must be met for reinforcement to be available on other occasions" (p. 142).

Layng and Andronis noted that the traditional approach to delusions and hallucinations assumes that disordered thoughts reflect a disordered private world. The traditional clinician therefore attempts to understand more about this private world. But a simpler, more scientific approach is possible. This approach assumes that delusions and hallucinations are operant behavior and are, like any other operant behavior, under the control of their consequences. As we have seen, effective treatment follows logically from this analysis.

SUMMARY

Although most people view thinking as fundamentally different from other human activities, thinking can be considered behavior. As with other forms of behavior, thinking apparently is subject to the influence of the environment.

Self-awareness may be viewed as the act of observing one's own behavior. We observe ourselves in much the same way that we observe others, and we do so because such observations allow us to behave in ways that are reinforced. Self-observation is encouraged by others who prompt us to make note of and comment upon our private experiences.

Seeing is a response to light emanating from objects in our environment, but it is not entirely innate. What we see is partly the product of our learning history. When we dream and when we imagine, we see things even though the object seen is not present.

When a learned response is not immediately forthcoming, we do things to prompt it. Such self-prompting is what is meant by remembering. Mnemonics aid later recall largely by providing prompts that will elicit the desired response.

When a problem solution is achieved suddenly after fruitless efforts, we often speak of insightful problem solving. But the insight does not explain the solution, it *is* the solution. The achievement of insight can be accounted for by previous learning and, in fact, we can produce insightful problem solving by training the organism to make the various responses that comprise the solution.

Delusions and hallucinations are bizarre forms of behavior that seem, at least initially, to occur independently of reinforcement. But more careful examination reveals that such behavior, like more ordinary behavior, is maintained by its consequences.

There are, of course, many kinds of thinking not treated here, but these topics are representative of what is meant by thinking. We can see that there is little reason to treat thinking as different in any fundamental way from other forms of behavior. Even when thinking is private, as in the case of silent speech, seeing, and feelings, it appears to be subject to modification in much the same way as public behavior.

To say that thinking is behavior is not to say that it is unimportant. Behavior of every kind has presumably evolved because it has survival value. Seeing and imagining allow us to respond more effectively to the world around us. If we can close our eyes and "see" the route to a place, we can better describe it to someone else. Being self-aware allows us to predict consequences and to obtain reinforcers and avoid aversive stimuli. The self-prompting we do when trying to remember allows us to produce responses that are not otherwise forthcoming. This has value not only for the 20th-century student taking tests in school but for the prehistoric cave-dweller finding a way home when lost in a fog. Similarly, achieving insight reinforces the effort that went into the learning experiences necessary for achieving it. And even such bizarre behavior as delusions and hallucinations help people survive in trying situations by prompting those around them to provide reinforcers they would otherwise withhold. Again and again in this text, we have seen that the function of behavior is to ensure survival. Apparently, this is as true of the covert behavior we call thinking as it is of any other behavior.

REVIEW QUESTIONS

1. Define the following terms:

the Cogito	thinking
self-awareness	insight
mnemonics	hallucination
Goldiamond's paradox	remembering

2. Explain the significance of the Cogito for psychology.

3. Defend the notion that thinking is behavior. Distinguish between overt and covert behavior, and explain why the distinction is arbitrary.

4. John says that people continue to use cocaine even after they know its dangers because they "crave it." Explain why this explanation is inadequate. (Hint: See question 13.)

5. John B. Watson said that thinking is largely covert speech. Explain why you agree or disagree with this definition.

6. How is self-awareness like the awareness that we have of others? How is it different?

7. Mary hypothesizes that people who are good at observing others are good at observing themselves. Design a study to test her hypothesis.

8. Some people are very good at seeing things that are not before them; others are not. Suppose a person asks you for help in improving his or her imaging ability. How would you go about it? (Hint: See Chapter 4.)

9. Gallup concludes that *"insofar* as self-recognition of one's mirror image implies a concept of self" (emphasis added), the fact that chimps will use mirrors demonstrates that they have self-concepts. *Does* mirror use imply a concept of self?

10. What is the significance of Turnbull's observations of Kenge?

11. Explain why people see what they expect to see. (Hint: What does "expect" mean?)

12. Conduct an experiment on remembering like that proposed by Lindsay and Norman. Encourage your subject to give as detailed an answer as possible and tape record his or her reply. Identify the different kinds of self-prompts the subject uses.

13. Why is "insight" not an adequate explanation for problem solving? (Hint: See question 4.)

14. How might intuition and creativity be accounted for in terms of instrumental conditioning?

15. Suppose you wanted to get a chimpanzee to solve Köhler's two-stick problem without actually training the animal to put the two sticks together. How would you go about it? (Hint: See how Epstein et al. got a pigeon to solve the box and banana problem.)

16. Professional boxing is an example of behavior that may appear bizarre until we consider the reinforcers it provides (Layng & Adronis, 1984). What is another example of "normal" behavior that might seem bizarre if its reinforcing consequences were unknown?

17. Goldiamond (1975) makes the point that to understand bizarre behavior, we have to consider the alternative sources of reinforcement for the individual. Why is this important?

18. Give an example of some behavior in which you engage that might be considered delusional. What reinforcer maintains this behavior?

19. Some delusions and hallucinations are at least partly due to organic impairment. Suppose a psychiatric patient believes he is

Napoleon. How could you determine whether this delusion is under the control of reinforcing consequences?

20. Why do people think? What role does thinking play in human survival?

SUGGESTED READINGS

Descartes's *Discourse on Method* (1637) is both interesting and an important historical document. You may find it dry, but give it a try.

B. F. Skinner is the leading spokesperson for the natural science approach to thinking. See especially his chapters on thinking in *Verbal Behavior* (1957), *Science and Human Behavior* (1953), and *About Behaviorism* (1974).

Other researchers are following Skinner's lead in treating thinking as behavior. See in particular the articles by Goldiamond (1975), Epstein and his colleagues (1981, 1984), and Layng and Andronis (1984) cited in this chapter. For more on the role of reinforcement in the etiology of "mental illness," see Benjamin Braginsky et al., *Methods of Madness: The Mental Hospital as Last Resort* (1971).

For an approach to thinking different from that offered in this chapter, see *Human Information Processing: An Introduction to Psychology* by Peter Lindsay and Donald Norman (1972). For more on animal thinking, see the text by Roitblat (1987).

TEN

■

The Limits of Learning

In the preceding chapters, we saw that learning plays a vital role in the behavior of animals and humans. It is clear, then, that to understand human nature—or the nature of chimpanzees, monkeys, giraffes, rats, pigeons, and many other animals—we must understand how behavior is modified by experience; that is, we must understand how learning occurs. But we must also understand the limits of learning. For while learning does contribute to the differences in behavior that distinguish one person from another, or a person from a chimpanzee, there are limits to what people and chimpanzees can learn. In this chapter, we will discuss some of these limitations.

PHYSICAL CHARACTERISTICS

Fish can't jump rope, humans can't breathe under water, cows can't coil up like snakes. The very structure of an organism's body makes certain kinds of behavior possible and other kinds of behavior impossible. What an organism can learn to do is therefore limited by what it is physically capable of doing. This is such an obvious fact that one might think it goes without saying. Indeed, it seldom is mentioned in the learning literature. But obvious generalizations are sometimes worth making because the particulars that lead to the generalization are not always so obvious.

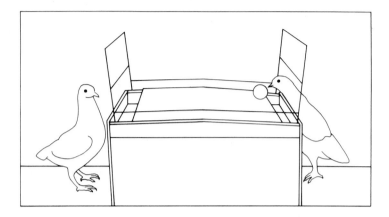

Figure 10-1 Physical characteristics and learning. Pigeons can't learn to play ping pong in the usual manner, but these two have learned to play a variation of the game. (From B. F. Skinner, "Two synthetic social relations," *Journal of the Experimental Analysis of Behavior*, 1962, 5, p. 531, figure 1. Copyright 1962 by the Society for the Experimental Analysis of Behavior, Inc. Reprinted by permission of the publisher and author.)

For instance, a dog will readily learn to respond differentially to two different sounds, but it may not learn to discriminate two different colors. The reason is that dogs may be partly or wholly color-blind. (Research on this issue has produced ambiguous results.) Similarly, a hawk's superb vision allows it to discriminate between heads and tails on a quarter at a distance of a quarter of a mile, whereas a person is unable to see the coin at all at that distance. Obviously, then, under certain circumstances, it would be far easier to teach a hawk a simple discrimination than it would be to teach a person that discrimination.

All sorts of physical structures set limits upon what organisms can learn. Some years ago, various attempts were made to teach chimpanzees to talk (see, for example, Hayes, 1951; Kellogg, 1968). These efforts were almost wholly unsuccessful and convinced many people that chimpanzees could not acquire language. The famous primatologist Robert Yerkes believed that this failure was due to the chimpanzee's lack of spontaneous imitation of vocal sounds. He found that chimps would imitate much of his behavior, but not his speech. "Obviously," Yerkes wrote, "an animal which lacks the tendency to reinstate auditory stimuli—in other words to imitate sounds—cannot reasonably be expected to talk" (quoted in Gardner & Gardner, 1969, p. 666). Yerkes believed that chimpanzees had the intelligence to learn language, but lacked the tendency of humans and some other animals to imitate it. "If the imitative tendency of the parrot could be coupled with the quality of intelligence of the chimpanzee, the latter undoubtedly could speak" (p. 666).

Other researchers doubted that the chimpanzee (or any other nonhuman creature) had the capacity to learn language. To them, language was the ultimate discriminator between humans and beasts, the one difference that continued to set us off from furrier creatures. But in 1966, Allen and Beatrice Gardner (1969) began teaching Washoe, a young female chimpanzee, the sign language of the deaf. In less than 2 years, Washoe had a vocabulary of over 30 signs, and by the time she was 7, her vocabulary was pushing toward 200 signs. Since the Gardner's first efforts, a number of other researchers have taught sign language to chimps. Whether these animals have really learned to communicate in the human sense is subject to debate (see, for example, Terrace, 1979). The point, however, is not that chimps are as adept as humans at learning language, but rather that the physical inability of chimps to speak misled us into believing that they were incapable of learning language. For it turns out that even humans would be incapable of speech if they had to use the kind of vocal structures that chimps have. The physical characteristics of an organism set important, but not always obvious, limits upon what the organism can learn.

INTELLIGENCE

The Brain

There is nothing about the gross anatomy of the chimpanzee (e.g., the way its arms and legs are put together) that keeps it from learning to solve algebra word problems. Yet it seems extremely unlikely that anyone will ever succeed in training a chimpanzee, or any other animal, to perform so sophisticated a skill. (Of course, a chimp might be trained to respond with the correct answer to a particular problem. But when we say that people can solve algebra word problems, we mean that they can respond correctly to problems they have never seen before. This is much more difficult.) Apparently, the principal reason that some people can master this sort of task, while no chimpanzee can, has to do with differences in their nervous systems. To put it simply, a human brain is a more powerful learning instrument than a chimpanzee brain. It is also clear that there are pronounced differences in the learning abilities of individuals within a given species, and it seems likely that differences in "brain power" are partly responsible.

Just what it is that makes one brain better at learning than another is a mystery. Comparisons of the brains of various species show very pronounced differences in size and weight. The earthworm's brain is little more than a nodule, about the size of a BB pellet, that sits on top of the spinal cord; the chimpanzee's brain is about the size of a softball. Surely the greater learning ability of the ape is in some way related to the greater size of its brain. Yet within a given species, size and weight turn out to be generally unrelated to learning ability. A list of highly gifted people will, for example, include some with unusually small brains, as well as many whose brains are no larger than average.

Efforts to identify the physical basis for differences in intelligence have included studies on the chemical composition of the brain. James McGaugh and his colleagues (1961) performed an experiment in which they tested the effects of a synthetic compound on three groups of rats that were known to vary in learning ability. Some of the rats in each group got the experimental drug, while the others got a placebo (an ineffective substance). The results showed that the drug improved the rate of learning in the duller rats, but not in the brightest ones. On the basis of this and other studies, it seems reasonable to assume that the anatomical and chemical structure of an organism's brain sets important limits on what the organism can learn. These brain characteristics are, in turn, determined by both hereditary and environmental influences.

Heredity

The influence of heredity on the brain was demonstrated many years ago by the research of Robert Tryon (1940). Tryon ran a large number of rats through a maze and recorded the number of errors each rat made on a series of trials. There was a great deal of variability among the rats in the total number of errors made, with some rats making over 20 times as many errors as others. Tryon then bred those rats that had made the fewest errors with each other, and those that had made the greatest number of errors with each other. Next, Tryon tested the offspring of these rats on the maze and again bred the brightest of the bright with each other and the dullest of the dull with each other. He continued this procedure for 18 generations, all the while keeping the environments of the two strains as much alike as

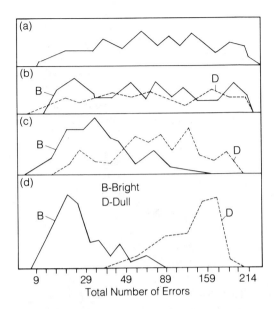

Figure 10-2 Heredity and maze learning. Tryon's original sample of rats showed wide variation in maze learning (a). The first generation of selectively bred rats showed considerable overlap (b), but the second generation showed clear differences in maze-learning ability (c). By the seventh generation there was a substantial difference in the average number of errors made by the two groups (d). (After Robert Tryon, "Genetic Differences in Maze-Learning Ability in Rats," in the Thirty-Ninth Yearbook of the National Society for the Study of Education, *Intelligence: Its Nature and Nurture, Part I: Comparative and Critical Exposition,* G. M. Whipple [Ed.], 1940, p. 113, figure 4. Copyright 1940 by the National Society for the Study of Education. Reprinted by permission of the publisher.)

possible. The average number of errors in maze running for the two groups got further and further apart with each generation (see Figure 10-2), thus suggesting that heredity was having an important impact on the animals' brains. This interpretation is supported by studies that compared the brain chemistry of descendants of Tryon's rats. Mark Rosenzweig and his colleagues (1960), for example, found that the brains of these rats differed in the amount of neurotransmitters they contained. (Neurotransmitters are chemicals involved in learning.)

Additional support for the role of heredity in learning ability comes from studies of sex differences. Most studies of sex differences have found that males are better at learning spatial and mathematical tasks and that females are better at learning verbal tasks (Maccoby & Jacklin, 1974). It is easy to speculate upon how such differences might have had survival value for our species. For instance, for thousands of years, males played the dominant role in hunting, for which spatial abilities may have been important, while women played the dominant role in foraging, for which the ability to communicate directions might have been helpful. But the extent to which these differences are due to inherited differences in brain structure or chemistry, on the one hand, and cultural variables, on the other, is hotly debated.

Environment

The influence of the environment on the brain and on learning ability has been demonstrated by the research of David Krech and Mark Rosenzweig and their colleagues (see, for example, Rosenzweig et al., 1962). These researchers have spent several years investigating the effects of environmental complexity on the brain. In a typical experiment, 3 rats, all from the same litter, are placed in different environments. In the control condition, the rat shares an ordinary laboratory cage with a few other rats; in the deprived condition, the rat lives alone in a cage; in the enriched condition, the rat lives in a large cage with several other rats and a variety of toys that are changed periodically. Examination of the animal's brains reveals that the complexity of the environment affects certain physical characteristics of the brain: the more complex the environment, the larger and heavier the brain. The ratio of the higher brain—the cortex—to the lower brain, or subcortex, is also greater. In addition, the brain's chemical makeup varies significantly with the complexity of the environment. Some research suggests that these physical differences in the brain are correlated with differences in learning ability.

Robert Cummins and his co-workers (1977) have proposed that such differences may be due to the deprived environment suppressing neurological development rather than to the enriched environment enhancing development. More recent research, however, supports the idea that complex environments modify the brain. Neurobiologist William Greenough has found that complex environments increase the number of connections among certain kinds of brain cells (reported in Hall, 1985). Greenough has also found that learning increases the number of connections. Thus, while it is customary to think that the quality of the brain sets limits upon learning, it may also be the case that learning helps to determine the quality of the brain.

RECIPE FOR GENIUS

Many of the world's geniuses have had unusually enriched environments. In fact, intellectual enrichment is a common element in the lives of people like Beethoven and Francis Galton. Could it be that an enriched environment actually improves the human brain and increases the individual's ability to learn? There are, unfortunately, no hard data that bear on this question. However, there is some very intriguing anecdotal evidence.

For instance, the 19th-century British philosopher John Stuart Mill had an incredibly enriched environment as a child. The boy's father, philosopher and historian James Mill, began tutoring him when he was still in the cradle. John was reading by age 3 and routinely answered questions from his father about what he had read. By the time John was 8 years old, he had already read most of the Greek classics (in Greek, incidentally), and as an adult, he went on to outdistance his father as a philosopher.

A more recent effort to improve ability by providing an enriched environment came from a man named Aaron Stern (1971). Too ill to work, Stern decided that he would devote his time toward the education of his daughter. When Edith was still an infant, Stern played classical music for her, showed her flash cards with numbers on them, read to her, and made a point of speaking to her slowly and in complete sentences. When she was 18 months old, Stern taught Edith math with an abacus, showed her words on flash cards, and taught her to read street signs. By age 2, Edith was reading books intended for children of 6 and 8; by age 4, she was reading *The New York Times* and playing chess; by age 5, she had read much, if not all, of the *Encyclopaedia Britannica*; by age 6, she was reading Dostoyevsky and Tolstoy; and by age 15, Edith had graduated from college and begun graduate work at Michigan State University.

Of course, neither of these examples provides any evidence that enriched environments actually change the anatomical or chemical composition of the brain. In fact, it is possible that the remarkable achievements of John Stuart Mill and Edith Stern had little to do with the special environments in which they were reared. Nevertheless, these and other cases leave open the possibility that environmental complexity can have important effects on the human brain and on the ability to learn.

PREPAREDNESS

In the 1960s, researchers began to notice that while a given animal might learn quite readily in one situation, it can seem downright stupid in a slightly different situation. The difference was not due to some subtle complexity of the learning task, but rather to a peculiar predisposition of the organism. Martin Seligman (1970) reviewed this research and proposed that the bizarre findings were due to a **continuum of preparedness:** An organism came to a learning situation biologically prepared to learn (in which case learning proceeded quickly), unprepared (in which case learning would proceed steadily but more slowly), or contraprepared (in which case the course of learning would be very slow and irregular [see Figure 10-3]). Some examples of the influence of preparedness will help clarify the concept.

Keller and Marion Breland, psychologists-turned-animal-trainers, used instrumental conditioning procedures to train hundreds of animals as performers in TV commercials and films and as attractions at shopping centers. The Brelands were expert animal trainers, yet they sometimes had great difficulty getting an animal to perform what seemed to be a simple task. In a classic article entitled, "The Misbehavior of Organisms" (1961), they describe some of the peculiar problems they encountered in their work. For instance, the Brelands wanted to train a raccoon to pick up some coins and put them in a metal box that served as a bank. Raccoons are sharp animals, so the trainers expected no difficulty. The raccoon quickly learned to pick up a coin and carry it to the box, but the Brelands report that the animal "seemed to have a great deal of trouble letting go of the coin. He would rub it up against the inside of the container, pull it back out, and clutch it firmly for several seconds" (p. 682). When the Brelands tried to teach the animal to pick up two coins and put them in the box, the raccoon became even more of a dunce. Instead of dropping the coins into the box, it would rub them together "in a most miserly fashion" (p. 682) and dip them in and out of the box. None of this behavior was reinforced by the trainers.

It might seem reasonable to conclude that the task was simply too difficult for the raccoon to master. But raccoons have no trouble learning other, equally complex tasks, so the idea that their misbehavior was due to stupidity just did not hold up.

Time and again, the Brelands had trouble getting animals to perform acts that should have been easy. In some cases, the Brelands managed to teach an animal to make the desired responses, only to

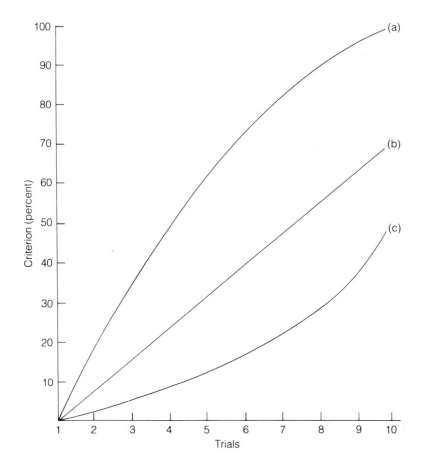

Figure 10-3   Preparedness and learning. Hypothetical learning curves for a task an organism is prepared to learn (a), unprepared to learn (b), and contraprepared to learn (c).

find that the act later broke down. For example, the Brelands taught a pig to make bank deposits in a manner similar to that of the raccoon. But after a time, the pig began to behave oddly; instead of picking up the large wooden coin and carrying it to the bank, the pig would drop the coin to the ground, push at it with its snout, throw it up into the air, nudge it again with its snout, and so on. None of this behavior was reinforced by the Brelands. In fact, the animal's errant behavior delayed reinforcement.

Why did such "misbehavior" occur? The Brelands theorized that innate behavior interfered with learning. In the wild, raccoons dip their prey into the water and then rub it between their paws, as if washing it. Some biologists speculate that this serves to break away the outer shell of the crayfish that often forms an important part of the raccoon's diet. In any case, it appears that this behavior interfered with teaching the raccoon to drop coins into a bank. Similarly, pigs dig their snouts into the ground to uncover edible roots, and this rooting behavior interfered with learning to carry coins to the bank.

The tendency of an animal to revert to a fixed action pattern sets limits on learning. If a particular act conflicts with a fixed action pattern, the animal will have trouble learning it. In Seligman's terms, the animal is contraprepared for learning that response. After the Brelands' discovery, other researchers began to report evidence that animals show peculiar talents for learning some things, but are peculiarly resistant toward learning others. The limitations that these oddities place on learning were nicely illustrated in a study of taste aversion in rats conducted by John Garcia and Robert Koelling (1966).

Garcia and Koelling set up four classical conditioning experiments in which they paired water with aversive stimuli. The water was made distinctive by being flavored and by having a light and a clicking noise come on whenever the rat drank. Thus, in one experiment, the rat drank water that was bright, noisy, and tasty, and later it became sick from exposure to X-radiation. In another experiment, if a rat drank the water, it later received an electric shock. After training, the experimenters gave the rats the opportunity to drink water that was either bright-noisy or tasty. They found that rats that had been made sick were more likely to avoid the *tasty* water; those that had been shocked were more likely to avoid the *bright-noisy* water (see Figure 10-4). According to Seligman's theory, these animals were biologically prepared to associate sickness with taste, and pain with light and sound. It is probably not coincidental that, in the rat's natural environment, sickness is more likely to be paired with certain tastes (e.g., tainted meat), than with lights and sounds, while pain is more likely to be paired with auditory and visual stimuli (e.g., the sight and sound of a cat). It is easy to see how the rat's preparedness would facilitate learning in its natural environment.

There are many other examples of preparedness in animals. Hardy Wilcoxon and his colleagues (1971) found, for instance, that while bobwhite quail could learn to avoid flavored water that made them sick, they were much more adept at learning to avoid water that had a distinctive color. Similarly, Jerzy Konorski (1967) had little difficulty teaching dogs to lick or scratch themselves, but he had a devil of a time getting them to yawn. Thorndike (1911) found that cats learned

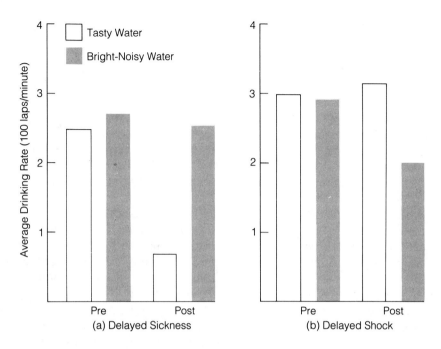

Figure 10-4   Preparedness and taste aversion. Rats were given the opportunity to drink bright-noisy and tasty water before and after conditioning. When drinking preceded sickness, rats later tended to avoid tasty water (a); when drinking preceded shock, the rats learned to avoid bright-noisy water (b). (After John Garcia & Robert Koelling, "Relation of cue to consequence in Avoidance Learning," *Psychonomic Science*, 1966, 4, p. 124, figure 1. Copyright 1966 by the Psychonomic Society. Reprinted by permission of the publisher and authors.)

to escape a box by scratching at a lever, but when scratching themselves had the same effect, the animals did not catch on.

The facility with which animals learn responses they are biologically prepared to perform is illustrated by a classic experiment conducted by Paul Brown and Herbert Jenkins (1968). These researchers put pigeons into Skinner boxes rigged so that periodically a disk would be illuminated. The disk would remain lit for 8 seconds, and when the light went off, a food tray would provide the pigeon with grain. As in Skinner's superstition experiment (see Chapter 4), the bird received food regardless of what it did; the only real difference was that the food was preceded by the illumination of the disk. The question was, What sort of superstitious behavior would the birds develop?

What happened was that all of the birds began pecking the disk. The experimenters noted that the birds went through characteristic stages before they pecked the disk. First, there was a general increase in activity level; second, the bird attended more and more to the disk when it was lit; third, the bird began to peck in the general area of the disk; fourth, the bird pecked the disk. These stages are similar to those that one might have observed if disk pecking had been shaped up through the reinforcement of successive approximations, so the experimenters called the phenomenon **autoshaping** (see Garcia et al., 1973, for a review).

The autoshaping research demonstrates that pigeons are so strongly prepared to peck that they readily develop superstitious pecking. Experiments by David and Harriet Williams (1969) showed that such pecking may be quite persistent. These researchers started with an experimental situation similar to that of the Brown and Jenkins study. In one condition, each time the bird pecked a lighted disk, the disk went dark and the bird got some grain. In another condition, pecking the lighted disk made it go dark but did not produce food. No effort was made to shape up disk pecking in either case, but in the first condition, disk pecking was reinforced when it occurred, whereas in the second case, disk pecking actually delayed food. The results showed that the birds pecked the lit disk, and continued pecking it, whether their efforts were reinforced or not.

There is evidence of preparedness in humans. Psycholinguists have argued that people are biologically prepared to learn language, noting that children readily learn language without any great effort on the part of adults. (Chimpanzees, however, learn sign language only through tedious instruction.) Psycholinguist Eric Lenneberg (1967, 1969) points out that language development follows a regular, predictable pattern around the world, which suggests that people are prepared to learn language in a certain way. In addition, Lenneberg notes that retarded children do not develop a bizarre language of their own, but rather their language freezes at a primitive stage of development: They are prepared to learn language in the same way as more intelligent people, though they cannot learn to the same level of complexity.

Seligman (1970) has proposed that phobias provide additional evidence of human preparedness (see also Ost & Hugdahl, 1985). Certain objects, he points out, are far more likely than others to become phobic stimuli. He adds that "the great majority of phobias are about objects of natural importance to the survival of the species" (p. 320). People are far more likely to fear sharks, spiders, snakes, and dogs than they are lambs, trees, houses, and cars. Martin Seligman and Joanne Hager (1972b) tell the story of a 7-year-old girl who saw a snake while playing in the park. Several hours later, the girl accidentally slammed a car door on her hand, after which she developed a fear of snakes. Obviously, the snake did not hurt her hand. The implication is that people are biologically prepared to acquire a fear of snakes but not a fear of cars, yet in this case, a car phobia would have made more sense. Seligman (1970) also observes that people are far more likely to form strong attachments to some objects than to others. As he notes, the cartoon character Linus carries a security *blanket*, not a security shoe.

It seems clear that in humans as well as in animals, learning depends partly upon whether the organism is prepared, unprepared, or contraprepared to learn the task in question.

CRITICAL PERIODS

Sometimes, organisms are especially prepared to learn a particular kind of behavior at one point in their lives but not at others; these stages for optimum learning are referred to as **critical periods**. For example, many birds are prepared to form an attachment to their mothers during a critical period soon after birth. If the mother is unavailable, the youngster will become attached to any moving object that happens to be handy, whether another animal of the same species, a mechanical object, or a human being. Konrad Lorenz (1952) was one of the first to study this phenomenon, which he called **imprinting**. He discovered that if you remove a newly hatched goose chick from an incubator, you will have inadvertently become a parent; the chick will follow you about and ignore its true mother. "If one quickly places such an orphan amongst a brood which is following its parents in the normal way," writes Lorenz, "the gosling shows not the slightest tendency to regard the old birds as members of its own species. Peeping loudly, it runs away and, should a human being happen to pass, it immediately follows this person; it simply looks upon human beings as its parents" (quoted in Thorpe, 1963, p. 405).

Imprinting has been demonstrated in coots, moorhens, turkeys, ravens, partridges, ducks, chickens, deer, sheep, buffalo, zebras, guinea pigs, baboons, and other organisms. Animals have been imprinted to species different from themselves, including humans, and to objects such as wooden decoys and electric trains. All that is necessary for imprinting to take place is that the young animal be able to view the "mother" and that the mother-object move.

Imprinting is not the only evidence for critical periods. John Scott

BOY OR GIRL? A CRITICAL QUESTION

When a baby is born, one of the first questions people ask is, "Is it a boy or a girl?" But the sex of a child is only partly determined by the physical equipment he or she inherits at birth. The subjective sense of maleness and femaleness, as well as masculine and femine mannerisms and preferences, are acquired by the child as it interacts with other people. In a very real sense, the child learns to be a boy or a girl.

The learning starts early. Studies have shown, for instance, that parents behave very differently toward male babies than they do toward female babies. They look at and talk to girls more often than to boys, and, at least after the first 6 months, generally touch girls more than boys. Male babies are encouraged to roam about, girls are encouraged to stay close. And parents expect different things from boys than they expect from girls. Jeff Rubin and his co-workers (1974) asked parents to rank their newborn babies on a number of characteristics. Objective measures showed no differences between boys and girls on these characteristics, but the parents of daughters rated their babies differently than did the parents of boys. For example, daughters were rated as softer and smaller than sons.

Similarly, Jerrie Will and her colleagues (1976) had mothers interact with a 6-month-old baby. Some mothers were led to believe that the baby was a boy, others that he was a girl. The researchers found that the supposed sex of the child influenced the kinds of toys the women invited the child to pay with. As a boy, the child was given a toy train; as a girl, he was handed a doll. Such differences in treatment are probably vital to the development of gender identity, the sense of being male or female.

There is considerable evidence that the first two or three years of life may be a critical period for the formation of gender identity. Many specialists in child development believe that a child's sense of maleness or femaleness is determined by age 3, and some believe the critical period is the first 18 months. Once the child's gender identity is formed, it is extremely difficult to change. If, for example, a male infant is treated as a girl for the first few years, he may never form a strong sense of masculine identity. Such people often feel that they have the right sexual identity, but the wrong sex organs.

We learn early what we are, male or female, and what we learn in that critical period sticks with us for a lifetime.

(1958) has shown that social behavior in the dog depends upon its experiences during certain critical periods. He points out, for example, that if a puppy is to become a good housepet, it must have contact with people when it is between 3 and 12 weeks old. Dogs completely deprived of human contact during this period behave like wild dogs, ever fearful of humans.

Maternal behavior may have to be learned during critical periods. Scott (1962) once bottle-fed a lamb for the first 10 days of its life and then put the lamb in with a flock of sheep. The lamb cared little for the sheep, preferring to be with people. More importantly, however, when this lamb gave birth, it was a poor mother: It allowed the lamb to nurse, but took no particular interest in other motherly activities.

Harry and Margaret Harlow (Harlow, 1958; Harlow & Harlow, 1962a, b) obtained similar results when they reared rhesus monkeys in isolation. In the Harlows' experiments, young monkeys were fed by a surrogate mother, a terry cloth–covered object that did nothing but provide food and warmth. The infants became very attached to these surrogate mothers and would cling to them for hours. If a monkey were exploring about the cage and became frightened, it would run to "mother" for protection. Later, when these monkeys were placed in cages with normally reared monkeys, they were terrified. They would run to a corner of the cage and roll up into a ball, sometimes sucking on a finger. As adults, these monkeys did not play or mate or rear young the way normally reared monkeys do. While it was possible for these animals to acquire some social skills as adults, they always seemed to be socially retarded. Apparently, the early part of their lives, when they ordinarily would have interacted with their mothers and young monkeys, was a critical period for acquiring social skills. They may learn them later on, but only with difficulty.

CONTINGENCY TRAPS

One limitation of learning stems from peculiarities in the ways organisms are affected by reinforcement contingencies. In discussions of instrumental conditioning, psychologists often speak of R-S contingencies (see Chapters 2 and 4). That is, the occurrence of some event, S, is contingent upon the occurrence of some response, R. Usually, the stimulus in question is an event that occurs soon after the response. But the fact is that responses can have both immediate and remote consequences, and sometimes the nature of these conse-

quences differs. If a response has immediate reinforcing consequences, for instance, but delayed punishing consequences, we may
behave in nonadaptive ways. Such situations are often referred to as
social traps (Cross & Guyer, 1980), though a better term might be
contingency traps, since it is the discrepant contingencies that form
the essence of the phenomenon.

The most widely cited example of a contingency trap is cigarette
smoking. The immediate consequences of smoking are, for the
smoker at least, reinforcing. Tobacco contains nicotine, a stimulant.
Moreover, there are social rewards for smoking: It is often a shared
activity; it gives one something to do with one's hands in awkward
social situations; it allows one to conform to the images of desirable
people in cigarette ads; and so on. There are, however, much less
desirable consequences of smoking: emphysema, lung cancer, stroke,
and other diseases. Obviously, these important negative consequences ought to outweigh the positive consequences: Looking
"cool" ought to be less reinforcing than staying alive. Yet many people smoke despite the fact that they know of its harmful effects. Why?

The explanation seems to be that immediate, high-probability
consequences outweigh remote, low-probability consequences. In the
case of smoking, the desirable consequences occur right away and are
almost certain; the undesirable consequences, by contrast, are more
distant (one doesn't die of cancer after smoking one cigarette) and
less certain (not everyone who smokes gets cancer). These are the
essential ingredients of contingency traps.

Contingency traps also help explain why people perform unsafe
acts, such as driving a car at excessive speeds. The reinforcing consequences (the excitement of driving fast, the fact that the driver
thereby resembles the attractive people in automobile ads) are immediate and certain, while the aversive consequences (having an accident) are unlikely to occur during any given ride. The same explanation seems to account for the tendency of workers to take
unnecessary chances on the job. One should never stand on the top
of a ladder, for example, yet people sometimes do, simply because
they usually get away with it (see Chance, 1981).

The implications of the frequency of such irrational behavior are
grim. Studies have indicated that the use of various drugs, including
alcohol and tobacco, by pregnant women can be injurious to their
unborn children. Smoking during pregnancy results in lower IQs of
the offspring, presumably by interfering with the neurological development of the fetus. Consumption of alcohol, especially during the

early stages of pregnancy, has even more devastating effects. These facts have been widely publicized in magazines and newspapers, yet one often sees pregnant women smoking or drinking. It is unlikely that these women would continue to smoke and drink if, upon doing so, they usually developed severe headaches. Nevertheless, they run the risk of far more aversive consequences (for themselves as well as for their children), apparently because the aversive consequences are uncertain and several months off, while the reinforcing consequences are certain and immediate.

In another kind of contingency trap, the problem is not the tendency to do something dangerous, but a *failure* to do something sensible. People often put off a visit to their physician, even though they have symptoms of what might be a serious illness, because such visits often produce discomfort and/or bad news, which are strongly aversive; by staying home, they avoid these events. The result is that people who have symptoms suggestive of a serious disease sometimes procrastinate until their discomfort has become severe. By this time, however, what might have been a curable disease may have become fatal.

Much more could be said about contingency traps (see, for example, Cross & Guyer, 1980; Hardin, 1968). For our purposes, the importance of contingency traps is that they interfere with learning. We often persist in nonadaptive and even self-injurious ways because of our tendency to be controlled more by immediate, high-probability events than by distant, low-probability events.

NONHERITABILITY OF LEARNED BEHAVIOR

Another limitation of learning is that learned behavior is not inherited. Reflexes and fixed action patterns are passed on from generation to generation, but behavior that is acquired through learning dies with the individual. This places a serious limitation on the ability of a species to benefit from experience, because it means that every individual is as ignorant at birth as its parents were when they were born. The lion cub must learn to stalk antelope just as its parents did; the rat must learn to avoid poisonous water; the child must learn to look for traffic before crossing streets.

The idea that learned behavior might be inherited has been thoroughly discredited and now seems quite absurd to most people. However, it wasn't so long ago that many people, including a number of scientists, believed that learning experiences might somehow benefit an organism's offspring. The idea grew out of a kind of evolutionary theory that preceded Darwin.

A French naturalist named Jean de Lamarck tried to account for the peculiarly adaptive physical features of many animals. The crane, for example, finds food by wading into shallow waters. How is it that the crane has such conveniently long legs, legs that ideally suit the bird to its habitat? Or take the giraffe, an animal that lives on the African plains where it feeds on the leaves of trees; were it not for its long neck, the giraffe would not be able to reach the highest leaves. How did the giraffe come by so sensible a physique? Lamarck, writing in the early 1800s, theorized that these and other physical characteristics were acquired adaptations that were passed on from generation to generation.

Consider the giraffe. Suppose the food supply is low, so that the giraffe has to stretch its neck in an effort to reach higher leaves. If the animal had to do this day after day, it might, Lamarck speculated, make a slight difference in the length of the giraffe's neck. If this slight change were inherited by the giraffe's offspring, then over the course of several hundred generations, the giraffe's neck might get longer and longer until it reached its present, very adaptive length. For Lamarck, evolution was the result of a given species' efforts at adapting to its environment.

The Lamarckian theory of evolution was replaced by Darwin's theory based on natural selection. But some scientists, most notably the eminent psychologist William McDougall, adopted a Lamarckian view of learned behavior. They argued that when experience modifies the behavior of an organism, it also modifies its genes in some way. This did not mean, of course, that if a person learned to read Latin, his or her offspring would be born knowing how to read Virgil. But McDougall and others did believe that, other things being equal, the offspring might have a slightly easier time mastering Latin than had the parent. McDougall was no armchair psychologist, and he spent years performing experiments to test his Lamarckian theory.

In a typical experiment, McDougall (1927, 1938) would train a number of rats to avoid electric shocks. Then he would train the offspring of these rats on the same task, and so on for several generations. The idea was that each generation should inherit more and more skill until, after many generations, the offspring would learn to avoid shock much more easily than their progenitors had. McDougall's research convinced him that his hypothesis held true. Other scientists, though they respected McDougall's integrity, doubted his data. They ran similar experiments with better controls than McDougall had used and found no evidence that succeeding generations of animals learned a task any more readily than their forebears (see, for example, Agar et al., 1954).

The nonheritability of learning would seem to be the severest of all limitations on learning. Certainly, anyone who has had a difficult time mastering parallel parking or memorizing the forms of the French verb *to be* will agree that being able to benefit from the learning experiences of one's parents would be helpful. It is possible, however, that if we did inherit learned behavior, we would not be entirely happy with the results. Had our ancestors been born expert hunters and gatherers, for example, they might never have invented agriculture, one of the most important developments in the history of civilization. And if children inherited their parents' skills, each succeeding generation would probably have become more and more specialized. In the past 20 years, there have been dramatic changes in the social roles of men and women in Western societies. It seems unlikely that such changes would have been possible if, over the past million years, men and women had inherited the roles of their parents. Inherited learning might also have slowed the advance of science. Had Copernicus been born *knowing* that the sun revolved about the earth, he might not have been able to develop the view that the earth revolves about the sun.

The value of learning is that it enables us to adapt to changes in our environment. If we inherited learned behavior that was once adaptive but no longer is, learning would be a hindrance. Yet it has to be admitted that the nonheritability of learning places severe limitations upon what any individual can learn in a lifetime.

PRACTICAL AND ETHICAL LIMITATIONS

A number of practical problems limit the value of learning. It is all very well to demonstrate in a laboratory that punishment suppresses behavior, and it is logical to conclude from such evidence that if criminal behavior were reliably and quickly followed by aversive events, the incidence of criminal behavior would fall almost to zero. The critical word, however, is *if*. Most criminal acts do not lead to the immediate arrest and conviction of the perpetrator. When conviction does result, it is often several months after the commission of the crime. So much for reliable and swift punishment.

Of course, punishment is not the only way of dealing with crime and other kinds of undesirable behavior. We might also use various forms of positive reinforcement. Police officers could give traffic citations for safe driving, citations that could be redeemed for cash or other prizes. State and federal governments could provide rebates to taxpayers who had *not* committed a crime in a given year, with bonuses to those who had gone 5 years without criminal activity. Such reinforcers might not alter the rate of violent crime such as assault, but they might result in a substantial reduction in other kinds of crime. But how does one solve the practical problem of getting taxpayers to pay now for benefits that will not be reaped for some time, if at all? (Here again we see the pernicious influence of contingency traps.)

We face the same sort of practical difficulties in other arenas. The therapist can use reinforcement principles to improve the self-image of a depressed client, but the therapist cannot control the events that occur in the client's natural environment, some of which will undermine the good effects of therapy. Institutionalization is one means of getting control over a person's environment, but this is an expensive option. And even institutional treatment has its limits, for once treatment is concluded, the client normally returns to the very same environment that produced the symptoms in the first place. This is also why efforts at the rehabilitation of drug abusers and criminals so often fail. Drug addicts, for example, may be removed from their natural environment, put into a therapeutic environment, taken off drugs, and taught various alternatives to drug use. But when they are released, they naturally go home; that is, they return to the same environment that produced their drug-use patterns (Chance, in press; Siegel, 1983). Those who do not relapse following release typically are those who avoid returning to the environment from which they came (Robins et al., 1974, 1975). One solution to the relapse problem, then, is to relocate rehabilitated addicts into new communities. But the cost of such an effort would be immense and would no doubt meet with resistance from a public that prefers to see such people returning to "their own kind." The point of all this is that while a study of learning principles suggests many concrete applications, there are practical problems that place restrictions upon the implementation of these principles.

There are also important ethical concerns that restrict the use of learning principles. For instance, it is possible to get around the difficulty of providing swift, certain punishment to law violators. Electronic surveillance devices are available and are now being used to keep tabs on those who have a record of criminal behavior. One device is a kind of ankle bracelet that sends out a signal to a surveillance team. The team knows where a subject is, though not what he or she is doing, every minute of the day. This does not, of course, prevent the subject from committing a crime, but if the subject were to commit a crime, the device would provide proof that he or she was at the scene at the time it was committed, and it would also aid in the person's capture. Removal of the device might be grounds for incarceration. Thus, such technologies help overcome certain practical limitations on the implementation of learning principles by greatly increasing the probability of punishment for misbehavior. But there is a catch. We cannot use such technology without invading the privacy of the individual under surveillance. Is this ethical? And if we decide that it is, how do we set limits upon its use? Do we electronically monitor criminals as an alternative to imprisonment? Do we monitor those who have served their sentences? Do we monitor those who have committed no offense but are judged to be in a "high-risk group" (i.e., likely to become criminals)?

Such questions arise in areas other than crime reduction. The treatment of the mentally ill, the education of children, the preservation of natural resources—all present ethical issues once we know how to use learning principles to modify behavior effectively. Some people worry that we are headed for a society in which some "Big Brother" monitors and controls our every move. Most psychologists feel that such concerns are unrealistic. In fact, it is likely that the dissemination of knowledge about the way the environment exerts control over behavior actually makes the prospects of a Brave New World *less* likely, since such knowledge gives the individual some protection against the abuse of these principles by governments, big businesses, and unscrupulous individuals. Nevertheless, the availability of a technology of behavior brings with it the need to wrestle with ethical questions concerning its use.

OVERADAPTABILITY

There is one final, paradoxical limitation of learning. The ability to learn is the ability to adapt to changing conditions, and no organism on earth is so adaptable as we human beings. Our plasticity—our tendency to be molded and remolded by the classical, instrumental, and vicarious experiences described in this text—is ordinarily viewed as a great boon. And so it is. Were it not for that great plasticity, civilization as we know it could not exist. What we are as individuals,

---

THE PRICE OF LEARNING

When Mark Twain (1917) was an apprentice pilot on a Mississippi steamboat, he found that learning to read the river took some doing. There were all sorts of stimuli, some indicating safe waters (S^Ds), others indicating danger ($S^\Delta s$). Navigating the river safely required a sophisticated level of stimulus discrimination. When Twain had mastered the task, he admitted that he had "made a valuable acquisition" (p. 78). But he had lost something too: "All the grace, the beauty, the poetry, had gone out of the majestic river! . . . that floating log means that the river is rising . . . ; that slanting mark on the water refers to a bluff reef which is going to kill somebody's steamboat one of these nights . . . ; those tumbling 'boils' show a dissolving bar and a changing channel there; the lines and circles in the slick water over yonder are a warning that that troublesome place is shoaling up dangerously; that silver streak in the shadow of the forest is the 'break' from a new snag . . ." (pp. 78–80). What had one been beautiful and romantic eyecatchers had turned into mere roadsigns!

The same sort of sophisticated discrimination may rob others as well. Does the astronomer see the same stars he viewed when he was a boy? Does the pianist hear Beethoven as she did before she spent hundreds of hours at the keys?

Learning gives us a great deal. But it may rob us as well.

---

as a society, and as a species depends greatly upon what we can learn. But that very ability to learn, to adapt to our environment, has its disadvantages.

Richard Powers (1971–1972) points out that we "endure the frustrations of subway or commuter trains, freeway driving . . . , ugliness, and smog. People in Tokyo, Japan allow others to push them so that they can be squeezed more 'economically' into commuter trains. . . . And Japanese traffic cops have to take regular breaks to breathe oxygen because the quality of air they breathe in the streets is so bad" (p. 103). Powers concludes that "all of these attempts to cope with unpleasant and dangerous conditions are discouraging in a very important way. They seem to suggest that no matter how miserable the living conditions, *people will adapt*" (p. 103, emphasis added).

The point is that we *learn* to endure such conditions. As Powers points out, if there were a sudden decline in the quality of life, we might do something about it. But as rapid as the changes are, they are still slow enough that we learn to cope with them. The world be-comes a little less beautiful, a little less friendly, a little sadder. And we adapt.

When people visit Southern California for the first time, they are often astonished by the smog. Why, they ask, do people tolerate such conditions? Part of the answer is that the smog didn't arrive over-night. The sky simply got a little grayer each day, and people learned to live with it. When people visit New York City for the first time, they are astounded by the security precautions that people take as a matter of routine. Often an apartment dweller will have a number of locks, bolts, and chains on each door, bars on the windows, and registration numbers on the TV set and other pieces of furniture. The visitor looks at this and wonders why people endure such conditions. Part of the answer is that the crime rate did not jump overnight. Your apartment is burglarized, so you put another lock on the door; some-one breaks into your neighbor's apartment through a window, so you follow their lead and put bars on all the windows. And so it goes, bit by bit, little by little, day by day.

We adapt. We learn to live with it, until one day we find our-selves driving in bumper-to-bumper traffic down a freeway at 20 miles an hour in smog so thick we cannot see 200 feet in front of us; or we find ourselves living in a city where we literally barricade our-selves in our home for protection. But if we were not so adept at learning, if we did not so readily adapt to the deterioration of our world, perhaps we might be better off. Perhaps we would design a better environment, a world without such intolerable conditions.

If only they *were* intolerable. The trouble is that we learn so well that we may adapt to increasingly adverse conditions. Our remark-able ability to learn can work against us, as well as for us.

SUMMARY

An understanding of learning is essential to an understanding of behavior, especially human behavior. There are, however, important limits on the ways in which learning can contribute to behavior.

The physical structure of an organism sets limits on what it can learn. Chimpanzees are apparently incapable of speech because of the nature of their vocal equipment.

The quality of an organism's nervous system affects what it can learn. It is not known precisely what chemical and/or anatomical properties make one nervous system better than another, but there is evidence that these properties are affected by both hereditary and environmental factors.

Another limitation on learning is the extent to which the organism is prepared to acquire some behavior. There seems to be a continuum of preparedness, with organisms being prepared to learn some things, unprepared to learn others, and contraprepared to learn still others. Preparedness has been demonstrated in a number of species, and there is some evidence of preparedness in humans.

There are certain critical periods during which certain kinds of behavior are particularly likely to be learned. Such periods appear to play an important role in social behavior and may be important in determining the sense of gender identity in humans.

Humans and animals tend to be more strongly affected by immediate, high-probability contingencies than by remote, low-probability contingencies. The result is a tendency to fall prey to contingency traps.

Learned behavior is not passed on to future generations, which means that each individual must learn many of the same skills acquired by its parents. This limits what any one individual can learn in its lifetime.

There are numerous practical and ethical limitations on the value of learning principles. While we may have the scientific skill to modify certain kinds of behavior through the use of learning principles, practical and ethical considerations may prevent us from making use of that knowledge.

Finally, the ability to learn may sometimes work against us. Human beings have an almost unlimited ability to adapt to adverse conditions. Were we not so adaptable, we might be more inclined to find ways of improving the conditions around us.

Some students read about the limits of learning, especially those with an organic origin, and conclude that learning is really of little importance after all. They decide that "It's really genetics that matters in behavior. Biology is destiny." But is it? In some sense, the answer is yes. Some behavior is largely, if not wholly, genetically determined. Like the behavior that emerges through instrumental conditioning, behavior emerges in a species as a result of the species' interactions with its environment. It is due to "the selective action of that environment during the evolution of the species" (Skinner, 1978, p. 97). Moreover, as we noted at the very beginning of this book, the ability to learn is itself a biologically evolved adaptation to the environment. In some sense, then, all behavior can be traced to biological forces, and those forces set limits upon what learning can accomplish.

We should not, however, lose sight of the value of an analysis of the way the environment affects behavior. The interactions of organisms with their environments are lawful, and understanding those laws is as useful as understanding the laws of genetics. To appreciate the importance of learning to the survival of hundreds of species, one need only consider what would happen if those species were to lose their ability to benefit from experience. In no species are the benefits more obvious than in humans. There is hardly any aspect of human existence, especially in industrialized societies, that could exist in its present form were humans less adept at learning.

No other species has accomplished so much as homo sapiens, and the credit goes to our ability to learn. But it is also true that no other species has put itself, and the fate of all other forms of life, in such peril, and the credit for that goes partly to our ability to learn. The foremost question before the world today is whether our species' formidable learning ability will ultimately do more harm than good. B. F. Skinner (1987), who has contributed so much to our understanding of learning, has expressed his doubts on this matter. He puts the question this way: "Can we," he asks, "create a culture that has the chance of a future before our present cultures destroy us?" (p. 50). It is a question that might have been asked hundreds of years ago. It is a question that may well be answered, one way or the other, in your lifetime.

REVIEW QUESTIONS

1. Define the following terms:

preparedness	autoshaping
overadaptability	critical period
imprinting	contingency trap

2. Sally buys a high-frequency whistle at a discount store. She attempts to train her dog to come on command using the whistle as a signal. She follows the correct conditioning procedures but is unsuccessful. What is the likely cause of the failure?

3. Explain why it is sometimes difficult to assess the intelligence of people who suffer from infantile paralysis and similar disorders.

4. Suppose that, because of its superior vision, a falcon can learn a discrimination task faster than a person. Mary believes this means the bird is smarter than the person. What reasons might she have for this idea?

5. Design a hypothetical experiment that would determine once and for all whether there are genetic differences in the learning abilities of men and women.

6. How might preparedness to learn be nonadaptive?

7. Explain the role of evolution in the findings of Garcia and Koelling.

8. In what sense might it be said that autoshaping represents preparedness to acquire a superstition?

9. Some people believe that it is important for a human infant to have intimate contact with the mother during the first few hours after birth (rather than being hurried off to a nursery). How could you determine if there is a critical period for the formation of a human-infant bond?

10. Describe a contingency trap that has "caught" you. Do not use any of the examples provided in the chapter.

11. Explain how whole societies can fall prey to contingency traps. Give an example.

12. Suppose you had inherited everything your parents and grandparents knew. How would you be different? Overall, would you be better off? Explain why or why not.

13. Identify a social problem not mentioned in this chapter that might, except for practical difficulties, be easily solved through the application of learning principles. Explain briefly what those difficulties are.

14. Many people see nothing wrong with punishing misbehavior, but object to reinforcing desirable behavior. They consider such use of reinforcement manipulative. What is the flaw in their logic?

15. A visitor to New York complained about the noise of the city. Her host replied, "Oh, you get used to it." Is the host better off adapting to the city, or would she be better off if she were not so adaptable? Justify your answer.

16. How could you determine whether humans really are biologically prepared to learn language? Would ethical problems prevent you from performing the experiment?

17. Roger McIntire (1973) recommends that people be required to undergo training in child-rearing before being allowed to have

children. What support for his position can you draw from the research of Harlow and Harlow?

18. What would it take to make our judicial system an effective instrument for reducing crime?

19. Explain why it would be desirable to have political leaders who understand basic learning principles.

20. What protection could the public have against the abuse of learning principles by political leaders?

SUGGESTED READINGS

Much of the discussion of the limits of learning has to do with biological factors. E. O. Wilson's *On Human Nature* (1978) deals with some of these issues. One of the classic works on the limits of learning is *Biological Boundaries of Learning*, edited by Martin Seligman and Joanne Hager (1972a). For a much briefer and less technical account, see Seligman and Hager (1972b).

For more on contingency traps, see *Social Traps* by John Cross and Melvin Guyer (1980).

Glossary

ABA design   A type of single subject research design in which behavior is observed before, during, and after an experimental manipulation.

Adventitious reinforcement   The coincidental occurrence of a reinforcer following a response.

Attentional processes   In Bandura's theory of vicarious learning, any activity by an observer that aids in the observation of relevant aspects of a model's behavior and its consequences.

Autoshaping   A procedure in which a stimulus is followed by a reinforcer regardless of what the organism does. The procedure often results in the shaping of superstitious behavior that the organism is biologically prepared to learn.

Backward conditioning   A classical conditioning procedure in which the US precedes the CS.

Baseline period   In an ABA design, the period of observation before experimental manipulation.

Behavioral economics   See experimental economics.

Blocking   Failure of a stimulus to become a CS when it is part of a compound stimulus that includes an effective CS.

CER   Abbreviation for conditioned emotional response.

Chaining   Establishing a sequence, or chain, of responses, the last of which is reinforced.

Chain schedule   A reinforcement schedule in which a response is under the control of two or more schedules, but reinforcement is delivered only upon completion of the last schedule.

Classical conditioning   See Pavlovian conditioning.

Compound stimulus   Two or more stimuli presented simultaneously, often as a CS.

Concept   Any class or group whose members share one or more defining features.

Concurrent schedule   A reinforcement schedule in which two or more schedules are available at once.

Conditional reflex   A reflex acquired through experience. Consists of a CS and a CR. (Cf. unconditional reflex.)

Conditional response   The response part of a conditional reflex. The CR is elicited by a CS. Often called conditioned response.

Conditional stimulus   The stimulus part of a conditional reflex. The CS elicits a CR. Often called conditioned stimulus.

Conditioned emotional response A classically conditioned emotional reaction due to pairing a neutral stimulus with an emotion-eliciting stimulus. When the emotion involved is positive (e.g., joy), there is an increase in the rate of ongoing behavior, called conditioned facilitation; when the emotion is negative (e.g., fear), there is a decrease in ongoing behavior, called conditioned suppression.

Conditioned facilitation See conditioned emotional response.

Conditioned suppression See conditioned emotional response.

Conditioned taste aversion An aversion, acquired through Pavlovian conditioning, to a food with a particular flavor.

Context theory Theory of forgetting that attributes forgetting to differences between the situation in which the response is learned and the situation in which recall is tested. Also called stimulus change theory.

Contiguity Nearness in time (temporal contiguity) or space (spatial contiguity).

Contingency Dependency between events. (Cf. stimulus contingency, response contingency.)

Contingency trap A response contingency in which a response has immediate consequences that are different from (sometimes the opposite of) the delayed consequences. Heretofore called a social trap, but need not be social.

Continuous reinforcement A reinforcement schedule in which a particular response is always reinforced. (Cf. intermittent reinforcement.)

Continuum of preparedness The hypothetical range in an organism's predisposition to learn various responses. The organism is said to come to a situation biologically prepared to learn, unprepared to learn, or contraprepared to learn.

Covert rehearsal In Bandura's theory of vicarious learning, any attempt to rehearse or act out modeled behavior without overtly performing the behavior.

CR Abbreviation for conditional response.

CRF Abbreviation for continuous reinforcement.

Critical period A period in the development of an organism during which it is especially likely to acquire a particular response.

CS Abbreviation for conditional stimulus.

CS+ In Pavlovian discrimination training, the stimulus that is regularly paired with a US. (Cf. CS−.)

CS− In Pavlovian discrimination training, the stimulus that regularly appears in the absence of the US. (Cf. CS+.)

Cue-dependent forgetting Forgetting that occurs because of the absence of cues that were present during learning.

Cumulative record A graphic record of responses over time. Changes in the slope of the resulting curve indicate changes in the response rate, which in turn reflect learning.

Cumulative recorder An apparatus that records every occurrence of a particular response. The record produced is a cumulative record.

Delayed conditioning   A classical conditioning procedure in which the neutral stimulus starts before, and then overlaps with, the US.

Delayed matching to sample   A method of testing for forgetting in which an organism is reinforced for responding to a stimulus that matches a stimulus (the sample) after a predetermined delay period.

Deprivation   A hypothetical state due to the withholding of a given reinforcer, such as food, for a given period of time.

Discrimination   The tendency for learned behavior to occur in the presence of stimuli present during training, but not in the presence of stimuli absent during training. (Cf. generalization.)

Discrimination training   A procedure for establishing a discrimination. In Pavlovian conditioning, it consists of presenting the CS+ with the US and presenting a CS− alone. In instrumental conditioning, it consists of reinforcing a response in the presence of an S^D, but not in the presence of an S^Δ.

Discriminative stimulus   In instrumental conditioning, any stimulus that indicates either that a response will be reinforced (an S^D) or that a response will be punished or go unreinforced (an S^Δ).

Disuse, theory of   See theory of disuse.

Drive   A physiological state (such as hunger) caused by a period of deprivation (as of food).

Drive-reduction theory   The theory of reinforcement that attributes a reinforcer's effectiveness to the reduction of a drive state.

Endogenous   Inherited. Literally, in the genes. (Cf. exogenous.)

Equilibrium theory   The theory of reinforcement that attributes a reinforcer's effectiveness in restoring a state of balance in the organism's activities.

Errorless discrimination training   A procedure by which discrimination is achieved with few or no errors.

Excitatory gradient   A generalization gradient showing an increased tendency to respond to the S^D or CS+ and stimuli resembling them.

Exogenous   Not genetic. Literally, outside of the genes. (Cf. endogenous.)

Experimental economics   The use of reinforcement schedules as a model for studying economic principles. Also called behavioral economics.

Experimental neurosis   Any bizarre or neurotic-like behavior induced through an experimental procedure.

Extinction   (1) In classical conditioning, the weakening of a CR with repeated presentation of the CS alone. (2) In instrumental conditioning, the weakening of a response by withholding the reinforcer that normally follows that response. Often confused with forgetting.

Extinction method   Method of measuring forgetting by comparing extinction of a response after a retention interval.

FI schedule   Abbreviation for fixed interval schedule.

Fixed action pattern   Any innate series of fairly complex, interrelated acts. Formerly called instinct. (Cf. inherited behavior trait.)

Fixed interval schedule A form of intermittent reinforcement in which a specified period of time must elapse between reinforced responses. (Cf. variable interval schedule.)

Fixed ratio schedule A form of intermittent reinforcement in which every *n*th response is reinforced. (Cf. variable ratio schedule.)

Forgetting A change in learned response following lack of opportunity to make the response. Usually implies a failure to make a response after an interval of time following training. Often confused with extinction.

Free recall method Method of measuring forgetting by requiring subject to produce a response after a retention interval. (Cf. prompted recall.)

FR schedule Abbreviation for fixed ratio schedule.

Frustration hypothesis The hypothesis that extinction phenomena can be attributed to frustration caused by nonreinforcement of previously reinforced behavior.

Generalization The tendency for learned behavior to occur in the presence of stimuli that were not present during training. (Cf. discrimination.)

Generalization gradient Any graphic representation of generalization.

Goldiamond's paradox The principle that in order for bizarre behavior to be reinforced, it must sometimes occur on occasions when it cannot be reinforced. Named after Israel Goldiamond.

Group design A research design in which a researcher provides some subjects (the experimental group) with a particular experience and compares their behavior with that of similar subjects (the control group) that have not had that experience.

Habituation A reduction in the strength of a reflex response brought about by repeated exposure to a stimulus that elicits that response.

Higher-order conditioning A classical conditioning procedure in which a neutral stimulus is paired with a well-established CS.

Imprinting The tendency of some animals, particularly birds, to follow the first moving objects they see after birth, usually their mothers.

Inherited behavior trait Any genetically based behavioral tendency. (Cf. fixed action pattern.)

Inhibitory gradient Generalization gradient showing a decreased tendency to respond to the S^D or CS$-$ and stimuli resembling them. (Cf. excitatory gradient.)

Instinct See fixed action pattern.

Instrumental conditioning Any procedure by which a response becomes more or less likely to occur, depending upon its consequences. Also called operant conditioning.

Interference theory Theory that attributes forgetting to the learning of responses that interfere with the response in question.

Intermittent schedule Any of several reinforcement schedules in which a response is sometimes reinforced. Also called partial reinforcement. (Cf. continuous reinforcement.)

Interstimulus interval   The interval between the CS and the US.

Intertrial interval   The interval separating the trials of any conditioning procedure.

ISI   Abbreviation for interstimulus interval.

ITI   Abbreviation for intertrial interval.

Latent inhibition   The tendency of a stimulus not to become a CS following its repeated appearance in the absence of a US.

Law of Effect   The principle that the probability of an operant response depends upon its effect on the environment.

Learned helplessness   The failure to escape an aversive stimulus following exposure to an aversive stimulus under circumstances that made escape impossible.

Learning   A relatively enduring change in behavior due to experience.

Matched sampling   Technique for reducing extraneous differences among subjects by matching those in the experimental and control groups on specified characteristics, such as age, sex, and weight.

Matching law   The principle that, given two or more concurrent schedules, the rate of responding on each schedule will match the rate of reinforcement on each schedule.

Mnemonic   Technique for improving recall.

Multiple schedule   A reinforcement schedule in which a response is under the control of two or more schedules, each associated with a particular stimulus.

Negative reinforcement   A reinforcement procedure in which a response is followed by the removal of, or a decrease in the intensity of, a stimulus. (Cf. positive reinforcement.)

Negative reinforcer   The stimulus that reinforces a response in negative reinforcement.

Observational learning   See vicarious conditioning.

Operant conditioning   See instrumental conditioning.

Operant behavior   Behavior mediated by striated muscles. Often referred to as willful, or voluntary, behavior, to distinguish it from innate behavior, especially reflexes. (Cf. respondent behavior.)

Overlearning   Continuing training trials beyond the point required to produce one errorless performance.

Overshadowing   Failure of a stimulus that is part of a compound stimulus to become a CS. The stimulus is said to be overshadowed by the stimulus that does become a CS. (Cf. blocking.)

Paired associate learning   A learning task involving pairs of words or other stimuli. The subject is presented with the first item of each pair and is expected to produce the second item.

Partial reinforcement   See intermittent schedule of reinforcement.

Partial reinforcement effect   The tendency of a response to be more resistant to extinction following partial reinforcement than following continuous reinforcement.

Pavlovian conditioning   Any procedure by which a neutral stimulus comes to elicit a response by being paired with a stimulus that regularly elicits that response. Also called classical, or respondent, conditioning.

Peak shift   The tendency following discrimination training for the peak of responding in a generalization gradient to shift away from the CS+ or S^D.

Positive reinforcement   A reinforcement procedure in which a response is followed by the presentation of, or an increase in the intensity of, a stimulus. (Cf. negative reinforcement.)

Positive reinforcer   The stimulus that reinforces a response in positive reinforcement.

Postreinforcement pause   A pause in responding following reinforcement; associated primarily with FI and FR schedules.

Premack Principle   The principle that high-probability behavior will reinforce low-probability behavior. Named after David Premack.

Preparatory response theory   Theory of Pavlovian conditioning that proposes that the CR prepares the organism for the occurrence of the US.

Preparedness   See continuum of preparedness.

Primary reinforcer   Any stimulus that is inherently reinforcing to all or nearly all members of a species. Examples include food and sexual stimulation. (Cf. secondary reinforcer.)

Proactive interference   Forgetting caused by learning that occurred prior to the response in question.

Prompt   A stimulus used to elicit a response. Also, the act of using a prompt to elicit a forgotten response.

Prompted recall   Method of measuring forgetting by presenting prompts. (Cf. free recall.)

Pseudoconditioning   The tendency of a neutral stimulus to elicit a CR when presented after a US has elicited a reflex response. Apparently due to sensitization.

Psychosomatic illness   Any organic disorder due partly or wholly to experience.

Punishment   The procedure of decreasing the probability of a response by following it with a punisher, usually an aversive stimulus.

Random assignment   Assignment of subjects to an experimental or control group in a random (nonsystematic) way.

Ratio strain   Disruption of the pattern of responding due to stretching the ratio of reinforcement too abruptly.

Reflex   Any simple, innate, involuntary reaction to a specific event. (Cf. reflex arc.)

Reflex arc   The anatomical structures through which a reflex is mediated. Consists at a minimum of receptors, sensory neurons, interneurons, motor neurons, and effectors (muscles or glands).

Regression   In psychoanalytic theory, the tendency to return to more primitive forms of behavior. (Cf. resurgence.)

Reinforcement   The procedure of increasing the probability of a response by following it with a reinforcer.

Relative value theory   Theory of reinforcement that considers reinforcers to be responses rather than stimuli and that attributes a reinforcer's effectiveness to its probability relative to other responses.

Relearning method   A method of measuring forgetting by resuming training after a retention interval. The more training required to achieve an earlier level of performance, the greater the amount of forgetting.

Releaser   Any stimulus that reliably elicits a fixed action pattern.

Respondent behavior   Behavior mediated by smooth muscles or glands. Often described as involuntary. (Cf. operant behavior.)

Respondent conditioning   See Pavlovian conditioning.

Response   Any specific action, or set of actions, performed by muscles or glands.

Response contingent   Depending upon the occurrence of a response. A response-contingent event occurs if and only if a particular response occurs.

Response cost   A type of punishment in which a response is followed by the removal of a positive reinforcer.

Resurgence   The reappearance of previously reinforced behavior during the extinction of more recently reinforced behavior. (Cf. regression.)

Retention interval   The time between training and testing for forgetting.

Retentional processes   In Bandura's theory of vicarious learning, any activity by an observer that aids recall of modeled behavior. Examples include covert rehearsal and symbolic coding.

Retroactive interference   Forgetting caused by learning that occurred subsequent to the response in question.

S^D Any stimulus that indicates that a particular response will be reinforced.

S^Δ Any stimulus that indicates that a particular response will either be punished or go unreinforced.

Satiation   The point at which a previously effective primary reinforcer is no longer an effective reinforcer.

Schedule of reinforcement   The schedule by which a particular response is reinforced.

Secondary reinforcer   Any stimulus that has acquired its reinforcing properties through association with other reinforcers. (Cf. primary reinforcer.)

Semantic generalization   Generalization based on the meaning of a stimulus rather than its physical properties.

Sensitization   The tendency of a weak stimulus to elicit a reflex response following the presentation of a strong stimulus.

Sensory preconditioning   A procedure in which two neutral stimuli are paired, after which one is paired with a US. The stimulus that is not paired with the US nevertheless sometimes elicits a CR.

Sequential theory   Theory that attributes extinction effects to the sequence of reinforced and nonreinforced responses prior to extinction.

Shaping   An instrumental conditioning procedure in which successive approximations of a desired response are reinforced.

Simultaneous conditioning   A classical conditioning procedure in which the neutral stimulus and US occur together in time.

Single subject design   A research design in which each subject's behavior is observed before and after an experimental treatment. Thus, each subject serves as both an experimental and control subject.

Size constancy   The apparent constancy of the size of an object whether it is nearby or far away.

Social trap   See contingency trap.

Spatial contiguity   The distance in space between two events. (Cf. temporal contiguity.)

Spontaneous recovery   The sudden reappearance of a learned response following extinction.

State-dependent learning   Learning that occurs during a particular physiological state (such as alcoholic intoxication) and is lost when that physiological state passes.

Stimulus   Any event that affects, or is capable of affecting, behavior.

Stimulus change theory   See context theory.

Stimulus contingent   Depending upon the occurrence of a stimulus. A stimulus-contingent event occurs if and only if a particular stimulus occurs.

Stimulus event   See stimulus.

Stimulus substitution theory   In Pavlovian conditioning, the theory that the CS substitutes for the US. Assumes that the CR is essentially the same as the UR. Now largely discredited.

Stretching the ratio   Gradually increasing the number of responses required for reinforcement.

Superstitious behavior   Any operant behavior due to adventitious reinforcement.

Symbolic coding   In Bandura's theory of vicarious learning, a retentional process in which the model's behavior is represented in some way.

Temporal contiguity   Distance in time separating two events. (Cf. spatial contiguity.)

Test trials   In Pavlovian conditioning, the procedure of presenting the CS on some occasions without the US to determine if learning has occurred.

Thinking   Behavior, but especially covert behavior such as inaudible speech and imaging.

Theory of disuse   Theory that attributes forgetting to the passage of time. Now largely discredited.

Trace conditioning   A classical conditioning procedure in which the neutral stimulus begins and ends before the US is presented.

Transposition The tendency, following discrimination training, to respond to any stimulus that resembles the S^D in its relationship to S^Δ.

Trial In conditioning, each presentation of the events that constitute the conditioning procedure. For example, in Pavlovian conditioning, each pairing of CS and US is one trial.

Unconditional reflex A synonym for reflex. The term was used by Pavlov to distinguish between innate and acquired reflexes. Often called "unconditioned reflex." (Cf. conditional reflex.)

Unconditional response The response part of an unconditional reflex. The UR is elicited by a US. Often called unconditioned response.

Unconditional stimulus The stimulus part of an unconditional reflex. The US elicits a UR. Often called unconditioned stimulus.

UR Abbreviation for unconditional response.

US Abbreviation for unconditional stimulus.

Variable interval schedule A form of intermittent reinforcement schedule in which, on the average, a specific period of time must elapse between reinforced responses. (Cf. fixed interval schedule.)

Variable ratio schedule A form of intermittent schedule in which, on the average, every nth response is reinforced. (Cf. fixed ratio reinforcement.)

VI Abbreviation for variable interval.

Vicarious classical conditioning Any procedure in which a subject observes as a model undergoes classical conditioning.

Vicarious conditioning Any procedure in which an organism learns through vicarious, as opposed to direct, experience.

Vicarious instrumental conditioning Any procedure in which a subject observes as a model undergoes instrumental conditioning.

VR Abbreviation for variable ratio.

Yoked control A control subject or group that is exposed to some of the same experiences as experimental subjects. An experimental subject may receive food each time it makes a particular response; a yoked control would also receive food at that moment, whether it made the response or not.

References

Agar, W. E., Drummond, F. H., Tiegs, O. W., & Gunson, M. M. Fourth (final) report on a test of McDougall's Lamarckian experiment on the training of rats. *Journal of Experimental Biology,* 1954, *31,* 307–321.

Alberts, E., & Ehrenfreund, D. Transposition in children as a function of age. *Journal of Experimental Psychology,* 1951, *41,* 30–38.

Alexander, T. Economics according to the rats. *Fortune,* December 1, 1980, 127–130, 132.

Alford, B. A. Behavioral treatment of schizophrenic delusions: A single-case experimental analysis. *Behavior Therapy,* 1986, *17,* 637–644.

American Heritage Dictionary. New York: American Heritage and Houghton Mifflin, 1971.

Amsel, A. The role of frustrative nonreward in continuous reward situations. *Psychological Bulletin,* 1958, *55,* 102–119.

Amsel, A. Frustrative nonreward in partial reinforcement and discrimination learning: Some recent history and theoretical extension. *Psychological Review,* 1962, *69,* 306–328.

Anderson, K. At first I was scared. *Time,* April 11, 1983, p. 27.

Axelrod, S. Introduction. In S. Axelrod & J. Apsche (Eds.), *The effects of punishment on human behavior.* New York: Academic Press, 1983.

Ayllon, T. Intensive treatment of psychotic behavior by stimulus satiation and food reinforcement. *Behavior Research and Therapy,* 1963, *1,* 53–61.

Azrin, N. H., Hutchinson, R. R., & Hake, D. F. Extinction-induced aggression. *Journal of the Experimental Analysis of Behavior,* 1966, *9,* 191–204.

Bachrach, A. J., Erwin, W. J., & Mohr, J. P. The control of eating behavior in an anorexic by operant conditioning techniques. In L. P. Ullmann & L. Krasner (Eds.), *Case studies in behavior modification.* New York: Holt, Rinehart & Winston, 1965.

Bachrach, A. J., *Psychological research: An introduction.* New York: Random House, 1962.

Baenninger, R. & Ulm, R. R. Overcoming the effects of prior punishment on inter-species aggression in the rat. *Journal of Comparative and Physiological Psychology,* 1969, *69,* 628–635.

Bahrick, H. P. Semantic memory content in permastore: Fifty years of memory for Spanish learned in school. *Journal of Experimental Psychology: General,* 1984, *113,* 1–29.

Bandura, A. Vicarious processes: A case of no-trial learning. In L. Berkowitz (Ed.), *Advances in experimental social psychology* (Vol. 2). New York: Academic Press, 1965.

Bandura, A. Analysis of modeling processes. In A. Bandura (Ed.), *Psychological modeling: Conflicting theories*. Chicago: Aldine-Atherton, 1971. (a)

Bandura, A. (Ed.) *Psychological modeling: Conflicting theories*. Chicago: Aldine-Atherton, 1971. (b)

Bandura, A. *Social learning theory*. New York: General Learning Press, 1971.(c)

Bandura, A. *Aggression: A social learning analysis*. Englewood Cliffs, NJ: Prentice-Hall, 1973.

Bandura, A. *Social learning theory*. Englewood Cliffs, NJ: Prentice-Hall, 1977.

Bandura, A., & Menlove, F. L. Factors determining vicarious extinction of avoidance behavior through symbolic modeling. *Journal of Personality and Social Psychology*, 1968, *8*, 99–108.

Bandura, A. & Rosehthal, T. L. Vicarious classical conditioning as a function of arousal level. *Journal of Personality and Social Psychology*, 1966, *3*, 54–62.

Bandura, A., Ross, D., & Ross, S. A. Vicarious reinforcement and imitative learning. *Journal of Abnormal and Social Psychology*, 1963, *67*, 601–607.

Bandura, A., & Walters, R. H. *Social learning and personality development*. New York: Holt, Rinehart & Winston, 1963.

Barnett, P. E., & Benedetti, D. T. *A study in 'vicarious conditioning.'* Paper presented at the annual meeting of the Rocky Mountain Psychological Association, Glenwood Springs, CO, May 1960.

Baum, W. M. Time allocation in human vigilance. *Journal of the Experimental Analysis of Behavior*, 1975, *23*, 43–53.

Berger, S. M. Conditioning through vicarious instigation. *Psychological Review*, 1962, *69*, 450–466.

Berger, S. M. Observer perseverance as related to a model's success: A social comparison analysis. *Journal of Personality and Social Psychology*, 1971, *19*, 341–350.

Berkowitz, L. Aggressive cues in aggressive behavior and hostility catharsis. *Psychological Review*, 1964, *71*, 104–122.

Berkowitz, L. Aversively stimulated aggression: Some parallels and differences in research with animals and humans. *American Psychologist*, 1983, *38*, 1135–1144.

Bernstein, I. L. Learned taste aversion in children receiving chemotherapy. *Science*, 1978, *200*, 1302–1303.

Blough, D. S. Delayed matching in the pigeon. *Journal of the Experimental Analysis of Behavior*, 1959, *2*, 151–160.

Bower, G. H. Analysis of a mnemonic device. *American Scientist*, 1970, *58*, 496–510.

Bower, G. H., Monteiro, K. P., & Gilligan, S. G. Emotional mood as a context for learning and recall. *Journal of Verbal Learning and Verbal Behavior*, 1978, *17*, 573–585.

Bower, G. H. & Hilgard, E. R. *Theories of learning* (5th ed.). Englewood Cliffs, NJ: Prentice-Hall, 1981.

Boyle, M. E., & Greer, R. D. Operant procedures and the comatose patient. *Journal of Applied Behavior Analysis*, 1983, *16*, 3–12.

Brady, J. V. Motivational-emotional factors and the intracranial self-stimulation. In D. Sheer (Ed.), *Electrical stimulation of the brain*. Austin: University of Texas Press, 1961.

Brady, J. V. Toward a behavioral biology of emotion. In L. Levi (Ed.), *Emotions: Their parameters and measurement*. New York: Raven Press, 1975.

Braginsky, B. M., Braginsky, D. D., & Ring, K. *Methods of madness: The mental hospital as a last resort*. New York: Holt, Rinehart & Winston, 1971.

Bransford, J. D. *Human cognition: Learning, understanding and remembering*. Belmont, CA: Wadsworth, 1979.

Braun, H. W., & Geiselhart, R. Age differences in the acquisition and extinction of the conditioned eyelid response. *Journal of Experimental Psychology*, 1959, *57*, 386–388.

Breland, K., & Breland, M. The misbehavior of organisms. *American Psychologist*, 1961, *16*, 681–684.

Bridger, W. H. Sensory habituation and discrimination in the human neonate. *American Journal of Psychiatry*, 1961, *117*, 991–996.

Brogden, W. J. Sensory pre-conditioning. *Journal of Experimental Psychology*, 1939, *25*, 323–332.

Brower, L. P. Prey coloration and predator behavior. In V. Dethier (Ed.), *Topics in animal behavior, topics in the study of life: The BIO source book, part 6*. New York: Harper & Row, 1971.

Brown, J. S. Factors determining conflict reactions in different discriminations. *Journal of Experimental Psychology*, 1942, *31*, 272–292.

Brown, P. L., & Jenkins, H. M. Auto-shaping of the pigeon's key-peck. *Journal of the Experimental Analysis of Behavior*, 1968, *11*, 1–8.

Brown, R. *Social psychology*. New York: Free Press, 1965.

Bruner, A., & Revusky, S. H. Collateral behavior in humans. *Journal of the Experimental Analysis of Behavior*, 1961, *4*, 349–350.

Bruner, J. S., Goodnow, J. J., & Austin, G. A. *A study of thinking*. New York: John Wiley, 1956.

Bruner, J. S., & Postman, L. J. On the perception of incongruity: A paradigm. *Journal of Personality*, 1949, *18*, 206–223.

Burgess, K. The behavior and training of a killer whale (*Orcinus orca*) at San Diego Sea World. *International Zoo Yearbook*, 1968, *8*, 202–205.

Burish, T. G., & Carey, M. P. Conditioned aversive response in cancer chemotherapy patients: Theoretical and developmental analysis. *Journal of Consulting and Clinical Psychology*, 1986, *54*, 593–600.

Capaldi, E. J. A sequential hypothesis of instrumental learning. In K. W. Spence & J. T. Spence (Eds.), *The psychology of learning and motivation* (Vol. 1). New York: Academic Press, 1967.

Capaldi, E. J. Memory and learning: A sequential viewpoint. In W. K. Honig & P. H. R. James (Eds.), *Animal Memory*. New York: Academic Press, 1971.

Capehart, J., Viney, W., & Hulicka, I. M. The effect of effort upon extinction. *Journal of Consulting and Clinical Psychology*, 1958, *51*, 505–507.

Carr, A. Adaptive aspects of the scheduled travel of *Chelonia*. In R. M. Storm (Ed.), *Animal orientation and navigation*, pp. 35-55. Corvallis: Oregon State University Press, 1967.

Catania, A. C. Concurrent operants. In W. K. Honig (Ed.), *Operant Behavior: Areas of research and application*. New York: Appleton-Century-Crofts, 1966.

Cautela, J. R. The problem of backward conditioning. *Journal of Psychology*, 1965, *60*, 135–144.

Chance, P. Why people take chances. *WE*, January/February 1981, 10–12.

Chance, P. Life after head injury. *Psychology Today*, October 1986, 62–69.

Chance, P. Conditional addiction. *Psychology Today* (in press).

Cheney, C. D. Personal communication, August 21, 1978.

Church, R. N. Response suppression. In B. A. Campbell & R. M. Church (Eds.), *Punishment and aversive behavior*. New York: Appleton-Century-Crofts, 1969.

Coleman, E. B. Sequential interference demonstrated by serial reconstruction. *Journal of Experimental Psychology*, 1962, *64*, 46–51.

Cooley, C. H. *Human nature and the social order*. New York: Charles Scribner's Sons, 1902.

Cordes, C. Studies support learning in utero. *APA Monitor*, March 1984, 28.

Cross, J. G., & Guyer, M. J. *Social traps*. Ann Arbor: University of Michigan Press, 1980.

Cummins, R. A., Livesey, P. J. Evans, J. G. M., & Walsh, R. N. A developmental theory of environmental enrichment. *Science*, 1977, *197*, 692–694.

Cuny, H. [*Ivan Pavlov: the man and his theories*] (P. Evans, Trans.). Greenwich, CN: Fawcett World Library, 1962.

Darwin, C. *On the origin of species*. London: J. Murray, 1859.

Darwin, C. *The descent of man*. London: J. Murray, 1871.

Dentan, R. K. *The Semai: A nonviolent people of Malaya*. New York: Holt, Rinehart & Winston, 1968.

Descartes, R. *Discourse on method*. (L. J. Lafleur, Trans.). Indianapolis, IN: Bobbs-Merrill, 1960. (Originally published in 1637.)

Descartes, R. *Treatise of man*. (T. S. Hall., Trans.). Cambridge, MA: Harvard University Press, 1972. (Originally published in 1662.)

deVilliers, P. A. In W. K. Honig & J. E. R. Staddon (Eds.), *Handbook of operant behavior*. Englewood Cliffs, NJ: Prentice-Hall, 1977.

Dews, P. B. Some observations on an operant in the octopus. *Journal of the Experimental Analysis of Behavior*, 1959, *2*, 57–63.

Dorsey, M. F., Iwata, B. A., & McSween, T. E. Treatment of self-injurious behavior in profoundly retarded persons using a water mist. Unpublished manuscript, 1978.

Dworkin, B. R., & Miller, N. E. Failure to replicate visceral learning in the acute curarized rat preparation. *Behavioral Neuroscience*, 1986, *100*, 299–314.

Eaton, G. G. The social order of Japanese macaques. *Scientific American*, 1976, *234*(4), 96–106.

Ebbinghaus, H. *Memory, a contribution to experimental psychology.* (H. A. Ruger, Trans.). New York: Columbia University Press, 1913. (Originally published in 1885.)

Eiseley, L. *The immense journey.* New York: Vintage Press, 1957.

English, H. B., & English, A. C. *A comprehensive dictionary of psychological and psychoanalytic terms.* New York: David McKay, 1958.

Epstein, R. Resurgence of previously reinforced behavior during extinction. *Behavior Analyst Letters,* 1983, *3,* 391–397.

Epstein, R. Spontaneous and deferred imitation in the pigeon. *Behavioral Processes,* 1984, *9,* 347–354. (a)

Epstein, R. Simulation research in the analysis of behavior. *Behaviorism,* 1984, *12,* 41–59. (b)

Epstein, R. Extinction-induced resurgence: Preliminary investigation and possible application. *Psychological Record,* 1985, *35,* 143–153. (a)

Epstein, R. The positive side of reinforcement: A commentary on Balsam & Bondy (1983). *Journal of Applied Behavior Analysis,* 1985, *18,* 73–78. (b)

Epstein, R., Kirshnit, C., Lanza, R., & Rubin, L. Insight in the pigeon: Antecedents and determinants of an intelligent performance. *Nature,* 1984, *308,* 61–62.

Epstein, R., Lanza, R. P., & Skinner, B. F. "Self-awareness" in the pigeon. *Science,* 1981, *212,* 695–696.

Erikson, E. H. *Identity: Youth & crisis.* New York: W. W. Norton, 1968.

Estes, W. K. The statistical approach to learning theory. In E. Koch (Ed.), *Psychology: A study of a science* (Vol. 2). New York: McGraw-Hill, 1959.

Estes, W. K., & Skinner, B. F. Some quantitative properties of anxiety. *Journal of Experimental Psychology,* 1941, *29,* 390–400.

Eysenck, H. J. *Sex and personality.* Austin: University of Texas Press, 1976.

Ferster, C. B., & Culbertson, S. *Behavior principles.* (3rd ed.). Englewood Cliffs, NJ: Prentice-Hall, 1982.

Ferster, C. B., & Skinner, B. F. *Schedules of reinforcement.* New York: Appleton-Century-Crofts, 1957.

Fisher, J. L., & Harris, M. B. The effects of three model characteristics on imitation and learning. *Journal of Social Psychology,* 1976, *98,* 183–199.

Fisher, J., & Hinde, R. A. The opening of milk bottles by birds. *British Birds,* 1949, *42,* 347–357.

Freedman, D. G. *Human infancy: An evolutionary perspective.* Hillsdale, NJ: Erlbaum, 1974.

Freud, S. *[Totem and taboo.]* (A. A. Brill, Trans.). New York: Moffat Yard, 1918. (Originally published in 1913.)

Fujita, K. Acquisition and transfer of a higher-order conditional discrimination performance in the Japanese monkey. *Japanese Psychological Research,* 1983, *25,* 1–8.

Fuller, J. L., & Scott, J. P. Heredity and learning ability in infrahuman mammals. *Eugenics Quarterly,* 1954, *1,* 28–43.

Gagne, R. M. The retention of a conditioned operant response. *Journal of Experimental Psychology,* 1941, *29,* 296–305.

Gallup, G. G. Chimpanzees: Self-recognition. *Science*, 1970, *167*, 86–87.

Gallup, G. G. Self-awareness in primates. *American Scientist*, 1979, *67*, 417–421.

Gantt, W. H. Introduction. In I. P. Pavlov, [*Lectures on conditioned reflexes and psychiatry* (Vol. 2).] (W. H. Gantt, Trans.). New York: International Publishers, 1941.

Gantt, W. H. Conditional or conditioned, reflex or response. *Conditioned Reflex*, 1966, *1*, 69–74.

Garb, J. L., & Stunkard, A. J. Taste aversion in man. *American Journal of Psychiatry*, 1974, *131*, 1204–1207.

Garcia, J. Tilting at the paper mills of academe. *American Psychologist*, 1981, *36*, 149–158.

Garcia, J., Clarke, J., & Hankins, W. G. Natural responses to scheduled rewards. In P. P. G. Bateson & P. Klopfer (Eds.), *Perspectives in ethology*. New York: Plenum Press, 1973.

Garcia, J., Kimeldorf, D. J., & Koelling, R. A. A conditioned aversion towards saccharin resulting from exposure to gamma radiation. *Science*, 1955, *122*, 157–158.

Garcia, J., & Koelling, R. A. Relation of cue to consequence in avoidance learning. *Psychonomic Science*, 1966, *4*, 123–124.

Gardner, R. A., & Gardner, B. T. Teaching sign language to a chimpanzee. *Science*, 1969, *165*, 664–672.

Gaudet, C. L., & Fenton, M. B. Observational learning in three species of insectivorous bats (*chiroptera*). *Animal Behavior*, 1984, *32*(2), 385–388.

Girden, E., & Culler, E. A. Conditioned responses in curarized striate muscle in dogs. *Journal of Comparative Psychology*, 1937, *23*, 261–274.

Gleitman, H. Forgetting of long-term memories in animals. In W. K. Honig & P. H. R. James (Eds.), *Animal memory*. New York: Academic Press, 1971.

Gleitman, H., & Bernheim, J. W. Retention of fixed-interval performance in rats. *Journal of Comparative and Physiological Psychology*, 1963, *56*, 839–841.

Gleitman, H., & Holmes, P. Retention of completely learned CER in rats. *Psychonomic Science*, 1967, *7*, 19–20.

Gleitman, H., Wilson, W. A., Herman, M. M., & Rescorla, R. A. Massing and within-delay position as factors in delayed-response performance. *Journal of Consulting and Clinical Psychology*, 1963, *56*, 445–451.

Goldiamond, I. Insider-outsider problems: A constructional approach. *Rehabilitation Psychology*, 1975, *22*, 103–116.

Golding, W. *Lord of the flies*. New York: Putnam, 1962.

Gorn, G. J. The effects of music in advertising on choice behavior: A classical conditioning approach. *Journal of Marketing*, 1982, *46*, 94–101.

Grant, D. Cognitive factors in eyelid conditioning. *Psychophysiology*, 1973, *10*, 75–81.

Green, G., & Osborne, J. G. Does vicarious instigation provide support for observational learning theories? A critical review. *Psychological Bulletin*, 1985, *97*(1), 3–17.

Grether, W. H. Pseudo-conditioning without paired stimulation encountered in attempted backward conditioning. *Journal of Comparative Psychology,* 1938, *25,* 141–158.

Grissom, R. J., Suedfeld, P., & Vernon, J. Memory for verbal material: Effects of sensory deprivation. *Science,* 1962, *138,* 429–430.

Guthrie, E. R. *The psychology of learning* (rev. ed.). Gloucester, MA: Smith, 1960.

Guttman, N. Laws of behavior and facts of perception. In S. Koch (Ed.), *Psychology: A study of a science* (Vol. 5). New York: McGraw-Hill, 1963.

Guttman, N., & Kalish, H. I. Discriminability and stimulus generalization. *Journal of Experimental Psychology,* 1956, *51,* 79–88.

Hall, C. S. Emotional behavior in the rat. *Journal of Comparative Psychology,* 1937, *24,* 369–75.

Hall, J. F. *Classical conditioning and instrumental learning: A contemporary approach.* New York: Lippincott, 1976.

Hall, S. S. The brain branches out. *Science 85,* June 1985, pp. 72–74.

Haner, C. F., & Whitney, E. R. Empathic conditioning and its relation to anxiety level. *American Psychologist,* 1960, *15,* 493. (Abstract)

Hanson, H. M. Effects of discrimination training on stimulus generalization. *Journal of Experimental Psychology,* 1959, *58,* 321–334.

Hardin, G. The tragedy of the commons. *Science,* 1968, *162,* 1243–1248.

Harlow, H. F. The nature of love. *American Psychologist,* 1958, *13,* 673–685.

Harlow, H. F., & Harlow, M. K. The effect of rearing conditions on behavior. *Bulletin of the Menninger Clinic,* 1962, *26,* 213–224. (a)

Harlow, H. F., & Harlow, M. K. Social deprivation in monkeys. *Scientific American,* 1962, *207,* 136–146. (b)

Hayes, C. *The ape in our house.* New York: Harper & Row, 1951.

Hearst, E. Discrimination learning as the summation of excitation and inhibition. *Science,* 1968, *162,* 1303–1306.

Herbert, M. J., & Harsh, C. M. Observational learning by cats. *Journal of Comparative Psychology,* 1944, *37,* 81–95.

Herrnstein, R. J. Relative and absolute strength of response as a function of frequency of reinforcement. *Journal of the Experimental Analysis of Behavior,* 1961, *4,* 267–272.

Herrnstein, R. J. Superstition: A corollary of the principle of operant conditioning. In W. K. Honig (Ed.), *Operant behavior: Areas of research and application.* New York: Appleton-Century-Crofts, 1966.

Herrnstein, R. J. On the law of effect. *Journal of the Experimental Analysis of Behavior,* 1970, *13,* 243–266.

Herrnstein, R. J., Loveland, D. H., & Cable, C. Natural concepts in pigeons. *Journal of Experimental Psychology: Animal Behavior Processes,* 1976, *2,* 285–311.

Hilgard, E. R. The nature of the conditioned response: I. The case for and against stimulus substitution. *Psychological Review,* 1936, *43,* 366–385.

Hilgard, E. R., & Humphreys, L. G. The retention of conditioned discrimination in man. *Journal of General Psychology,* 1938, *19,* 111–125.

Hilgard, E. R., & Marquis, D. G. Acquisition, extinction and retention of conditioned lid responses to light in dogs. *Journal of Comparative Psychology*, 1935, *19*, 29–58.

Hinde, R. A., & Fisher, J. Some comments on the re-publication of two papers on the opening of milk bottles in birds. In P. H. Klopfer & J. P. Hailman (Eds.), *Function and evolution of behavior*. Reading, MA: Addison-Wesley, 1972, 377–378.

Ho, B. T., Richards, D. W., & Chute, D. L. (Eds.). *Drug discrimination and state dependent learning*. New York: Academic Press, 1978.

Hoffman, H. S., Fleshler, M., & Jensen, P. Stimulus aspects of aversive controls: The retention of conditioned suppression. *Journal of the Experimental Analysis of Behavior*, 1963, *6*, 575–583.

Holland, J. C. Behaviorism: Part of the problem or part of the solution? *Journal of Applied Behavior Analysis*, 1978, *11*, 163–174.

Honig, W. K., & Urcuioli, P. J. The legacy of Guttman and Kalish (1956): Twenty-five years of research on stimulus generalization. *Journal of the Experimental Analysis of Behavior*, 1981, *36*, 405–445.

Hovland, C. I. The generalization of conditioned responses: I. The sensory generalization of conditioned responses with varying frequencies of tone. *Journal of General Psychology*, 1937, *17*, 125–148. (a)

Hovland, C. I. The generalization of conditioned responses: IV. The effects of varying amounts of reinforcement upon the degree of generalization of conditioned responses. *Journal of Experimental Psychology*, 1937, *21*, 261–276. (b)

Hull, C. L. The rat's speed-of-locomotion gradient in the approach to food. *Journal of Comparative Psychology*, 1934, *17*, 393–422.

Hull, C. L. *Principles of behavior*. New York: Appleton-Century-Crofts, 1943.

Hull, C. L. *Essentials of behavior*. New Haven, CT: Yale University Press, 1951.

Hull, C. L. *A behavior system*. New Haven, CT: Yale University Press, 1952.

Hunter, W. S. The delayed reaction in animals and children. *Behavior Monographs*, 1913, *2*, 1–86 (whole no. 1).

Hursh, S. R. Economic concepts for the analysis of behavior. *Journal of the Experimental Analysis of Behavior*, 1980, *34*, 219–238.

Hursh, S. R. Behavioral Economics, *Journal of Experimental Analysis of Behavior*, 1984, *42*, 435–452.

Huxley, A. *Ape and essence*. New York: Harper, 1948.

Jenkins, J. C., & Dallenbach, K. M. Obliviscence during sleep and waking. *American Journal of Psychology*, 1924, *35*, 605–612.

Jenkins, H. M., & Harrison, R. H. Effect of discrimination training on auditory generalization. *Journal of Experimental Psychology*, 1960, *59*, 246–253.

John, E. R., Chesler, P., Bartlett, F., & Victor, I. Observational learning in cats. *Science*, 1968, *159*, 1489–1491.

Joncich, G. *The sane positivist: A biography of Edward L. Thorndike*. Middleton, CN: Wesleyan University Press, 1968.

Jones, M. C. The elimination of children's fears. *Journal of Experimental Psychology*, 1924, *7*, 382–390. (a)

Jones, M. C. A laboratory study of fear: The case of Peter. *Pedagogical Seminary*, 1924, *31*, 308–315. (b)

Kamin, L. J. Predictability, surprise, attention and conditioning. In B. A. Campbell & R. M. Church (Eds.), *Punishment and aversive behavior*. New York: Appleton-Century-Crofts, 1969.

Kawamura, S. The process of sub-cultural propagation among Japanese macaques. In C. H. Southwick (Ed.) *Primate Social Behavior*. New York: Van Nostrand, 1963.

Keen, S. *Faces of the enemy*. New York: Harper & Row, 1986.

Keith-Lucas, T., & Guttman, N. Robust single-trial delayed backward conditioning. *Journal of Comparative and Physiological Psychology*, 1975, *88*, 468–476.

Kellogg, W. N. Communication and language in the home-raised chimpanzee. *Science*, 1968, *162*, 423–427.

Kettlewell, H. B. D. Darwin's missing evidence. *Scientific American*, 1959, *200*(3), 48–53.

Kimble, G. A. Conditioning as a function of the time between conditioned and unconditioned stimuli. *Journal of Experimental Psychology*, 1947, *37*, 1–15.

Kimble, G. A. *Hilgard and Marquis' conditioning and learning*. New York: Appleton-Century-Crofts, 1961.

Kleinknecht, R. A. The origins and remission of fear in a group of tarantula enthusiasts. *Behavioral Research and Therapy*, 1982, *20*, 437–443.

Köhler, W. *The mentality of apes* (2nd ed.). New York: Liveright, 1973. (Originally published in 1927.)

Köhler, W. Simple structural function in the chimpanzee and the chicken. In W. A. Ellis (Ed.), *A sourcebook of Gestalt psychology*. New York: Harcourt Brace, 1939.

Konorski, J. *Integrative activity of the brain*. Chicago: University of Chicago Press, 1967.

Krech, D., & Crutchfield, R. S. *Elements of psychology*. New York: Knopf, 1961.

Lacey, J. I., Smith, R. L., & Green, A. Use of conditioned autonomic responses in the study of anxiety. *Psychosomatic Medicine*, 1955, *17*, 208–217.

Lane, H. L., & Shinkman, P. G. Methods and findings in an analysis of a vocal operant. *Journal of the Experimental Analysis of Behavior*, 1963, *6*, 179–188.

Larsen, O. N., Gray, L. N., & Fortis, J. G. Achieving goals through violence on television. In O. N. Larsen (Ed.), *Violence and the mass media*. New York: Harper & Row, 1968.

Lashley, K. S. The mechanism of vision: I. A method of rapid analysis of pattern-vision in the rat. *Journal of Genetic Psychology*, 1930, *37*, 453–640.

Lashley, K. S., & Wade, M. The Pavlovian theory of generalization. *Psychological Review*, 1946, *53*, 72–87.

Layng, T. V. Joe, & Andronis, P. T. Toward a functional analysis of delusional speech and hallucinatory behavior. *The Behavior Analyst*, 1984, 7(2), 139–156.

Lenneberg, E. *The biological foundations of language*. New York: John Wiley, 1967.

Lenneberg, E. On explaining language. *Science*, 1969, *164*, 635–643.

Lepper, M. R., & Greene, D. Intrinsic motivation: How to turn play into work. *Psychology Today*, September 1976, 49–54.

Lepper, M. R., & Greene, D. *The hidden costs of reward: New perspectives on the psychology of human motivation*. Hillsdale, NJ: Erlbaum, 1978.

Lightfoot, L. O. Behavioral tolerance to low doses of alcohol in social drinkers. Unpublished Ph.D. thesis, Waterloo University, 1980.

Lindsay, P. H., & Norman, D. A. *Human information processing: An introduction to psychology*. New York: Academic Press, 1972.

Locke, J. *An essay concerning human understanding* (P. H. Nidditch, Ed.). Oxford, England: Clarendon Press, 1975. (Originally published in 1690.)

Logan, F. A. *Incentive*. New Haven, CN: Yale University Press, 1960.

Logue, A. W. Taste aversion and the generality of the laws of learning. *Psychological Bulletin*, 1979, *86*, 276–296.

Logue, A. W., Logue, K. R., & Strauss, K. E. The acquisition of taste aversion in humans with eating and drinking disorders. *Behavioral Research and Therapy*, 1983, *21*, 275–289.

Logue, A. W., Ophir, I., & Strauss, K. E. The acquisition of taste aversion in humans. *Behavior Research and Therapy*, 1981, *19*, 319–333.

Lorenz, K. *King Solomon's ring*. New York: Crowell, 1952.

Lovaas, O. I. Behavioral treatment and normal educational and intellectual functioning in young autistic children. *Journal of Consulting and Clinical Psychology*, 1987, *55*, 3–9.

Lubow, R. E. Latent inhibition: Effects of frequency of nonreinforced preexposure of the CS. *Journal of Comparative and Physiological Psychology*, 1965, *60*, 454–457.

Lubow, R. E., & Moore, A. V. Latent inhibition: The effect of nonreinforced pre-exposure to the conditional stimulus. *Journal of Consulting and Clinical Psychology*, 1959, *52*, 415–419.

Luria, A. R. *The mind of a mnemonist*. (L. Solotaroff, Trans.). New York: Basic Books, 1968.

Maccoby, E. E., & Jacklin, C. N. *The psychology of sex differences*. Stanford, CA: Stanford University Press, 1974.

Malinowski, B. *Argonauts of the western Pacific*. New York: E. P. Dutton, 1922.

Malott, R. W., & Malott, M. K. Perception and stimulus generalization. In W. C. Stebbins (Ed.), *Animal psychophysics: The design and conduct of sensory experiments*. New York: Appleton-Century-Crofts, 1970.

Masserman, J. H. *Behavior and neurosis: An experimental-psychoanalytic approach to psychobiologic principles*. New York: Hafner, 1943.

McDougall, W. *An introduction to social psychology*. London: Methuen, 1908.

McDougall, W. An experiment for the testing of the hypothesis of Lamarck. *British Journal of Psychology*, 1927, *17*, 267–304.

McDougall, W. Fourth report on a Lamarckian experiment. *British Journal of Psychology,* 1938, *28,* 321–345.

McGaugh, J. L., Westbrook, W., & Burt, G. Strain differences in the facilitative effects of 5-7-Diphenyl-1-3-Diazadamantan-6-OL (1757 I. S.) on maze learning. *Journal of Comparative and Physiological Psychology,* 1961, *54,* 502–505.

McGeoch, J. A. Forgetting and the law of disuse. *Psychological Review,* 1932, *39,* 352–370.

McGuigan, F. J. *Cognitive psychophysiology: Principles of covert behavior.* Englewood Cliffs, NJ: Prentice-Hall, 1978.

McIntire, R. W. Parenthood training or mandatory birth control: Take your choice. *Psychology Today,* October 1973, 34f.

Mead, G. H. *Mind, self and society.* Chicago: University of Chicago Press, 1934.

Merrill, M. K., & Kewman, D. G. Training of color and form identification in cortical blindness: A case study. *Archives of Physical Medicine and Rehabilitation,* 1986, *67,* 479–482.

Miller, N. E. Biofeedback and visceral learning. *Annual Review of Psychology,* 1978, *29,* 373–404.

Miller, N. E. The value of behavioral research on animals. *American Psychologist,* 1985, *40,* 423–440.

Miller, N. E., & Carmona, A. Modification of a visceral response, salivation in thirsty dogs, by instrumental training with water reward. *Journal of Comparative and Physiological Psychology,* 1967, *63,* 1–6.

Miller, N. E., & DiCara, L. Instrumental learning of heart rate changes in curarized rats: Shaping and specificity to discriminative stimulus. *Journal of Comparative and Physiological Psychology,* 1967, *63,* 12–19.

Miller, N. E., & Dollard, J. *Social learning and imitation.* New Haven, CN: Yale University Press, 1941.

Minami, H., & Dallenbach, K. M. The effect of activity upon learning and retention in the cockroach (*Periplaneta americana*). *American Journal of Psychology,* 1946, *59,* 1–58.

Mowrer, O. H. *Learning theory and behavior.* New York: John Wiley, 1960.

Newsom, C., Flavall, J. E., & Rincover, A. Side effects of punishment. In S. Axelrod & J. Apsche (Eds.), *The effects of punishment on human behavior.* New York: Academic Press, 1983.

Nichols, J. R., & Hsiao, S. Addiction liability of albino rats: Breeding for quantitative differences in morphine drinking. *Science,* 1967, *157,* 561–563.

Ost, L., & Hugdahl, K. Acquisition of blood and dental phobia and anxiety response patterns in clinical patients. *Behavior Research and Therapy,* 1985, *23,* (1), 27–34.

Overmier, J. B., & Seligman, M. E. P. Effects of inescapable shock upon subsequent escape and avoidance learning. *Journal of Comparative and Physiological Psychology,* 1967, *63,* 23–33.

Overton, D. A. State-dependent or "dissociated" learning produced by pentobarbital. *Journal of Consulting and Clinical Psychology*, 1964, *57*, 3–12.

Pavlov, I. P. [*Conditioned reflexes.*] (G. V. Anrep, Ed. and Trans.). London: Oxford University Press, 1927.

Pavlov, I. P. Reply of a physiologist to psychologists. *Psychological Review*, 1932, *39*, 91–127.

Pavlov, I. P. [*Lectures on conditioned reflexes* (Vol. 2).] (W. H. Gantt, Ed. and Trans.). New York: International Publishers, 1941.

Pierce, W. D., & Epling, W. F. Choice, matching, and human behavior: A review of the literature. *The Behavior Analyst*, 1983, *6*, 57–76.

Pipitone, A. Jury to decide if sex obsession pushed man over edge. *Evening Sun* (Baltimore) April 23, 1985, pp. D1, D2.

Pisacreta, R., Redwood, E., & Witt, K. Transfer of matching-to-sample figure samples in the pigeon. *Journal of the Experimental Analysis of Behavior*, 1984, *42*, 223–237.

Polenchar, B. E., Romano, A. G., Steinmetz, J. E., & Patterson, M. M. Effects of US parameters on classical conditioning of cat hindlimb flexion. *Animal Learning and Behavior*, 1984, *12*, 69–72.

Powell, D. A., & Creer, T. L. Interaction of developmental and environmental variables in shock-elicited aggression. *Journal of Consulting and Clinical Psychology*, 1969, *69*, 219–25.

Powers, R. B. *Change.* Paper presented at a colloquium on land use planning sponsored by Environment and Man Program, Utah State University, Logan, October 1971–February 1972.

Premack, D. Toward empirical behavioral laws: I. Positive reinforcement. *Psychological Review*, 1959, *66*, 219–33.

Premack, D. Reversibility of the reinforcement relation. *Science*, 1962, *136*, 255–257.

Premack, D. Reinforcement theory. In D. Levine (Ed.), *Nebraska Symposium on Motivation* (Vol. 13). Lincoln: University of Nebraska Press, 1965.

Prokasy, W. F., & Whaley, F. L. Inter-trial interval range shift in classical eyelid conditioning. *Psychological Reports*, 1963, *12*, 55–88.

Pryor, J. W., Haag, R., & O'Reilly, J. The creative porpoise: Training for novel behavior. *Journal of the Experimental Analysis of Behavior*, 1969, *12*, 653–661.

Rachlin, H. *Behavior and learning.* San Francisco: W. H. Freeman, 1976.

Razran, G. A quantitative study of meaning by a conditioned salivary technique (semantic conditioning). *Science*, 1939, *90*, 89–90.

Razran, G. Extinction re-examined and re-analyzed: A new theory. *Psychological Review*, 1956, *63*, 39–52.

Reed, T. Challenging some "common wisdom" on drug abuse. *International Journal of Addiction*, 1980, *15*, 359.

Rescorla, R. A. Pavlovian conditioning and its proper control procedures. *Psychological Review*, 1967, *74*, 71–80.

Rescorla, R. A. Probability of shock in the presence and absence of CS in fear conditioning. *Journal of Comparative and Physiological Psychology*, 1968, *66*, 1–5.

Rescorla, R. A. Evidence of "unique stimulus" account of configural conditioning. *Journal of Comparative and Physiological Psychology*, 1973, *85*, 331–338.

Rescorla, R. A., & Holland, P. C. Behavioral studies of associative learning in animals. In M. R. Rosenzweig & L. W. Porter (Eds.), *Annual Review of Psychology*, 1982, *33*, 265–308.

Rescorla, R. A., & Wagner, A. R. A theory of Pavlovian conditioning: Variations in the effectiveness of reinforcement and nonreinforcement. In A. H. Black & W. F. Prokasy (Eds.), *Classical conditioning, II: Current research and theory*. New York: Appleton-Century-Crofts, 1972.

Revusky, S. H., & Garcia, J. Learned associations over long delays. In G. H. Bower & J. T. Spence (Eds.), *The psychology of learning and motivation, IV*. New York: Academic Press, 1970.

Rilling, M., & Caplan, H. J. Extinction-induced aggression during errorless discrimination learning. *Journal of the Experimental Analysis of Behavior*, 1973, *20*, 85–91.

Riordan, C. A., & Tedeschi, J. T. Attraction in aversive environments: Some evidence for classical conditioning and negative reinforcement. *Journal of Personality and Social Psychology*, 1983, *44*(4), 683–692.

Robins, L. N., Davis, D. H., & Goodwin, D. W. Drug use by U. S. Army enlisted men in Vietnam: A follow-up on their return home. *American Journal of Epidemiology*, 1974, *99*, 235.

Robins, L. N., Helzer, J. E., & Davis, D. H. Narcotic use in southeast Asia and afterwards. *Archives of General Psychiatry*, 1975, *32*, 955.

Roitblat, H. L. *Introduction to comparative cognition*. New York: W. H. Freeman, 1987.

Rosekrans, M. A., & Hartup, W. W. Imitative influences of consistent and inconsistent response consequences to a model on aggressive behavior in children. *Journal of Personality and Social Psychology*, 1967, *7*, 429–434.

Rosenzweig, M. R., Krech, D., & Bennett, E. L. A search for relations between brain chemistry and behavior. *Psychological Bulletin*, 1960, *57*, 476–492.

Rosenzweig, M. R., Krech, D., Bennett, E. L., & Diamond, M. Effects of environmental complexity and training on brain chemistry and anatomy: A replication and extension. *Journal of Comparative and Physiological Psychology*, 1962, *55*, 429–437.

Rozin, P., & Kalat, J. W. Specific hungers and poison avoidance as adaptive specializations of learning. *Psychological Review*, 1971, *78*, 459–486.

Rubin, J. Z., Provensano, F. J., & Luria, S. The eye of the beholder: Parents' view on sex of newborns. *American Journal of Orthopsychiatry*, 1974, *44*, 512–519.

Rundquist, E. A. Inheritance of spontaneous activity in rats. *Journal of Comparative Psychology*, 1933, *16*, 415–38.

Russell, D. E. H. *The secret trauma: Incest in the lives of girls and women.* New York: Basic Books, 1986.

Russell, M., Dark, K. A., Cummins, R. W., Ellman, G., Callaway, E., & Peeke, H. V. S. Learned histamine release. *Science,* 1984, *225,* 733–734.

Schneirla, T. C. A unique case of circular milling in ants, considered in relation to trail following and the general problem of orientation. *American Museum Novitiates,* 1944, *1253,* 1–26.

Schuett, G. W., Clark, D. L., & Kraus, F. Feeding mimicry in the rattlesnake *Sistrurus catenatus,* with comments on the evolution of the rattle. *Animal Behavior,* 1984, *32,* 624–629.

Schwartz, B. *The psychology of learning and behavior* (2nd ed.). New York: W. W. Norton, 1984.

Schwartz, B., & Lacey, H. *Behaviorism, science, and human nature.* New York: W. W. Norton, 1982.

Schwartz, B., & Reilly, M. Long-term retention of a complex operant in pigeons. *Journal of Experimental Psychology: Animal Behavior Processes,* 1985, *11,* 337–355.

Schwartz, B., Schuldenfrei, R., & Lacey, H. Operant psychology as factor psychology. *Behaviorism,* 1978, *6,* 229–254.

Scott, J. P. *Animal behavior.* Chicago: University of Chicago Press, 1958.

Scott, J. P. Critical periods in behavioral development. *Science,* 1962, *138,* 949–958.

Seligman, M. E. P. On the generality of the laws of learning. *Psychological Review,* 1970, *77,* 406–418.

Seligman, M. E. P. Phobias and preparedness. *Behavior Therapy,* 1971, *2,* 307–320.

Seligman, M. E. P. *Helplessness: On depression, development, and death.* San Francisco: W. H. Freeman, 1975.

Seligman, M. E. P., & Hager, J. L. (Eds.). *Biological Boundaries of Learning.* New York: Appleton-Century-Crofts, 1972. (a)

Seligman, M. E. P., & Hager, J. L. Biological boundaries of learning: The sauce-béarnaise syndrome. *Psychology Today,* August 1972, 59–61, 84–87. (b)

Selye, H. *The stress of life* (rev. ed.). New York: McGraw-Hill, 1976.

Shepher, J. Mate selection among second-generation kibbutz adolescents and adults: Incest avoidance and negative imprinting. *Archives of Sexual Behavior,* 1971, *1,* 293–307.

Sherry, D. F., & Galef, B. G., Jr. Cultural transmission without imitation: milk bottle opening in birds. *Animal Behavior,* 1984, *32* (3), 937–938.

Siegel, S. Evidence from rats that morphine tolerance is a learned response. *Journal of Comparative and Physiological Psychology,* 1975, *89,* 498.

Siegel, S. Morphine analgesic tolerance: Its situation specificity supports a Pavlovian conditioning model. *Science,* 1976, *193,* 323–325.

Siegel, S. Classical conditioning, drug tolerance, and drug dependence. In R. G. Smart, F. B. Glaser, Y. Israel, H. Kalant, R. E. Popham, & W.

Schmidt (Eds.), *Research advances in alcohol and drug problems* (Vol. 7). New York: Plenum, 1983.

Siegel, S. Pavlovian conditioning and heroin overdose: Reports by overdose victims. *Bulletin of the Psychonomic Society*, 1984, *22*, 428–430.

Siegel, S., Hinson, R. E., Krank, M. D., & McCully, J. Heroin "overdose" death: Contribution of drug-associated environmental cues. *Science*, 1982, *216*, 436–437.

Siqueland, E., & Delucia, C. A. Visual reinforcement on non-nutritive sucking in human infants. *Science*, 1969, *165*, 1144–1146.

Siipola, E. M. A study of some effects of preparatory set. *Psychological Monographs*, 1935, *46*, No. 210.

Silverman, P. *Animal behavior in the laboratory*. New York: Pica Press, 1978.

Skinner, B. F. *The behavior of organisms: An experimental analysis*. New York: Appleton-Century-Crofts, 1938.

Skinner, B. F. Superstition in the pigeon. *Journal of Experimental Psychology*, 1948, *38*, 168–172. (a)

Skinner, B. F. *Walden two*. New York: Macmillan, 1948. (b)

Skinner, B. F. Are theories of learning necessary? *Psychological Review*, 1950, *57*, 193–216.

Skinner, B. F. How to teach animals. *Scientific American*, 1951, *185*, 26–29.

Skinner, B. F. *Science and human behavior*. New York: Free Press, 1953.

Skinner, B. F. A case history in scientific method. *American Psychologist*, 1956, *11*, 221–233.

Skinner, B. F. *Verbal behavior*. New York: Appleton-Century-Crofts, 1957.

Skinner, B. F. Two 'synthetic' social relations. *Journal of the Experimental Analysis of Behavior*, 1962, *5*, 531–533.

Skinner, B. F. Behaviorism at fifty. *Science*, 1963, *134*, 566–602.

Skinner, B. F. *The technology of teaching*. Englewood Cliffs, NJ: Prentice-Hall, 1968.

Skinner, B. F. *Contingencies of reinforcement: A theoretical analysis*. New York: Appleton-Century-Crofts, 1969.

Skinner, B. F. *About behaviorism*. New York: Knopf, 1974.

Skinner, B. F. The shaping of phyologenic behavior. *Journal of the Experimental Analysis of Behavior*, 1975, *24*, 117–120.

Skinner, B. F. *Particulars of my life*. New York: Knopf, 1976.

Skinner, B. F. *The shaping of a behaviorist*. New York: Knopf, 1977.

Skinner, B. F. *Reflections on behaviorism and society*. Englewood Cliffs, NJ: Prentice-Hall, 1978.

Skinner, B. F. Selection by consequences. *Science*, 1981, *213*, 501–504.

Skinner, B. F. *A matter of consequences*. New York: Knopf, 1983. (a)

Skinner, B. F. Taking the future seriously. Invited address, Association for the Advancement of Behavior Therapy annual convention, Washington, DC, December 1983. (b)

Skinner, B. F. The evolution of behavior. *Journal of Experimental Analysis of Behavior*, 1984, *41*, 217–21.

Skinner, B. F. *Upon Further Reflection*. Englewood Cliffs, NJ: Prentice-Hall, 1987.

Smith, K. "Drive": In defence of a concept. *Behaviorism*, 1984, *12*, 71–114.

Spelt, D. K. The conditioning of the human fetuses in utero. *Journal of Experimental Psychology*, 1948, *38*, 338–346.

Spence, K. W. The nature of discrimination learning in animals. *Psychological Review*, 1936, *43*, 427–449.

Spence, K. W. The differential response in animals to stimuli varying within a single dimension. *Psychological Review*, 1937, *44*, 430–444.

Spence, K. W. Learning and performance in eyelid conditioning as a function of intensity of the UCS. *Journal of Experimental Psychology*, 1953, *45*, 57–63.

Spence, K. W. *Behavior theory and learning*. Englewood Cliffs, NJ: Prentice-Hall, 1960.

Spetch, M. L., Wilkie, D. M., & Pinel, J. P. J. Backward conditioning: A reevaluation of the empirical evidence. *Psychological Bulletin*, 1981, *89*, 163–175.

Staats, A. W., & Staats, C. K. Attitudes established by classical conditioning. *Journal of Abnormal and Social Psychology*, 1958, *57*, 37–40.

Staats, C. K., & Staats, A. W. Meaning established by classical conditioning. *Journal of Experimental Psychology*, 1957, *54*, 74–80.

Staddon, J. E. R., & Simmelhag, V. L. The 'superstition' experiment: A reexamination of its implications for the principles of adaptive behavior. *Psychological Review*, 1971, *78*, 3–43.

Steincrohn. Health. *Evening Sun* (Baltimore), September 21, 1984.

Stern, A. *The making of a genius*. Miami: Hurricane House, 1971.

Stone, I. *The origins*. New York: Doubleday, 1980.

Taylor, J. A. The relationship of anxiety to the conditioned eyelid response. *Journal of Experimental Psychology*, 1951, *41*, 81–92.

Terrace, H. S. Wavelength generalization after discrimination learning with and without errors. *Science*, 1964, *144*, 78–80.

Terrace, H. S. Discrimination learning and inhibition. *Science*, 1966, *154*, 1677–1680.

Terrace, H. S. By-products of discrimination learning. In G. H. Bower (Ed.), *The psychology of learning and motivation (Vol. 5)*. New York: Academic Press, 1972.

Terrace, H. S. *Nim*. New York: Knopf, 1979.

Thomas, G. V., Lieberman, D. A., McIntosh, D. C., & Ronaldson, P. The role of marking when reward is delayed. *Journal of Experimental Psychology*, 1983, *9*, 401–411.

Thorndike, E. L. Animal intelligence. *Psychological Review Monographs*, 1898, *2*(8).

Thorndike, E. L. The mental life of the monkeys. *Psychological Review Monograph*, 1901, *3*(15).

Thorndike, E. L. *Animal intelligence: Experimental studies*. New York: Hafner, 1911.

Thorndike, E. L. *Human learning*. Cambridge, MA: MIT Press, 1968. (Originally published in 1931.)

Thorndike, E. L. Autobiography. In C. Murchison (Ed.), *A history of psychology in autobiography* (Vol. 3). Worcester, MA: Clark University Press, 1936.

Thorpe, W. H. *Learning and instinct in animals*. London: Methuen, 1963.

Thune, L. E., & Underwood, B. J. Retroactive inhibition as a function of degree of interpolated learning. *Journal of Experimental Psychology*, 1943, *32*, 185–200.

Timberlake, W. A molar equilibrium theory of learned performance. In G. H. Bower (Ed.), *The psychology of learning and motivation* (Vol. 14). New York: Academic Press, 1980, pp. 1–58.

Timberlake, W., & Lucas, G. A. The basis of superstitious behavior: Chance contingency, stimulus substitution, or appetitive behavior? *Journal of the Experimental Analysis of Behavior*, 1985, *44*, 279–299.

Timberlake, W., & Allison, J. Response deprivation: An empirical approach to instrumental performance. *Psychological Review*, 1974, *81*, 146–164.

Tinbergen, N. *The study of instinct*. Oxford: Clarendon Press, 1951.

Tinbergen, N. *Social behavior in animals*. New York: John Wiley, 1962. (Originally published in 1953.)

Todorov, J. C., Hanna, E. S., & De Sa, M. C. N. B. Frequency versus magnitude of reinforcement: New data with a different procedure. *Journal of the Experimental Analysis of Behavior*, 1984, *41*, 157–167.

Tryon, R. C. Genetic differences in maze-learning ability in rats. In National Society for the Study of Education Yearbook, *Intelligence: Its nature and nurture: I. Comparative and critical exposition*. Public School Publishing Co., 1940.

Tulving, E. Cue-dependent forgetting. *American Scientist*, 1974, *62*, 74–82.

Turnbull, C. Some observations regarding the experiences and behavior of the BaMbuti Pygmies. *American Journal of Psychology*, 1961, *74*, 304–308.

Twain, M. *Life on the Mississippi*. New York: Harper and Brothers, 1917.

Ulrich, R. E. Pain as a cause of aggression. *American Zoologist*, 1966, *6*, 643–62.

Ulrich, R. E., & Azrin, N. A. Reflexive fighting in response to aversive stimuli. *Journal of the Experimental Analysis of Behavior*, 1962, 511–20.

Underwood, B. J. Retroactive and proactive inhibition after 5 and 48 hours. *Journal of Experimental Psychology*, 1948, *38*, 29–38.

Underwood, B. J. Interference and forgetting. *Psychological Review*, 1957, *64*, 49–60.

Underwood, B. J. *Experimental psychology*. New York: Appleton-Century-Crofts, 1966.

Van Houton, R. Punishment: From the animal laboratory to the applied setting. In S. Axelrod & J. Apsche (Eds.), *The effects of punishment on human behavior*. New York: Academic Press, 1983.

Wagner, A. R., & Rescorla, R. A. Inhibition in Pavlovian conditioning: Application of a theory. In R. A. Boakes & M. S. Halliday (Eds.), *Inhibition and learning*. London: Academic Press, 1972.

Wallace, P. Animal behavior: The puzzle of flavor aversion. *Science*, 1976, *193*, 989–991.

Warden, C. J., Fjeld, H. A., & Koch, A. M. Imitative behavior in cebus and rhesus monkeys. *Journal of Genetic Psychology*, 1940, *56*, 311–322.

Warden, C. J., & Jackson, T. A. Imitative behavior in the rhesus monkey. *Journal of Genetic Psychology*, 1935, *46*, 103–125.

Watson, J. B. Imitation in monkeys. *Psychological Bulletin*, 1908, *5*, 169–178.

Watson, J. B., & Rayner, R. Conditioned emotional reactions. *Journal of Experimental Psychology*, 1920, *3*, 1–4.

Weil, J. L. The effects of delayed reinforcement on free-operant responding. *Journal of the Experimental Analysis of Behavior*, 1984, *41*, 143–155.

Wells, H. K. *Pavlov and Freud: I. Toward a scientific psychology and psychiatry*. London: Lawrence and Wishart, 1956.

Wilcoxon, H. C., Dragoin, W. B., & Kral, P. A. Illness-induced aversions in rat and quail: Relative salience of visual and gustatory cues. *Science*, 1971, *171*, 826–828.

Will, J. A., Self, P. A., & Datan, N. Maternal behavior and perceived sex of infant. *American Journal of Orthopsychiatry*, 1976, *46*, 135–139.

Williams, C. D. The elimination of tantrum behavior by extinction procedures. *Journal of Abnormal and Social Psychology*, 1959, *59*, 269.

Williams, D. R., & Williams, H. Auto-maintenance in the pigeon: Sustained pecking despite contingent nonreinforcement. *Journal of the Experimental Analysis of Behavior*, 1969, *12*, 511–520.

Williams, J. E. Connotations of racial concepts and color names. *Journal of Personality and Social Psychology*, 1966, *3*, 531–540.

Williams, J. E., & Edwards, C. D. An exploratory study of the modification of color concepts and racial attitudes in preschool children. *Child Development*, 1969, *40*, 737–750.

Williams, S. B. Resistance to extinction as a function of the number of reinforcements. *Journal of Experimental Psychology*, 1938, *23*, 506–522.

Wilson, E. O. *Sociobiology: The new synthesis*. Cambridge, MA: Harvard University Press, 1975.

Wilson, E. O. *On human nature*. Cambridge, MA: Harvard University Press, 1978.

Wolfe, J. B. Effectiveness of token-rewards for chimpanzees. *Comparative Psychology Monographs*, 1936, *12*(5).

Yerkes, R. M., & Morgulis, S. The method of Pavlov in animal psychology. *Psychological Bulletin*, 1909, *6*, 257–273.

Zeiler, M. D. The sleeping giant: Reinforcement schedules. *Journal of the Experimental Analysis of Behavior*, 1984, *42*, 485–493.

Zener, K. The significance of behavior accompanying conditioned salivary secretion for theories of the conditioned response. *American Journal of Psychology*, 1937, *50*, 384–403.

Name Index

■

Subject Index

∎

The terms in **boldface** are defined in the glossary.

DATE DUE